# Employment Relations in a Changing Society

# Employment Relations in a Changing Society

## Assessing the Post-Fordist Paradigm

Edited by

Luis Enrique Alonso

and

Miguel Martínez Lucio

Selection and editorial matter © Luis Enrique Alonso and
Miguel Martínez Lucio 2006
Individual chapters © contributors 2006

All rights reserved. No reproduction, copy or transmission of this
publication may be made without written permission.

No paragraph of this publication may be reproduced, copied or transmitted
save with written permission or in accordance with the provisions of the
Copyright, Designs and Patents Act 1988, or under the terms of any licence
permitting limited copying issued by the Copyright Licensing Agency,
90 Tottenham Court Road, London W1T 4LP.

Any person who does any unauthorized act in relation to this publication
may be liable to criminal prosecution and civil claims for damages.

The authors have asserted their rights to be identified as the authors of this
work in accordance with the Copyright, Designs and Patents Act 1988.

First published 2006 by
PALGRAVE MACMILLAN
Houndmills, Basingstoke, Hampshire RG21 6XS and
175 Fifth Avenue, New York, N.Y. 10010
Companies and representatives throughout the world

PALGRAVE MACMILLAN is the global academic imprint of the Palgrave
Macmillan division of St. Martin's Press, LLC and of Palgrave Macmillan Ltd.
Macmillan® is a registered trademark in the United States, United Kingdom
and other countries. Palgrave is a registered trademark in the European Union
and other countries.

ISBN-13: 978–0–333–97037–9
ISBN-10: 0–333–97037–3

This book is printed on paper suitable for recycling and made from fully
managed and sustained forest sources.

A catalogue record for this book is available from the British Library.

Library of Congress Cataloging-in-Publication Data
Employment relations in a changing society : assessing the post-Fordist
    paradigm / edited by Luis Enrique Alonso & Miguel Martínez Lucio
        p. cm.
    Includes bibliographical references and index.
    ISBN 0–333–97037–3 (cloth)
        1. Labor market. 2. Labor policy. 3. Industrial relations. 4. Industrial
    sociology. 5. Industrial organization—Social aspects. 6. Organizational
    change. I. Alonso Benito, L. E. (Luis Enrique) II. Martínez-Lucio, Miguel,
    1960–
HD5706.E52 2005
331.1–dc22                                                    2005043423

10  9  8  7  6  5  4  3  2  1
15 14 13 12 11 10 09 08 07 06

Printed and bound in Great Britain by
Antony Rowe Ltd, Chippenham and Eastbourne

*This book is dedicated to the memory and legacy of the community of Spanish political exiles from fascism in the United Kingdom, and to the volunteers from Ireland and the United Kingdom who fought for the Republic and liberty in Spain during the 1930s and for other views regarding internationalization*

# Contents

| | |
|---|---|
| List of Figures and Tables | ix |
| Preface | x |
| Notes on the Contributors | xi |

## Part I  Introduction

1 Introduction: Employment Relations in a Changing Society — 3
   *Miguel Martínez Lucio*

2 Fordism and the Genesis of the Post-Fordist Society: Assessing the Post-Fordist Paradigm — 18
   *Luis Enrique Alonso*

## Part II  The Labour Market

3 Flexible Enterprises: An Analysis of their Institutional Standing — 35
   *José Manuel Lasierra*

4 The Degradation of Employment in Spain: From the Salaried Employment Norm to the Entrepeneurial Employment Norm — 52
   *Carlos Prieto*

5 The Myth of Decentralization and the New Labour Market — 69
   *Robert MacKenzie and Chris Forde*

## Part III  The State

6 Are We Moving Towards a Post-Fordist State? Full Employment of the European Workforce — 89
   *Daniel Albarracín*

7 Employability and the Flexible Economy: Some Considerations of the Politics and Contradictions of the European Employment Strategy — 104
   *Ian Greenwood and Mark Stuart*

8 Post-Fordism and Organizational Change in State Administration — 120
   *Ian Kirkpatrick*

## Part IV  Labour and Society

9  Feminization and Inequality in the New Regime of Work:
From Exclusion by Design to Exclusion by Default              139
*Jean Gardiner and Miguel Martínez Lucio*

10  A Post-Fordist Consumption Norm? Social Fragmentation,
Individualization and New Inequalities                        153
*Luis Enrique Alonso*

11  The Feminization of Work, Changes in Family Structure and
the Transformation of the Welfare State in the Post-Fordist
Environment                                                   169
*Gerardo Meil Landwerlin*

12  Individualism and Collectivism in the Sociology of the
Collective Worker                                             182
*Paul Stewart*

13  Trade Unionism and the Realities of Change: Reframing
the Language of Change                                        200
*Miguel Martínez Lucio*

14  Flexible Rigidities: A Model for Social Europe?           215
*Richard Hyman*

*Index*                                                       223

# List of Figures and Tables

**Figures**

| | | |
|---|---|---|
| 6.1 | Employment rate, Spain, 1987–2001 | 91 |
| 6.2 | Employment rate, EU 1997 | 91 |

**Tables**

| | | |
|---|---|---|
| 3.1 | The use of atypical employees in three EU countries, 1985–99 | 45 |
| 3.2 | Reasons for the use of subcontracting and atypical workers | 46 |
| 3.3 | Employment systems and their effects on job characteristics | 47 |
| 11.1 | Type of first union entered into by women, selected European countries, 1995 | 172 |
| 11.2 | Fertility among women born in 1941–45 and 1961–65, 2003 | 173 |
| 11.3 | Divorce rate and length of broken marriages in the EU, 1959–61 and 1996–98 | 173 |
| 11.4 | Employment rate of women aged 20–49 by number of children, second quarter of 2001 | 174 |
| 13.1 | Two interpretations of change | 210 |

# Preface

The book brings together authors from Spain and the United Kingdom who work on the subject of social and employment change. They are part of a critical constituency of academics who are concerned with the way in which new forms of employment and social organization are being interpreted and understood.

The two editors have previously collaborated on the subjects of flexibility and the shifts in the traditional Fordist production system. They have viewed developments in the United Kingdom and Spain with concern, as these economies have experienced some of the most serious changes in employment practised in Europe. Whilst their employment systems differ, they have both experienced high levels of work intensification and job insecurity.

This book sets out to do two things: to challenge the assumption that such changes bring positive experiences in terms of employment; and to analyze the tensions and political nature of the changes.

In this respect the contributors highlight the ironies of change and the manner in which they bring new social and economic costs and new forms of conflict. They also critique the political discourse of neoliberalism, which parallels the new systems of employment regulation.

The editors wish to thank the contributors for their insights and independent approach. They would also like to thank Jacky Kippenberger and Rebecca Pash of Palgrave Macmillan and Tricia Steele of the University of Bradford for their support and help. They especially thank Beth Gelb, who translated the chapters by the Spanish contributors, and Keith Povey for copy-editing. Robert MacKenzie is thanked for his illustration and general assistance, as is Paul Stewart.

LUIS ENRIQUE ALONSO
MIGUEL MARTINEZ LUCIO

# Notes on the Contributors

**Daniel Albarracín** is a researcher at the CIREM Foundation in Madrid and a coordinator for the European Industrial Relations Observatory. His main research interests are industrial relations and social policies, the sociology of consumption and qualitative methodology.

**Luis Enrique Alonso** is Professor of Sociology at the Universidad Autonóma de Madrid. His previous works include *Historia del consumo en España* (Madrid, 1994), *La mirada cualitativa en Sociología* (Madrid, 1998), *Trabajo y ciudadanía* (Madrid, 1999) and *Trabajo y postmodernidad*, (Madrid, 2001). He has lectured and published widely on subjects relating to labour processes, social movements and consumption.

**Chris Forde** is Lecturer in Industrial Relations at the Work and Employment Relations Division, Leeds University Business School. His research interests are the character and development of non-standard employment, particularly agency work; the nature and impact of employee participation mechanisms; and the social and economic consequences of restructuring in the steel industry.

**Jean Gardiner** is Senior Lecturer at the University of Leeds and Deputy Director of the Centre for Interdisciplinary Gender Studies. She is also a member of the Centre for Policy Studies in Education and the Centre for Research on Family, Kinship and Childhood. Her research focuses on the dynamic development of gender relations in labour markets, families and education systems. Her current interests include human resource strategies for parental employment, future employment trends in the context of changing gender relations, the flexibilization of labour and learning, and the interconnections between informal learning, gender and skills.

**Ian Greenwood** is Lecturer in Industrial Relations and Human Resource Management at the Work and Employment Relations Division, Leeds University Business School. His current research interests include developments in workplace learning, social partnership and its impact on collective bargaining, and the socioeconomic impact of restructuring in the steel industry. He is currently concluding research for an EU Framework 5 project on the role that lifelong learning can play in the restructuring of the European steel and metal sector.

**Richard Hyman** is Professor of Industrial Relations at the London School of Economics and Political Science (LSE) and is founding editor of the *European Journal of Industrial Relations*. He has written extensively on the themes of industrial relations, collective bargaining, trade unionism, industrial conflict and labour market policy, and is author of a dozen books (notably *Strikes* and *Industrial Relations: A Marxist Introduction*) as well as numerous journal articles and book chapters. His comparative study *Understanding European Trade Unionism: Between Market, Class and Society* was published in 2001 and is widely cited by scholars working in this field.

**Ian Kirkpatrick** is Senior Lecturer in Organisation Behaviour at Leeds University Business School. He has also taught at Cardiff University and the Universitat Pompeu Fabra in Barcelona. His main research interests are the restructuring of public service management, employment flexibility and changing work regimes in professional service firms. Recent works includes *The New Managerialism and Public Service Professions* (with Stephen Ackroyd and Richard Walker) and a chapter in the *Oxford Handbook of Work and Organisation*.

**Jose Manuel Lasierra** is Lecturer in Applied Economy at Zaragoza University and former Visiting Research Fellow at Leeds University. His published works include *Labour Market and Employer Strategies*.

**Robert MacKenzie** is Senior Lecturer in Industrial Relations at Leeds University Business School. His research interests include regulation of the employment relationship and industrial restructuring. He has written on subcontracting in the telecommunications industry and the use of contingent employment in construction. More recently he has conducted research into the social and economic impact of the restructuring of the steel industry in the UK.

**Miguel Martínez Lucio** is Professor of Industrial Relations and Human Resource Management at the School of Management Bradford University. Formerly he was a Reader at Durham University and has lectured at Leeds, Cardiff and Keele Universities since the 1980s. His work involves the nature of employment cooperation in capitalist societies, the crisis and renewal of trade unionism, the nature of regulation and economic change, the transformation of the public sector and the relation between worker identity and organized labour.

**Gerardo Meil Landwerlin** is Professor of Sociology at the Universidad Autónoma de Madrid. He was previously a visiting researcher at the University of Bielefeld and a Fellow of the Hanse Institute for Advanced Sciences in Delmenhorst, Germany. He is author of several books, including *The Postmodernization of the Spanish Family*, *Family Policy in Spain* and *Cohabitation in Spain* (all in Spanish), as well as numerous articles on family change, family solidarity, social policy, family policy and population trends.

**Carlos Prieto** is Professor of the Sociology of Labour Relations at the School of Political Science and Sociology, Complutense University, Madrid, Director of the journal *Cuadernos de Relaciones Laborales*, a member of the Editorial Board of *Travail et Emploi*, and a member of the Orientation Board of *Sociologie du Travail*. His publications include *Las Condiciones de Trabajo. Un enfoque renovador de la sociologia del trabajo* (coauthored with J. J. Castillo), *Trabajadores y condiciones de trabajo*, *Las Relaciones de Empleo en España* (coauthored with F. Miguelez), *La Crisis del Empleo en Europa* and *Collective Bargaining and the Social Construction of Employment* (coauthored with M. Alaluf).

**Paul Stewart** is Professor of the Sociology of Work and Employment at ESRU, Bristol Business School, University of the West of England. He has written widely on employment restructuring, trade union renewal and the labour process, and until recently was editor of *Work, Employment and Society*. He is a member of the Conference of Socialist Economists.

**Mark Stuart** is in the Work and Employment Relations Division at Leeds University Business School and Professor of Human Resource Management and Industrial Relations. His research focuses on organizational restructuring, employee development and social dialogue. He is the coeditor of *Partnership and Modernisation in Employment Relations* (with Miguel Martínez Lucio), a board member of *Work, Employment and Society* and an Associate Fellow of the ESRC Centre for Skills, Knowledge and Organisational Performance (SKOPE) at Oxford and Warwick Universities.

# Part I
# Introduction

# 1
# Introduction: Employment Relations in a Changing Society

*Miguel Martínez Lucio*

## Introduction

The ways in which we work and live have undergone major changes in the last three decades. The organized pattern of employment, with its hierarchies and established political and social roles, has been challenged by a variety of factors. The stable market situation of the postwar era has been eroding due to increasing globalization and market uncertainty. The regulatory framework of the Keynesian welfare state has been under pressure as a caretaker of and platform for capitalist development. Labour markets are marked by uncertainty, short-term arrangements, insecurity and fragmentation. This is a very different situation from that anticipated in the 1960s and 1970s, when more comforting views of a new postindustrial world prevailed.

The changes we have witnessed have therefore challenged our notions of stability and progress, and to make things worse we have been subjected to political and academic speculation and uncertainty in respect of interpreting such developments. It is unclear whether there has been a substantive shift in the social and economic structures of our societies, or whether these changes have emerged from ideological shifts and the exhaustion of the political projects that governed work and social relations in the postwar period. Therefore any study of changes in the relationship between work, organizations and society has the unenviable task of confronting the problem of what is meant by change and how it should be interpreted. Since the 1970s – the point at which the crisis of the postwar model of regulation emerged – we have seen scholars grapple with the extent and significance of changes. The debate on Post-Fordism has been the main conduit for such discussions. This is because Post-Fordism is not solely concerned with developments in the workplace and the labour market *après* Ford, but also with the economic and social context of work and the workplace (see Peck, 1996).

This book confronts the legacy of change by evaluating the new models of work and regulation that form the ideological and institutional platforms of the Post-Fordist movement. Four key questions will be addressed:

- To what extent have European labour markets and organizational forms changed?
- How have the language and practices of the state as a labour market player and employer influenced these developments?
- To what extent are changes in working relationships due to changing gender relations, family structures and forms of consumption?
- How has labour collectivism been reshaped politically and institutionally by such developments?

These questions are integral to understanding the manner in which the new regimes of work are underpinned and supported. This attention to different levels of change is based on a broader understanding of what changing workplace regimes are founded on and how they function. Such discussions of work do not solely address the end of mass production, but also draw attention to the often ignored issues of changes in mass consumption and the relations and structures that underpin the experiences and actions of citizens as more than just producers.

The chapters of this book show how developments in new forms of work, social organization, political regulation and labour activity have contradictory qualities that do not dissolve the role of organizations and politics but actually strengthen them. The reader is presented with arguments on the intensification of exploitative relations based on insecurity and uncertainty: these emerge as either breaks with modern forms of work and social relations and/or the reintroduction and intensification of premodern and ultramodern forms of social and organizational relations. There has not been a straightforward move to an individualized, market-oriented, high-commitment workplace and social context. However nor has there been a simple continuity of social relations, organizational processes and workplace identities.

There has been a sharpening of political dissonance and the new regime of work is not without tensions. Understanding how this dissonance is organized, understood and politically mediated is a major challenge. Whilst the now dominant language of neoliberalism has affected the ways in which we work and live and how these are regulated, a series of challenges and ironic twists suggest that a new equilibrium has not been reached. If anything, as various contributors to this book point out, new boundaries appear to be reinforcing the role of bureaucratic and traditional or even pretraditional working practices.

Whilst this book aims to discuss the European experience of change in general, it mainly draws from the work of British and Spanish authors.

Both sets of authors are citizens of countries that, while different in their political and regulatory characteristics (see Blyton and Martínez Lucio, 1995), have witnessed extraordinary changes in their labour markets. In the UK part-time work and flexible working practices have become commonplace (Bunting, 2004), whilst in Spain temporary contracting has reached some of the highest levels in Europe (Recio, 1999). At the same time, since the early 1980s both countries have undergone some of the most extensive industrial restructuring in Europe. Marketization and neoliberalism have predominated in both countries, albeit under the new right and then 'third way' social democracy in the UK and market-adapting social democracy (Smith, 1998) and centre-right governments in Spain. While the common obsession of the Spanish conservatives and the British Labour Party with deregulation and liberalization has been quite remarkable, the contributors approach the topic from the standpoint that change has not been easily contained, mediated and managed by the market or more flexible and market-oriented systems of regulation. These very systems themselves appear to be the object of change, although within the contributions there are varying positions as to the extent of their fragility and internal conflict.

## The new economic systems: background and history

Concern with change and the ending of mass production, based on a standardized producer/consumer/citizen, was not solely a phenomenon of the 1970s, with its economic crises and labour uprisings on pay and control. Countercurrents had existed previously and political discourses had questioned the ethical and social value of a system based on hierarchy and conformity. The Peruvian poet Octavio Paz (1987) has written of Leon Trotsky and the surrealist poet Andre Breton flirting in the 1930s with the possibility of challenging the prevailing understanding of value and use in economic analysis as the keys to challenging contemporary capitalism and Taylorist/ Stalinist communism. This brief, and perhaps naïve, venture shows us that we are not the first with our concerns about change and the manner in which we work, let alone its philosophical underpinnings.

The 1960s saw the first real signs that the quality and character of capitalist organizations were likely to change and that modern capitalist organization would always be undergoing a process of renewal. In the 1960s and 1970s two schools of thought emerged – one with an Anglo-Saxon perspective and the other with a French one. Both saw significant ruptures in the industrial logic of capitalism. Bell (1973) was one of the first to point to a shift away from manufacturing to services in terms of both supply and demand. As Noon and Blyton (1997) have noted, Bell also paid attention to cultural changes and the fact that the Taylorist work ethic was being challenged by such developments (see Bell, 1974). Within the French perspective the changes were broadened in terms of their political consequences.

For Gorz (1980), for example, in postindustrial society there was a collapse of traditional patterns of work, with the working class being subjected to changes in social and economic organization. This provided the potential for liberation, although how this was to occur was uncertain (see Hyman, 1983). In fact for some political observers the changes represented a collapse of work itself and a crisis of adjustment in a society that was increasingly based on reduced employment possibilities (Jenkins and Sherman, 1979).

Emerging from this early set of discussions was the realization that social science would have to account for a variety of societal relationships and dimensions if it was to grapple with the nature of change at work and the transformations besetting workers. However from the initial insights into the changing nature of employment and social relations it was clear that speculation and generalities would be central to the discussion (see Chapter 2 of this volume for a discussion and overview).

## Post-Fordism and its costs

Post-Fordism is a term used to capture the broader nature of change facing workers and consumers. The academic starting point was the French regulation school and their British counterparts. Aglietta (1979) was concerned with the inherent instability of socioeconomic systems. The tensions created by developments in specific capitalist relations and social structures were seen to lead to instability and an attempt to control or regulate these tensions through an ensemble of institutional bodies and agents (Jessop, 1990). The discussion therefore tended to focus on the nature of Fordism, with its highly structured and expansive economic organizations, mass production and mass markets. The Keynesian welfare state, with its relatively centralized systems of regulation and political control, acted as a guarantor of mass consumption through state expenditure, as a facilitator of mass production through its role as employer, purchaser and producer, and as an overall regulator through legislation and alliances with key social actors. The positive contribution of regulation theory is that for all its concern with functional characteristics (Bonefeld, 1987) it was able to link together the roles of different actors and processes in an explanatory framework that emphasized the interconnectedness of consumption, production, social structure and regulation. Within these macro-level relations there was a systematic link with micro-level employment relations in the form of Taylorist production systems, with their emphasis on routine, supervision and monitoring – that is, direct control.

Jessop (2002) sees Fordism as existing at four interconnected levels. First it was a labour process based on mass production and the ethos of Taylorism – an industrial paradigm. Second, it was a stable system of macroeconomic management based on mass production, maintaining aggregate demand and sustaining the supply side of industry – a regime of accumulation. Third, it involved the separation of ownership from control within capitalism in the form of multidivisional organizations that afforded a degree of autonomy in economic decision making on issues such as wage bargaining, for example. Finally, there were forms of social organization based on standardized consumption and stable social structures such as the nuclear family – 'societalization'.

The crisis of this system has been a topic of considerable discussion (Ruigrock and van Tulder, 1995). For some the point of change was the globalization of capitalist relations and the undermining of the closed economic system, with its protected labour and product markets. For others it was the changing nature of consumption due to a desire for less standardization, combined with the increasing financial demands made by workers through collective bargaining in the 1960s and 1970s (Piore and Sabel, 1984). Then there are those who have pointed to the inherent contradictions in the state itself, as its logic became ambiguous in the context of greater marketization and social change (O'Connor, 1973; Offe, 1984). Whatever its source, the crisis reflected a lack of congruence between economic processes and the roles of regulatory actors (Torfing, 1990).

The search for an institutional solution or panacea preoccupied social scientists and policy makers for some time. One proposed solution was Toyotism and flexible manufacturing (see Chapter 3 of this volume). Where once there were unified markets there would be dissected markets; where once there was a unified workforce there would be a specialized, variable and flexible workforce; and where once there was an interventionist state there would be a 'facilitative' state, nurturing the knowledge basis of the economy from below and focusing its more directive capacities for social supervision and control on the edges of society (Jessop, 2002). In Spain and the UK these views became popular due to the sheer extent of change.

Atkinson (1984) developed a model of employment that consisted of a functionally flexible core workforce and a periphery of subcontracted and temporary workers to meet the increasingly diverse needs of the product market through a differentiated approach to employment. Atkinson drew much of his inspiration from Japan, which had turned to a dual system of employment. This was a more mechanical view of the French academic version of Toyotism. It was nurtured by a political context of neoliberalism and Conservative governments (1979–97) that shifted the economic debate.

Alongside this model there emerged within the Anglo-Saxon tradition a concern with the preponderance of ready-made alternatives to Fordism in the form of greater worker differentiation, consumption change, state withdrawal and a broad cultural move to individualization. The perceived problem with the 'flexible firm model' (see Pollert, 1988) is that it failed to comprehend the limits of temporary contracting and certain types of flexible working, which furthermore were neither novel nor specific to Post-Fordism. The protected core has not been so flexible, the changes to mass production and markets have been overstated, and the new strategies have very little that is *strategic* and thought-out about them, despite arguments to the contrary by some (Procter *et al.*, 2004). In fact it is not uncommon for these to lead to new 'rigidities' in such practices as teamwork, due to limited work rotation, the prevalence of multitasking rather than multiskilling, the lack of broad job mobility, and the presence of inherent contradictions between numerical and functional flexibility, with the former at times limiting the development of the latter (Blyton and Morris, 1992; Martínez Lucio *et al.*, 2000). Moreover the growth of part-time work in the UK has been based primarily on female employment, and the growth of temporary work in Spain has been based on female and young workers. Work is in part allocated on the basis of gender-typing and the location of women in certain roles and professions (Lovering, 1990). That is to say, whilst women are now entering the labour market in greater numbers, jobs continue to be gendered, with work such as marketing and human resource management, for example, being viewed as more 'suited to women' (see Chapter 9 of this volume).

In addition, then, there are the social costs of flexibility: job insecurity, diminishing status and the decline of supportive relationships (Heery and Salmon, 2000). Rifkin (1995) and Sennett (1998) captured considerable attention when they highlighted the social costs of job insecurity and its denigrating effects, but in many respects they were merely reasserting in a populist manner a concern that had been raised by social and employment analysts for over a decade: that declining job security and fundamental social changes were undermining the fabric of society. According to Rifkin (1995, p. 184), new forms of workplace pressure were resulting from teamworking and the mimicking of the once exalted Japanese model: 'management [in Japan] often relies on its work teams to discipline members ... [and] continually pressure recalcitrant or slow workers to perform up to par'. Then there were the pressures brought about by technology: 'The new computer based technologies have so quickened the volume, flow and pace of information that millions of workers are experiencing mental "overload" and "burnout". The physical fatigue generated by the fast pace of the older industrial economy is being eclipsed by the mental fatigue generated by the nanosecond pace of the new information economy' (ibid., pp. 186–7). Hence discussions of the new workplace culture were replete with references to and biographies of individuals living burnt-out lives in a society drunk on the aspirations of a new managerial culture (Sennett, 1998; Bunting, 2004). (For this reason some prefer to use the term neo-Fordism due to the ongoing, and accelerated, features of controlled surveillance at work: Noon and Blyton, 1997: 119–20.)

These developments at work in terms of 'burn-out' were prompted by increasing labour intensification and the emergence of a new form of 'exploitation' (Garrahan and Stewart, 1992). The Marxist critique of change in employment and work links the new forms of control to shifts in global capital. Alternatives within this paradigm – along the lines of employer strategies to tie employee involvement and welfare to effective production and service delivery systems (Applebaum and Batt, 1994) – are criticized as evidence suggests that the social side of these developments are legitimation devices for further exploitation (Richardson *et al.*, 2004).

Added to these physical pressures is the cultural and psychological impact of flexibility, even if some claim that there is no clear evidence of a systematic move towards long-term job insecurity (Doogan, 2001). There is a 'manufactured uncertainty' created by the exposure of individuals to the rhetoric of market forces and corporate mergers, demergers and takeovers, and the decline of state social support systems. So *talk* of job insecurity has as great an effect as the *reality* of it. Guest (2000) considers whether the blame for such developments can be placed on the shoulders of management. Many of the changes discussed above may emerge from the failure of management to cope with structural pressures within the product and labour markets, which have become much more volatile. Lowe (1993), in a study of line management/supervision, points to the problem of increasing workloads, the impact of performance measurement and the way in which failure to coordinate change has impacted on supervisors and middle managers. Management has been as much a focus of restructuring as any other constituent (Lowe, 1993; Worall *et al.*, 2000). So there is a need for a more nuanced and critical approach to change, and for analyses based on a clearer observation of what is actually happening in the sphere of employment:

> [T]he dangers of developing a stylized account of the changing world of work by appealing to simple dualisms, such as the old (industrial) and the new (knowledge-intensive) economies, are transparent. Complexity, unevenness and the enduring features in the structure and relations of employment are crowded out by visions of universal paradigm shifts. (Nolan and Wood, 2003, p. 173)

This is echoed by Thompson (2003) who argues that there are contingencies and problem of 'connectedness' in terms of the current 'disconnected capitalism'.

### The arrival of a new order

In the 1990s there was a new wave of arguments that drew heavily from the concepts and futurism of Post-Fordist scholars, with the changes facing societies and workers being located in an unfolding social context based on fragmentation and disorder. A number of scholars have begun to talk in terms of risk. At the heart of this approach is the belief that the changing nature of labour markets, the degree of economic uncertainty and the ongoing social effects of destandardization and social disembedding means that the individual has to internalize risk:

> [T]he exhaustion, dissolution and disenchantment of collective and ground-specific sources of meaning (such as belief in progress, class consciousness) of the culture of industrial society (whose lifestyles and ideas of security have also been fundamental to the Western democracies and economic societies until well into the twentieth century) leads to all the work of definition henceforth being expected or imposed on individuals themselves. (Beck, 1996, p. 29)

Individuals must take on some of the broader roles of social regulation in terms of individual negotiation, financial planning and support (for example personal pensions), and social action (through reflexive behaviour in civil society and in respect of consumption). Yet within this academic approach the role of collective agencies is unclear. Ironically this failure to conceptualize collective agency also applies to the work of Castells (1996), who has built on the 1980s' notions of change by focusing on its spatial and virtual dimensions. It has served as a central interpretation of the way in which the new information economy has established new types of social relation based on complex relationships and socioeconomic synergies. At the heart of this development is the network – the new archetypal feature of work and social relations.

While the individual and his or her existential crisis is central to Beck's (1996) analysis, for Castells (1996) the relations themselves are the conduit for regulation. And within this new context the impact on workers is in great part similar to those discussed in the arguments of various Post-Fordists. Castells dualizes work in a similar way to the ideas of Atkinson and the Post-Fordist view of labour market segmentation. Castells notes that there are victims of the new economy, but their fate is out of their hands in a world of privileged networks with dominant nodes and hierarchies. These two schools of thought (on the risk society and the network society) have also been central to new variants of social democracy that are market oriented, intellectually driven by entrepreneurial values and that focus on individual responsibility (Findlayson, 2003).

These approaches are similar to those of Post-Fordism in terms of their fondness for functionalism (Bonefeld, 1987). It is not clear where agency fits in the Post-Fordist view. What are the capacities of individuals and groups of individuals in the new world being described? The ability to respond to and influence change appears to be a marginal consideration. This is understandable given the crisis of theories on social change and of discourses on social engagement, but the new approaches recreate a new economic reductionism in terms of market change and organizational mutation into networks. The individual is exogenous to and a passive recipient of these changes, being viewed as devoid of history and memory. There is another problem which emerges, therefore: the role of conflict around new and ongoing issues is rarely central to the discussion.

These problems are partly due to the fact that one of the main contributions of Post-Fordism is ignored – that is, the manner in which different social and economic activities and relations that were once tied together by regulations and intervention have become uncoupled and incongruent. Any attempt to analyze change, conflict and contradictions in society should start with the view that change is multilayered and that changes in one layer or relation provide a new set of challenges and constraints for another. The contributors to this book investigate the ironic twists that occur during the formation of the 'new', the manner in which organizational responses reassert traditional bureaucratic values, and the fact that there are tensions and instability in the discursive and practical changes taking place. New forms of conflict are indeed emerging to challenge the normative and material basis of change. In the Post-Fordist view of the world the boundaries between production and consumption, between state and civil society and between organizational levels (in firms and unions for example) are dissolving, but there are new tensions arising from the manner in which these boundaries are being rearranged (Martínez Lucio and MacKenzie, 2004; Mackenzie and Martínez Lucio 2004, 2005). This book studies these tensions from four standpoints: (1) the labour market and organizations; (2) the role of the state as a labour market player and employer; (3) changing gender relations, family structures and consumption patterns; and (4) the impact on labour organizations and collectivism.

## The structure of the book

In chapter 2 Luis Enrique Alonso examines Post-Fordism and argues that, for all the changes it has wrought on traditional forms of regulation, it can be viewed 'as a fragile, contradictory model of regulation that still requires a large degree of Fordist-type production, control and consumption'. The Fordist model, in terms of the mass production of standardized products and a mass consumption norm, is still pertinent to current lifestyles regardless of the changes so often referred. This has created instability and contradictions in capitalist relations.

The contributions in Part I focus on the labour market and organizations. The decentralization and fragmentation of labour markets and firms has received considerable attention, although there has been a failure to appreciate the complex dynamics underpinning the development of organizations and the organization of employment in terms of the divergent paths taken by organizations in different national contexts (Rubery and

Grimshaw, 2003), even if the extent of such changes has been well documented (Pollert, 1988).

In Chapter 3 José Manuel Lasierra argues that there has been a profound reorganization of production in Europe, driven by a variety of technical, organizational, economic and sociopolitical factors. He describes how firms have utilized various types of contract to undermine the traditional terms of employment, based on a minimalist and contractualist vision that fails to understand the broader capacities and creativity of labour. He considers flexible working practices from a Spanish perspective and points out that the new production regime rests on a short-term, instrumental view of labour. This is further developed in Chapter 4, where Carlos Prieto challenges the normative basis of the new flexible forms of working. Underpinning this development is the shift from a salary-based employment relation, founded on social norms and social concerns, to a business-oriented notion of employment. Employment practices have been realigned in economic, social and political terms to the immediate requirements of the market. Both chapters therefore highlight the political readjustment of employment and not just its economic transformation, and the fundamental tensions that emerge subsequently.

This shift in employment relations has not been accompanied by corporate decentralization. In Chapter 5 Robert MacKenzie and Chris Forde point out that the use of subcontractors and staff from temporary employment agencies, as two pillars of Post-Fordist employment, indicates the absence of decentralization. On the contrary firms have been further bureaucratized through highly structured subcontracting and monitoring arrangements. Meanwhile temporary employment agencies have developed from facilitators to large employers and labour market coordinators in their own right. The supposed re-emergence of the small firm and decentralized employer networks is challenged by these authors, who also question the belief that flexible employment, for example in the form of short-term employment contracts, is merely a reflection of uncertain product markets.

Part III addresses the role of the state in employment. In Chapter 6 Daniel Albarracín provides a detailed account of developments in Europe in this regard. Regulation is increasingly subject to two pressures. The first is the neoliberal attempt—in the interest of flexible employment—to limit direct state intervention in employment relations and social practices in the workplace. The second pressure arises from the EU's inability to develop a model of regulation that is both effective and consistent. According to Ian Greenwood and Mark Stuart (Chapter 7), neoliberalism in the EU is determining not just broad economic policy but also labour market policy. An obsession with cost containment and productivity based on wage controls appears to be a feature of EU rhetoric. The EU employment strategy has infused labour market policy with a supply-side orientation that transfers responsibility for training and learning to an increasingly individualized workforce. Policies are aimed at equipping individuals with the skills and knowledge required to make them more flexible and ensure that the concept of flexibility prevails over social considerations. Increasingly discernible in this strategy is the view that voluntary arrangements between employers and workers are the preferred vehicle for workplace developments.

The concept of flexibility is also evident in the restructuring of state administration. However in Chapter 8 Ian Kirkpatrick points to the need for caution when discussing the role of the state due to the complexity of its development within the EU. Using the UK as an example, Kirkpatrick shows that the state is increasingly using its roles as purchaser, auditor and monitor to rein back decentralization. This mirrors the claim made in Chapter 5 by MacKenzie and Forde that the firm is not shedding its bureaucratic identity, rather it is taking measures to ensure the effectiveness of its bureaucracy. Hence the state and the firm are not passive subjects of the pressures exerted by the new product and labour markets, but are modernizing their bureaucracies and utilizing labour in quite strategic ways. Deliberate action and strategy remain a part of the story of labour markets and their administration.

Part IV considers the social dimensions of labour market changes. The political realignment of labour market regulation may seem to be reinforcing the move towards a more individualized society, but it may also indicate two other developments. First, the extent of social change may challenge the norms and effectiveness of regulation and new forms of firm and state behaviour because workers and consumers have become more reliant on paid employment for social protection. Second, workers and consumers may in fact be integrated into the new employment or consumption processes through the use of traditional, modern and even premodern processes and identities. These developments could be a source of instability and conflict within the new regimes of work.

Jean Gardiner and Miguel Martínez Lucio (Chapter 9) discuss labour market change in terms of gender relations. Whilst women constitute a growing proportion of the workforce their inclusion in the labour market remains partial and uneven. They find themselves on the edge of the labour market and underrepresented in an age of flexibility and change. In certain cases the jobs women are offered reflect an outdated understanding of their roles: hence employment practices still rest fundamentally on 'gender-typing'. This problem is exacerbated by changes to the traditional family structure. In Chapter 11 Gerardo Meil Llandwerlin points to the decline of the family and the lack of support for children by welfare regimes that are increasingly ill-equipped to cater to fragmented family units. The tensions and social problems this has generated have become a focus of political concern, even if in countries such as the UK and Spain it has not always led to an expansive social policy. Child poverty remains a widespread problem and working women who have family responsibilities are experiencing new forms of discrimination.

In Chapter 10 Luis Enrique Alonso considers social developments in the area of consumption. At the heart of Post-Fordist analysis is the notion that consumption has moved beyond the bounds of mass production. As in employment and society, the product market has undergone fragmentation, specialization and differentiation. However this is based on a marketized view of the individual, for whom the purpose of consumption is to gratify immediate needs. Therefore consumption is 'desperate', void of any rational calculation and it is short term.

These social shifts are not easily associated with a new individualization. Paul Stewart (Chapter 12) views such changes from the point of view of collective conflict and collective subjects at work. The notion that workplace conflict has been replaced by the more minimalist notion of 'organizational misbehaviour' is questionable in Stewart's view. He rejects the claim that methodological individualism and individual identity are the keys to understanding the ontological nature of individual motivation and action, and asserts that individual identity cannot be viewed as autonomous from the conditions of the labour process, both internally and more broadly in the wider political economy. A 'new politics of production' is emerging, based on work intensification versus quality of life at work, company-sponsored collectivism versus employee disaffection, and employee/individual responsibility versus collectivism in everyday life. In Chapter 13 Miguel Martínez Lucio echoes this in the case of trade unions. The latter have been written out of the Post-Fordist script, being seen as old social movements and at best only relevant when adopting enterprise–union identities. Martínez Lucio focuses on different features of trade union decline and argues that these do not constitute absolute challenges to the labour movement but relative challenges to the boundaries of its traditional activities. Seen from this perspective, the shifts in work and consumption in terms of the workplace, its social context, and relations with management, for example, do not make the labour movement irrelevant. Instead there is a possibility of a new politics of labour that will link these spheres together in novel ways. Such links will depend on a new vision from labour interms of principles and social agendas. What is being challenged is the model of labour regulation, not labour regulation *per se*. Hence, Richard Hyman's final chapter raises issues regarding what this means in terms of European regulation and the political logic and approach required for a progressive social Europe.

In this book change is found to be inextricably linked to conflict and instability. There is no new age of individuality and flexibility, but an unstable system of production and consumption that serves to constrain social enhancement and a richer form of citizenship. The chapters highlight the social costs of this in terms of skill formation, experiences of social life, dignity at work and social consumption. In many respects flexibility is political. It is driven as much by ideological and political motives as by structural and economic considerations. It has been constructed, and in this respect it is creating a new politics of work, employment and consumption that will test the view of change and inevitability in Post-Fordist interventions and managerialist interpretations. As Daly (1991) puts it, the decline of an organized economic and political space does not mean that there is no need for intervention and countermobilization which in turn will reflect the contradiction and tensions within changes. What we appear to be witnessing is an age of disorganized debate, politics and counter, mobilization. These do not carry clearly articulated utopias, but they do alert us to the reality that there are contradictions even in these most difficult moments of social and economic existence. Perhaps the answers rest in a study not of Fordism, modernity, and Keynesian welfare regimes, but of earlier times when individuals were subject to the fundamental contradictions of social and economic life under capitalism and developed ethical and social values to make sense of their lives and aspirations. The contradictory and problematic aspects of the new developments in work and employment can only be understood if they are discussed alongside the relevant regulatory, social and political factors. When they are, it becomes clear that we may be moving away from Fordism but we are far from the point at which economic progress and social justice are balanced. Moreover, this calls for approaches to the study of change that transcend the boundaries of the way we approach regulation and work. It also echoes O' Donnell's (1993) pioneering insights on Post-Fordisim: we cannot be deflected from ongoing critique by the fatal attraction of believing we can regulate discreet elements of capitalism and competitive relations in isolation of a broader understanding of this socio-economic system.

## References

Aglietta, M. (1979) *A Theory of Capitalist Regulation* (London: New Left Books).
Applebaum, E. and R. Batt (1994) *The New American Workplace* (Ithaca, NY: ILR Press).
Atkinson, J. (1984) 'Manpower strategies for flexible organisation', *Personnel Management*, August, pp. 97–125.
Beck, U. (1996) 'Risk Society and the Provident State', in S. Lash, B. Szerszyhski and B. Wynne (eds), *Risk, Environment and Modernity* (London: Sage).
Bell, D. (1973) *The Coming of Post Industrial Society* (New York: Basic Books).
Bell, D. (1974) *The Cultural Contradictions of Capitalism* (London: Heinemann).
Blyton, P. and M. Martínez Lucio (1995) 'Constructing the Post Fordist State? The Politics of Labour Market Flexibility in Spain', *West European Politics*, 18 (2), pp. 340–60.
Blyton, P. and J. Morris (1992) 'HRM and the Limits of Flexibility', in P. Blyton and P. Turnbull (eds), *Reassessing Human Resource Management* (London: Sage).
Bonefeld, W. (1987) 'Reformulation of State Theory', *Capital and Class*, 33, pp. 96–127.
Bunting, M. (2004) *Willing Slaves* (London: HarperCollins).

Castells, M. (1996) *The Rise of the Network Society* (Oxford: Blackwell).
Daly, G. (1991) 'The Discursive Construction of Economic Space', *Economy and Society*, 20 (1) pp. 79–102.
Doogan, K. (2001) 'Insecurity and Long-term Employment', *Work, Employment and Society* 15 (3), pp. 419–41.
Findlayson, A. (2003) *Making Sense of New Labour* (London: Lawrence and Wishart).
Garrahan, P. and P. Stewart (1992) *The Nissan Enigma* (London: Mansell).
Gorz, A. (1980) *Farewell to the Working Class* (London: Pluto).
Guest, D. (2000) 'Managing the Insecure Workforce', in E. Heery, and J. Salmon (eds), *The Insecure Workforce* (London: Routledge).
Heery, E. and J. Salmon (2000) 'Introduction' in E. Heery, and J. Salmon (eds), *The Insecure Workforce* (London. Routledge).
Hyman, R. (1983) 'Andre Gorz and his Disappearing Proletariat', in R. Miliband and J. Saville (eds), *The Socialist Register 1983* (London: Merlin).
Jenkins, C. and B. Sherman (1979) *The Collapse of Work* (London: Eyre Methuen).
Jessop, B. (1990) *State Theory* (Oxford: Polity Press).
Jessop, B. (2002) *The Future of the Capitalist State* (Oxford: Polity Press).
Lovering, J. (1990) 'A Perfunctory Sort of Post-Fordism: Economic Restructuring and Labour Market Segmentation in Britain', *Work, Employment and Society*, 4 (2), pp. 9–28.
Lowe, J. (1993) 'Manufacturing Reform and the Changing Role of the Production Supervisor', *Journal of Management Studies*, 30 (6), pp. 739–58.
MacKenzie, R. and M. Martínez Lucio (2004) 'The Realities and Diversity of "Re-regulation": Accommodation, Negotiation and Colonisation', paper presented to the conference on Work, Employment and Society, Manchester, September.
MacKenzie, R. and M. Martínez Lucio (2005) 'Accomodation, Negotiation or Colonisation? The realities of regulatory change', *Sociology* 39 (3) 519–37
Martínez Lucio, M. and R. MacKenzie (2004) 'Unstable Boundaries? Evaluating the "New Regulation" within Employment Relations', *Economy and Society*, 33, pp. 77–97.
Martínez Lucio, M., M. Noon and M. Jenkins (2000) 'The Flexible–Rigid Paradox of the Employment Relationship at Royal Mail', *British Journal of Industrial Relations*, June, pp. 277–98.
Nolan, P. and S. Wood (2003) 'Mapping the Future of Work', *British Journal of Industrial Relations*, 41 (2), pp. 165–74.
Noon, M. and P. Blyton (1997) *The Realities of Work* (London: Macmillan).
O'Connor, J. (1973) *The Fiscal Crisis of the State* (New York: St. Martin's Press).
O' Donnell, K. (1993) 'The New Competition: A Review Article', *International Review of Applied Economics*, 7 (1).
Offe, C. (1984) *Contradictions of the Welfare State* (London: Hutchinson).
Paz, O. (1987) *Los Hijos del Limo* (Barcelona: Biblioteca de Bolsillo).
Peck, J. (1996) *Workplace* (New York: Guilford).
Piore, M. and C. Sabel (1984) *The Second Industrial Divide* (New York: Basic Books).
Pollert, A. (1988) 'The "Flexible Firm": Fixation or Fact', *Work, Employment and Society*, 2(3), pp. 281–316.
Procter A. J., M. Rawlinson, L. McCardle, J. Hassard and P. Forrester (1994) 'Flexibility, Politics and Strategy: In Defence of the Model of the Flexible Firm', *Work, Employment and Society*, 8 (2), pp. 221–42.
Recio, A. (1999) 'La Segmentación del Mercado de Trabajo en España', in F. Miguélez and C. Prieto (eds), *Las Relaciones Laborales en España* (Madrid: Siglo Veintiuno).

Richardson, M., P. Stewart, A. Danford, S. Tailby and M. Upchurch (2004) 'Employees' experiences of workplace partnership in the private and public sector', in M. Stuart and Martínez M. Lucio (eds), *Partnership and Modernisation in Employment Relations* (London: Routledge).
Rifkin, J. (1995) *The End of Work* (New York: G. P. Rufman).
Rubery, J. and D. Grimshaw (2003) *The Organisation of Employment* (London: Palgrave).
Ruigrock, W. and R. van Tulder (1995) *The Logic of International Restructuring* (London: Routledge).
Sennett, R. (1998) *The Corrosion of Character* (London: W. W. Norton).
Smith, W. R. (1998) *The Left's Dirty Job: The Politics of Industrial Restructuring* (Pittsburgh: University of Pittsburgh Press).
Stewart, P. (1996) 'Introduction', in P. Stewart (ed.), *Beyond Japanese Management: The End of Modern Times?* (London: Frank Cass).
Thompson, P. (2003). 'Disconnected capitalism: or why employers can't keep their side of the bargain', *Work, Employment and Society*, 17(2), pp. 359–78.
Torfing, J. (1990) 'A Hegemony Approach to Capitalist Regulation', in R. B. Bertramsen, J. P. Thomson and J. Torfing (eds), *State, Economy and Society* (London: Unwin Hyman).
Worall, L., C. Cooper and F. Campbell (2000) 'The New Reality of UK Managers', *Work, Employment and Society*, 14 (4), pp. 647–668

# 2
# Fordism and the Genesis of the Post-Fordist Society: Assessing the Post-Fordist Paradigm

*Luis Enrique Alonso*

> A production model is finally constructed through a largely unintentional process of making policy-products, the organisation of production, and wage relations congruous with the profitability strategy pursued. (Boyer and Freyssenet, 2000, p. 23)

## Introduction

Fordism, the regulation mode[1] that began to be developed at the time of the First World War to meet wartime needs, took root with the growth of the market for durable consumer goods. This required manufacturers to be able to produce a large volume of standard products at considerable speed and relatively low cost, and therefore the technology and organizational principles used in manufacturing had to be remodelled. The solution was provided by F. W. Taylor's 'scientific rationalization and organization of work' and Henry Ford's mass production system (Braverman, 1974; Coriat, 1982; Littler 1982).

Thus capitalist manufacturing was transformed by the gradual implementation of Taylor's 'scientific management', in which the planning of tasks was separated from their execution, work was broken down into its most elementary constituents, and working methods and tools were standardized, based on the principle of finding the 'single best way' of performing a task. All of this was facilitated by Ford's automated assembly line, whereby the standardized parts of standardized products were assembled by workers stationed along the moving assembly line. The workers' activities were organized according to Taylorist time and motion studies, which were aimed at achieving maximum effective movement in the minimum length of time. Strict management control over the work process was accompanied by an attempt to control workers' home lives through mandates on acceptable forms of living and consumption.

## Fordist production

The economic consequences of this production revolution were spectacular. Work productivity increased, output mushroomed, and costs fell, partly because poorly qualified, low-cost workers could be used as the skills needed for production were reduced. In short mass production guaranteed an increase in the total value produced at a lower cost per unit. Thus relatively cheap mass produced goods became widely available. This broke the traditional dichotomy between aristocrat's luxury goods and workers' basic commodities by introducing a large range of everyday goods that were still related to need but were primarily defined by their functional and symbolic characteristics (Gauron and Billaudot, 1987).

According to Freeman *et al.* (1982, pp. 71–2), the assembly line struck a hard blow to the equilibrium of the mercantile structure of the time:

> The decisive step taken by American firms (as a result of competitive pressure within the industry) was to reduce the manufacturing costs of a gasoline motor car by more than 50 per cent in just a few years. The price of the Model T fell from 850 dollars in 1908 to 360 in 1916, sales increased twofold and the market share increased from 10 per cent in 1909 to 60 per cent in 1921, net value profit increases were up to 300 per cent and, thanks to this fact, the United States attained a dominant position in world export markets.

Another dimension of this development was demand. Boosting demand was at the heart of the remodelling of pay systems. When Henry Ford increased his workers' pay to five dollars a day in 1914 he claimed that it was because he wanted all his workers to have the chance to buy the company's Model T. However it has since been shown that Ford's assertion was mere propaganda, and that rather than wanting his workers to be able to afford a car, wages were increased to encourage workers to stay on the assembly lines and endure the dreadful working conditions. Moreover, far from being applied across the board the wage increase was contingent on highly restrictive conditions imposed by management.

Despite this totalitarian paternalism on the part of management (which was reflected in one of the harshest actions against strikes by the American workers' movement, with management hiring professional strikebreakers plus police to inspect factories and workers' settlements), the idea of turning the working class – again in Ford's own words – into a well-off class capable of absorbing the enormous fruits of production indicates the trend to instil wages with a status they had never had in the past. Wages had merely been about remuneration for work, or at best an incentive to improve productivity (the most refined implementation of this philosophy was Taylor's 'differential salary according to parts'). However, wages became something much more complex. They structured not only the immediate realm of production, but also consumption and the reconstruction of the workforce. Both on and off the factory floor Taylor's and Ford's rationalization acted as a powerful catalyst in transformating the working class and its reproduction (Nadworny, 1955; Raff, 1995). This led to a new rudimentary and authoritarian mode of regulation, as vividly described by Antonio Gramsci (1980) at the end of the 1920s. There were factory inspectors, company stores, company communities, direct management control over the reproduction of the workforce and so on. But working conditions were gradually socialized and institutionalized and forms of collective bargaining were established.

Throughout the nineteenth century and well into the twentieth century there was little commodification. Accumulation was incomplete and only came from producing the means of production. Lifestyle was merely contingent, and was not integrated into the mercantile logic. In fact the main function of the consumer was not to ensure the reproduction of the workforce but to enable value to be realized through the export of goods (British textiles is a good example) in exchange for income for the bourgeoisie and petit bourgeoisie. The need to integrate mercantile logic into demand led to the creation of a strong advertising and sales promotion sector that created 'captains of conscience' who were as rich and powerful as the captains of industry. Overcoming the austere puritan resistance to consumption, the proclivity to save and guilt about purchasing non-essentials became the principal mission of the new market research and promotion sector, which consecrated consumerism as the new logic of capitalism.[2]

In order to prepare the economic groundwork for accumulation, capitalist production relations had to penetrate all spheres of life, far beyond the shadowy bounds of the traditional factory. The social reproduction model therefore had to be fitted to the material production model. The construction of this new economic order resulted in workers' movements calling for the radical rationalization and modernization of their working and living conditions. All social spheres previously lying outside capitalist production began to fall within its dynamic. Yet at the same time, they were a product of the social reform of living conditions imbued with the values of a new modernization. Capitalist consumption was also the arena in which various social groups struggled in terms of distribution. This is why the term consumer society has a far more complex, multidimensional meaning.

Encouraging a new lifestyle meant establishing a new relationship between the workforce and the factors that reproduced it. The mass manufacture of consumer goods, the new wage structure and the division of labour laid the groundwork for a new mode of regulation. Through mechanization and rationalization, came a new social existence: factory society, when mechanization took control of social imagery and shaped social struggles.

Under these conditions mercantilism was introduced into all social relations. Consumption was therefore standardized according to the logic stemming from the organization of work, its technical requirements and the production structure it generated. This is what the French economist Michel Aglietta (1979) called the 'worker's consumption social norm', a term he used to describe a new form of consumption based on the mass purchase of traditional subsistence goods (food, clothing and other essential items) and new goods (cars, furniture, household appliances, durable consumer goods and so on) that just a decade earlier had either not existed or had only been available to the well-off. Thus standardized durable consumer goods were made affordable through mass production. It was their symbolic value that mattered most. A dynamic was therefore established whereby aspirations were created and classified. This radical change in lifestyle in the United States during the 1920s gradually made its way to the most prosperous countries of Europe, eventually bringing to an end a period in which insecurity did not allow consumer habits to be established in their own right (Castel, 1995).

On the whole the 'worker's condition' was subject to a process of rationalization. According to the philosopher Simone Weil (1964), this rationalization was imbued with a scientific, Cartesian discourse that concealed profound dehumanization and a lack of interest in anything other than increased productivity, and by extension, increased consumption, which became synonymous with material well-being. However the taste for mechanization that so seduced film-makers, industrial designers, decorative artists, architects, fascist futurists and partisans of proletariat socialist realism ensured that this was the terrain in which the struggle for the political meaning being the ideal of progress and rationality in the working world took place.

This labour order, typical of the period between the two World Wars, soon entered into crisis. Productivity and profitability grew at the same intensity as social narrowness and authoritarianism on the part of management. Strict control by management (of production, of workers' accommodation and of consumption) generated a demand crisis in the Keynesian sense of the term. The democratic and social democratic response in Europe to the crisis of under-consumption in the 1930s, and the purpose of the New Deal in the United States, was to take social reform to the ultimate by institutionalizing national collective bargaining and creating a strong infrastructure for collective consumption (the welfare state). Social reform from the top downwards resulted in the totalitarianism of Nazism and fascism. The ensuing expansion of international capitalism, perhaps the most spectacular in history, was at the root of the resolution of this conflict.

## Fordism's golden age

The decoupling of the production of goods and management of the necessary conditions for workforce reproduction, was a factor, amongst others, that triggered the Great Depression at the end of the 1920s.

The consumption norm therefore had to be re-established in order to enable the reconstruction of the productive order as an expansive way out of the 1929 crash and the war's effects during the early 1940s. This brought about mechanisms based on remodelling preceding economic forces in order to achieve a new balance in accumulation. These regulating mechanisms were the ones that served to turn Fordism from a simple organization of work and industrial relations model (the reflection of a direct, individualized, disciplinary mode of production and consumption) into a globalizing social form dominating the general conditions for creating and distributing value, in other words, for setting wage relations in an institutional context, enlarging the system's production and reproduction.

The front line in the transformation of regulation was the widespread technological reordering of the production system. The destructive and innovative consequences of the second World War produced a wave of technical transformation that would soon be integrated into work organization and the design of consumer objects. Semi-automation, digital control, the first processes in programming, chemical synthesis, and the use of plastics therefore developed the Fordist production model. This also positioned labour as a commodity in another disciplinary code, that of technical 'depersonalization'. This form of control was integrated in technological mechanisms and the direct control processes used over the workforce. Fordism thus found the new social and technical groundwork it needed for its growth and for forming a new generic disciplinary code (Friedman, 1977; Gaudemar, 1982).

This leads us immediately to the second mechanism regulating mass consumption determined by the remodelling of formal aspects of the values of use that were adapted to the needs of economic circulation and accumulation. The automation principle was projected on the form-object, flexibilizing and stepping up the penetration of a new 'machinist' logic into lifestyle. This aspect marked the functional and generalized constitution of a new, expansive consumer structure contrary to the direct, authoritarian forms prevalent during the introductory stage of pioneer Fordism. This generated a host of social dynamics that drove demand for consumer goods and constituted the basic element that stablized a path of growth absorbing subconsumption and stagnation tendencies in the long term. Consumption thus became the product of an industrial/mercantile process based on new technical supports and growing markets sustained by an institutional network that tended to create a model of standardization and uniformization. This became the formula for the growth of the system's economic production and its technical capacity.

Once the early Talyorist and Fordist stage of productive order had begin to decline, consumption entered into the general order of signifiers in which symbolic dimensions tended to envelope and totalize any purchasing practice. Society went from isolated objects to systems of objects, from simple goods to the 'standard package' (the set of indispensable goods in new post-traditional homes), from needs to desires, and from functionality of use to functionality of representation within a social system of aspirations.[3] The constitution of consumer merchandise was no longer solely what was derived from the rationalization of how it was produced. It was the stimulation of demand, and demand increasingly associated with larger and larger chains of complementary purchasing. Generating demand became as necessary as generating supply.

The supply-side productivist rationale that proved to be the last expression for Protestant Puritanism during early Fordism went on to be overtaken by a new hedonistic culture of consumption that was projected on all aspects of life. Reprogramming and enlarging Protestant work culture in order to turn it into a fluent consumerism was both the direct mission of advertising and packaging processes and the indirect function of product design and the entertainment industry. Comfort, aerodynamic design, colour saturated styles, built-in obsolescence, the acceleration of fashions, ongoing styling and the restyling of objects, and the complementarity of all of these dimensions, built an integrated regime of signs, an international style. This was based on private expenditure and an increasingly broad base of both tangible and intangible goods leading to social recognition based on a generalised materialism.

This aesthetics of opulence that served as a framework for the increasing furnishing of durable goods represented, in the symbolic order, the need to fit mass consumption into the specifications of a new model of economic growth (Hoffenberg and Lapidus, 1997). Symbolic oversizing, programmed motivation, the aspiration of being integrated into large groups of social reference by consuming brands and objects validated by a new consumption culture, were all indications that functionality was being radically transformed during this period. Merchandise was of use, but primarily to reproduce general status, to demarcate differentiated social groups and, most of all, to materially develop an immense set of complementary and substitutive types of potential consumption.[4] In this mature, functional Fordism (unlike early, pioneer, authoritarian, and management dominated Fordism) it was the integration of the general social order underpinned by productivity that facilitated individual inclusion into this new social universe of merchandise. Therefore, although luxury goods were maintained and even enhanced (as were situations of social exclusion) it was the discourse of mass consumption goods, the taste of the middle class, and generalized leisure goods or modern life that came to replace the old forms of popular or working-class life.

The intensified working day was therefore complemented with a codified leisure (consumption) day related to the universe of merchandise. Towns and cities were organized in terms of new, large-scale consumer networks: cars and home ownership in turn structured consumption as an ongoing, renewable system of objects. The new Fordist consumer was not the direct outcome of production relations. Instead, with a certain degree of autonomy, it reproduced a general order of (economic, symbolic and cultural) capital and merchandise that reproduced social inequality, but also took up the struggles for the repositioning and redistribution of power. This is how Fordist consumption was constituted as a code for controlling and reproducing status (as well as conditioning and framing conflict). However, by functioning as a *habitus* – a social grammar generating practices (Bourdieu, 1972) – it was also a sphere for struggles over distribution in terms of the attempt to regulate mass consumption in the most advantageous way possible.

This Fordist organization of time, objects, social subjects and working lives, of commercial areas and homes, was rooted in an economic growth regime based on an unequal but real distribution of earnings from productivity between those with incomes and those with profits from capital. Distribution was codified by a social state in terms of policies based on stable purchasing and the framework of wage relations. This synthesis between wage relations and standardized purchasing also emerged through a new type of consumption based both on traditional objects, and the works and objects designed by the *avant-garde* to generate a new style for the professional class which was constituted as a contrast to the triumph of mass consumption. Cultural and artistic consumption became distinctive insignias of the emerging urban professional classes that assimilated their differential taste with the construction of a new, modern style lying outside serial produced objects.

In Fordist 'organized' capitalism, state intervention was fundamental in terms of a public element of social citizenship being added to the private dimension of the Fordist producer/consumer.[5] This social citizenship underpinned and collectively developed wage relations. During this period, state intervention was therefore a direct mechanism (a 'producer of social relations') of this model of economic development. It was within the realm of the state that conflicts deriving from struggles for distribution were partially and unequally integrated, and it was also in this same realm that social consumption, indispensable for maintaining mass consumption, was generated. We therefore find ourselves with an ensemble of regulation mechanisms clustered around the state management of the workforce. This management was not without contradictions. While indispensable in the development of productive forces and in ensuring both the conditions of production and the realization of value, it could not be properly absorbed and supported by individual capitals since their structural position was that of the constant quest to maximize profits within a competition scenario (Offe, 1990, 1992).

In this complex set of regulatory instruments and policies two major types of state intervention linked to the consumption norm could be found. The legal systems enabled controlled integration of workers' wage claims into the state's economic management apparatus (income policy, collective bargaining, social pacts and so on). This turned aspects of trade union activity into complements for rationalizing the contemporary economy, because they acted along the lines set out by the social expansion of capital itself and took care of reaching agreements on the price of the workforce that could ensure the realization of value. Second indirect wages, which came on the scene as citizenship's social rights and as a response to labour's claims for positive liberties, were, at the same time, seen as the way to materially socialize the collective basis for private consumption. We therefore find a network of social consumption that organized, socialized and codified the costs of the reproduction of the workforce.

These costs basically developed in two different directions. First there were infrastructure costs for the settlement, education, and mobility of labour (housing, schooling, qualification, urban remodelling, public transportation, communications, and so forth). Second, there were programmes aimed at protection from economic insecurity through the collective management of risk (unemployment, disability, old age and retirement insurance, and so on) with the added effect of eradicating the excess elements of working-class poverty. In both of these cases, at that point in history, these indirect wages and forms of social consumption became part of the mass consumption that developed during postwar capitalism (Giraud, 1996). (They became its complements and even a basis for its organization.)

This importance of a decommodifying state in the organization of consumption went far beyond the supply of non-individualized goods, which did not directly clash with the regime of the profitable production of private merchandise. The decommodifying state was the 'social organizer' of lifestyles that enabled the materialization of the working class as a structural force. This made the postwar regulation model one whose role fostering workforce reproduction was public and nationally oriented. Commercially speaking, the Keynesian order was therefore multinational and highly integrated on a worldwide scale, but institutionally speaking, its social regulation was played out at the state/nation level. The world economy was forged during this golden age of Fordism and based on a new configuration economically led by the United States (since the First World War when it displaced the British imperial order typical of the nineteenth century) and ideologically driven by it as well in terms of culture and lifestyle, the American way of life.

## The crisis of Fordism

Postwar growth and the associated consumer boom deteriorated and faced a crisis during the 1970s. It has been noted that each decade has its general characteristics conferring it with a specific meaning. While the 1950s for instance was a period of boundless growth and the 1960s became known as the 'prodigious decade', the 1970s has gone down in history as the decade of 'crisis'. And indeed, it would be difficult to find another period in time in which the feeling of crisis applied to the broadest and most diverse realms of social existence. The 1970s was the decade of the 'economic crisis', the 'energy crisis', the 'urban crisis' and the 'citizenship crisis', to name just a few. But these crises even took on absolute dimensions when they were encompassed by the 'ecology crisis' or the 'crisis of civilization' itself. To a great extent, the force with which these crises pervaded lifestyles as of the mid and late 1970s, turning the consumption crisis into crisis consumption, was nearly perfectly mirrored by the spectacular drive of the economy during the preceding decades which witnessed the greatest economic boom in universal history and which gave an increasing number of workers access to an increasing number of durable consumer goods. As Arendt (1985) stated, the crisis as an indefinable gap, that nevertheless exists between the past and the future, changed and reorganized the subjectivity of social actors. It led to the transformation of the ways in which work processes and forms of consumption were articulated leading to social dynamics that contributed a different mode of regulation.

During this period, the crisis played the role both of expressing limitations and reorganizing the function performed by each factor in the geographical, social and sectorial configuration of the world economy. It can be said that it was in these periods of crisis that the trends for articulating a new structure of production/consumption begin to materialize. We therefore saw a redeployment of different industrial sectors that came to replace one another to form dominant models of production and substantially modify salary relations. The chronology of these adjustments and the replacement of prevailing technological and industrial sectors is well known: from 1815 to 1840 the steam engine and the loom, from 1850 to 1870, the railroad and steel industry, from 1890 to 1914, electricity, oil and the internal combustion engine, and finally, from 1945 to 1973, the manufacturing of durable consumer goods, semi-automated industries and the functional urban planning that came hand in hand with this process. The preponderance of industrial consumer goods in this cycle beginning during the Second World War lead many authors to speak of a 'consumer capitalism,' as compared with traditional nineteenth and early twentieth century production capitalism, that became depleted and saturated during the 1970s. In order to overcome this saturation, the development of a computerized robotic productive model was gestating along with a set of new forms of social regulation (or deregulation) mechanisms (Arrighi, 1999).

This depletion was not only a technological issue. It also marked the disorganization of a social process and a work process (wage relations process) involving mass consumption and the welfare state itself. The structure of labour costs made the linear organization of work rooted in Taylorism unsustainable. The structural strength of the working classes reduced industrial capital's expectations of oversized profits while the mechanical organization of production was unable to continue to sustain growth in productivity since it hit up against physical and mercantile limits to the profitable use of the workforce. The model also showed alarming signs of depletion on the demand side. Markets in objects became fragmented and saturated. The long uniform series of products became commercially unviable just as the social representation of middle class status was constrained and the *homo democraticus* as a consumer ceased to be profitable. The highly unified organization of markets and the depletion of the ways of presenting average products to passive consumers proved unlikely to be efficient at bringing about expansion. It was therefore the industrial model on the whole which, over the 1970s, was unable to generate growth and profitability rates similar to those of the earlier years *any longer*. This was also driven by a deceleration in the growth of labour's direct productivity.

Taylorism and Fordism's technical, political and social limits in ensuring profitable reproduction in the most advanced markets could not be concealed. Runaway inflation coupled with stagnation during the 1970s was already clear proof of the limits in Fordist regulation. Real productivity stagnated, the inflation of demand politics became grotesquely distorted and the defensive reaction of various groups in the form of struggles for distribution spectacularly distorted the mass consumer norm that, in its traditional form, now proved to be insufficient to support the reproduction of the workforce. The consumption norm, in its Fordist, industrialist configuration, became one of the major political areas of struggle for the social appropriation of surplus. Moreover, this occurred in both private consumption and social consumption, the first mechanisms to show their structural weakness in this context.[6]

One can therefore actually speak of a true weakening of the Keynesian state since its role as a regulator of imbalances between production and consumption began to be undermined. The political system's mechanisms therefore lost their ability to adjust to economic imbalances, instead state action appear to generate the contrary of what they would have needed to. They conveyed, extended and expanded the struggles for redistribution. The outstanding role that the public sector had played in advanced capitalist countries both in socializing the foundations (and the cost) of production (by generating industrial infrastructure, supplying collective consumption, financing technological development, and so on), and in upholding the welfare consensus began to face a variety of objective limitations. First, there were limits brought by the scale of the state. The social forces that had driven growth had ended up generating an enormous public sector that clashed with private accumulation. Second, there were *financial* limits that manifested themselves in a structural fiscal crisis in which the difficulties in increasing income clashed with trends towards excessive expenditure generated by attempts to resolve and internalize conflicts in distribution, and this triggered the acceleration of inflationary pressure. Third, there were *political* limits and limits in terms of *governability*, since the structure of corporate representation became too distributive and, according to neoconservative thought, the state itself became too democratic as it took up the demands and the needs of a variety of groups, social movements and citizens' institutions that had not been validated by the competitive party democratic system. Fourth, there were limits to *efficiency* given that the Keynesian welfare state typically intervened in a rational-legal way in the Weberian sense of the term, and this implicitly almost always leads to bureaucratization which is systematically internalised by the state and de-stabilized. The volume of demands thus grew exponentially while the financial and organizational possibilities did not keep up with this pace. Meanwhile, a large portion of resources was allocated to generating new agencies with an enormous bureaucratic weight that deepened the crisis in the intervention model instead of solving it.

## Conclusion

During the 1970s and early 1980s the mechanisms regulating industrialist Fordism were undermined. Neither the articulation of production and consumption nor the stabilizing, decommodification measures taken by interventionist neocapitalism could ensure possibilities for profitable growth. *Stagflation* was a sign that the regulatory model had reached its limits and that by shifting the problems of private capital accumulation over to the public sector, the public sector ended up succumbing to a disorganization. It was also just at this time when the transition towards a new mode of regulation articulating geographical, technological, social and other mechanisms (as yet unknown) began to forge a new post-Fordist model for regulation.[7] The model being implemented was less 'brilliant' than what its postmodern apologists began to tout, and it was not free of unconcealable social costs either.

As a mode of regulation, Fordism was able to build a mass consumer norm congruous with standardized mercantile production. This norm worked as a partially and unstable, yet effective, way to solve the conflict in distribution originating in the labour process. However, to present this mass consumption norm specifically, or the Fordist mode of regulation on the whole, as a closed, harmonic or idyllic process would be to belittle the historical manner of its formulation, development and functioning as a surplus distribution system as it created a relatively organized framework for struggles for the distribution of material wealth and for their symbolic expression, even if this model neither eliminated the basic social contradictions (the conflict between capital and labour), nor ceased to generate other added contradictions (the ecological conflict, the confrontation between the public and private spheres). Nor was it too effective in acknowledging conflicts of a broader nature, such as gender conflicts, generational conflicts, or ethnic conflicts, all previously hidden and subjugated to the constitution of a central model of citizen (a male, industrial, older, benefit-accruing, Fordist consumer with a dependent family).

Just as Fordism was not seamless and contradiction-free in adjusting production and consumption, so so-called Post-Fordism is not behaving as a clear leap beyond the Fordist model with its de-materialization of the economy and society's hypersymbolism. The picture is rather one of fragmentation, differentiation and deinstitutionalization of the *uses* to which the workforce is put, with a parallel process of fragmentation, segmentation and in many cases systematic degradation of consumer models and lifestyles which are taken to the very limit of a new, institutionalized social insecurity (Castel, 2003). Changes in geographical scale, technological fetishism and the furthering of commodification mechanisms (what we euphemistically call globalization) in the production and the accumulation processes have over-run in the areas of regulation and lifestyle.

Post-Fordisim, it might be said, is therefore a fragile, contradictory model of regulation that still requires a large degree of Fordist-type production, control and consumption to generate a social foundation for segments of highly information-intensive production and services, technological design, and financial availability associated with the emerging lifestyle of the new cosmopolitan 'classes'. Increasingly, significant segments of social exclusion remaining outside the increasingly demanding code of normality in production have also come on the scene. The Fordist foundation, that is, the production of large, standardized series with an adjusted mass consumption norm, is still the major material basis of current lifestyles. But the new mechanisms flexibilizing the production process in geographical, technological, social and legal terms have generated a diverging contemporary social structure consisting of consumption strategies with highly fragmented social meanings

## Notes

1. Here 'regulation mode' or 'mode of regulation' refers to the ensemble of regulatory schemes and social conventions that socially reproduce the preconditions for the production of goods and the accumulation of capital. Aglietta's (1979) pioneering work established this concept as the core explanatory model of capitalist

growth and production, and there after the regulation school became one of the main generators of social theories, with concepts such as Fordism and Post-Fordism deriving from it. See Brenner and Glick (1991) Boyer and Saillard (1994), Sebaï and Vercellone (1994) and Jessop (2001).
2. During the 1920s there was an organized campaign to put an end to the Protestant savings ethic. At the same time as strikebreakers and thugs were waging a harsh attack on American workers a new 'economic gospel of consumption' was proclaimed in American business circles in an attempt to equate consumption with patriotism. The aim, in order to feed the new economic machine, was to create a new narcissistic, individualistic anti-thrift culture to replace the old protestant determinism. This social and psychological aspect of the transformation of consumption and its consequences are analyzed by Lasch (1984), Cross (1993) and Wernick (2000).
3. Various classical views of the consumption society are presented in Aldridge (2003).
4. The issue of new systemic functionality and generally the functionality of consumption and its structuring as a complete, complex social language going beyond mere productivist instrumentalism is the classical approach of the structuralist authors. See for instance Baudrillard (1969, 1993), or for a critical view, Pretecelle and Terrail (1988).
5. We must still cite T. H. Marshall's classical theorization (see Marshall and Bottomore, 1992) about citizenship. This consideration has been taken up in several controversial works summarized by Steenbergen (1994) and Faulks (2000). In Alonso (1999) an in-depth study is presented on the relations between Marshallian and Fordist social citizenship.
6. The crisis in the Keynesian cycle as well as the crisis in the articulation between its model of production, monetary system and territorial framework can be read in Vergopoulos (2002) and Gauron (2002).
7. For a general view of this subject see Amin (1994) and Boyer and Durand (1998). For the relationship between production and the development of postmodern culture see Harvey (1989) and Alonso (2001).

## References

Aglietta, M. (1979) *Regulación y crisis del capitalismo. La experiencia de Estados Unidos* (Madrid and Mexico: Siglo XXI).
Aldridge, A. (2003) *Consumption* (Cambridge: Polity Press).
Alonso, L. E. (1999) *Trabajo y ciudadanía. Estudios sobre la crisis de la sociedad salarial* (Madrid: Trotta).
Alonso, L. E. (2001) *Trabajo y posmodernidad. El empleo débil* (Madrid: Fundamentos).
Amin, A. (ed.) (1994) *Post-fordism. A Reader* (Oxford: Blackwell).
Arendt, H. (1985) *Between Past and Future. Eight Exercises in Political Thought* (Harmondsworth: Penguin).
Arrighi, G. (1999) *El largo siglo XX* (Madrid: Akal).
Baudrillard, J. (1969) *El sistema de los objetos* (Madrid: Siglo XXI).
Baudrillard, J. (1974) *La sociedad de consumo* (Barcelona: Plaza y Janés).
Bourdieu, P. (1972) *Esquisse d'une théorié de la pratique* (Geneva: Droz).
Boyer, R. and J.-P. Durand (1998) *L'Après-fordisme* (Paris: Syros).
Boyer, R. and M. Freyssenet (2000) *Les modèles productifs* (Paris: La Découverte).
Boyer, R. and D. Saillard (eds.) (1994) *Théorie de la regulation. L'état de Savoirs* (Paris: La Découverte).
Braverman, H. (1974) *Labor and Monopoly Capital* (New York: Monthly Review Press).

Brenner, R. and M. Glick (1991) 'The Regulation School: Theory and History', *New Left Review*, 188, pp. 5–90.
Castel, R. (1995) *Las Metamorphoses de la question sociale* (Paris: Fayard).
Castel, R. (2003) *L'insecurité sociale* (Paris: Seuil).
Coriat, B. (1982) *El taller y el cronómetro. Ensayo sobre el taylorismo, el fordismo y la producción en masa* (Madrid: Siglo XXI).
Cross, G. (1993) *Time and Money. The Making of Consumer Culture* (London: Routledge).
Faulks, K. (2000) *Citizenship* (London: Routledge).
Freeman, C., J. Clark and L. Soete (1982) *Unemployment and Technical Innovation* (London: Frances Pinter).
Friedman, A. L. (1977) *Industry and Labour* (London: Macmillan).
Gaudemar, J.-P. de (1982) *L'ordre et la production. Naissance et forme de la discipline de usine* (Paris: Dunod).
Gauron, A. (2002) *L'empire de l'argent* (Paris: Descléé de Brouwer).
Gauron, A. and B. Billaudot (1987) *Crecimiento y crisis* (Madrid: Siglo XXI).
Giraud, P.-N. (1996) *L'inegalité du monde* (Paris: Gallimard).
Gramsci, A. (1980) 'Americanismo y fordismo', in *Notas sobre Masquiavelo, sobre la política y sobre el Estado moderno* (Buenos Aires: Nueva Visión).
Harvey, D. (1989) *The Condition of Postmodernity* (Oxford: Blackwell).
Hoffenberg, A. and A. Lapidus (1977) *La société du design* (Paris: PUF).
Jessop, B. (2001) *Regulation Theory and the Crisis of Capitalism,* 5 vols (Cheltenham: Edward Elgar).
Lasch, C. (1984) *The Minimal Self* (New York: W. W. Norton).
Littler, C. R. (1982) *The Development of the Labour Process in Capitalist Societies* (London: Heinemann).
Marshall, T. H. and T. Bottomore (1992) *Citizenship and Social Class* (London: Pluto).
Mumford, L. (1969) *El mito de la máquina* (Buenos Aires: Emecé).
Mumford, L. (1971) *Técnica y civilización* (Madrid: Alianza).
Nadworny, M. (1955) *Scientific Management and the Unions (1900–1932)* (Cambridge, Mass.: Harvard University Press).
Offe, C. (1990) *Contradicciones del Estado del Bienestar* (Madrid: Alianza).
Offe, C. (1992) *La sociedad del trabajo. Problemas estructurales y perspectivas del futuro* (Madrid: Alianza).
Preteceille, E. and J.-P. Terrail (1985) *Capitalism, Consumption and Needs* (Oxford: Blackwell).
Raff, D. M. (1995) *Buying the Peace: Wage Determination Theory, Mass Production, and the Five-Dollar Day at Ford* (Chicago, Ill.: University of Chicago Press).
Sebaï, F. and C. Vercellone (eds) (1994) *École de la régulation et critique de la raison économique* (Paris: L'Harmattan).
Steenbergen, B. van (ed.) (1994) *The Condition of Citizenship* (London: Sage).
Vergopoulos, K. (2002) *Mondialisation. La fin d'un cycle* (Paris: Séguier).
Weil, S. (1964) *La condition ouvrière* (Paris: Gallimard/Idées).
Wernick, A. (2000) 'The Promotional Condition of Contemporary Culture', in M. J. Lee, *The Consumer Society Reader* (Oxford: Basil Blackwell), pp. 300–18.

# Part II
# The Labour Market

# 3
# Flexible Enterprises: An Analysis of their Institutional Standing

*José Manuel Lasierra*

## Introduction

During the last quarter of the twentieth century, most developed countries suffered from the effects of widespread unemployment in the wake of what came to be known as the golden age of the world economy. During this period economic growth went hand in hand with high levels of unemployment, contained inflation rates and public policies that provided strong safety nets against economic uncertainty for society as a whole.

Analyzing labour transformation over the last quarter of a century cannot be done without taking into account the ensemble of factors deriving from that economic and social situation. In other words the economic dimension of production change is a salient aspect of the configuration of new labour relations, and the role played by technological innovations and social changes must also be examined. These issues are analyzed in the second section of this chapter. The third section considers the relationship between transformations in production and labour fragmentation, and discusses the models used and the general reasons for their adoption. The fourth section provides a brief empirical analysis of the different jobs linked to flexible enterprise, and the fifth analyzes the impact of labour fragmentation on labour relations and other aspects of the job market. The chapter ends with some brief conclusions.

## Factors for change in production: revision at the end of a cycle

### Unemployment

The large and persistent imbalance in the labour market following the energy crisis in the mid 1970s explains to a great extent the transformation of labour relations. Institutional factors affected labour's capacity and strength to determine the quality, quantity and price of labour, particularly in the long term, and market forces worked to worsen working conditions and salaries by generally reducing workers' capacity to negotiate and defend their interests. It might be thought that once the labour markets returned to full employment, labour relations in certain countries with full employment would return to the former model, but this has not occurred.

## The restructuring of production

The restructuring of production has resulted not only from economic pressure on the supply side, with greater competition in terms of the number of competitors and the type of competition, but also from pressures on the demand side, with international product marketing requiring increased standardization and, paradoxically, the rapid and flexible production of more customized products in smaller batches for smaller groups of consumers.

The restructuring of production has been principally, although not exclusively, based on technology. Organizational and technological innovations have significantly changed the way in which companies organize production. The industrial relations implications of this can be seen in changes in skills, relations between companies and their employees, the organization of work and the disappearance of boundaries in companies (Campbell, 1996).

Finally, the size of the tertiary economy has grown considerably over the decades, therefore any study of the job market and the reorganization of production should take account of the enormous quantitative and qualitative dimensions of the service sector. Some of this sector's traits differ from those of the industrial sector. First, the ratio between work and output is higher than in the industrial sector in terms of total labour costs and in terms of contribution to the final product. Second, the difficulty of measuring inputs and outputs means that the possibility of control and supervision is less than in the industrial production process. Third, the variety of activities in the service sector translates into a clear dualization of labour, materializing in repetitive activities with little added value versus highly skilled activities with high added value. In turn, the service sector as a whole has a high rate of female work as well as atypical or non-standard and contingent work. Both these factors have lowered the rates of union membership and the possibility of collective action.

## Social changes

Various dimensions of social change can be observed. First, there has been a considerable increase in the proportion of women joining the job market and occupying various jobs and job categories. The proportion of women in part-time work is particularly significant (Cully et al., 1999). There have also been many cultural changes, leading to new lifestyles, higher levels of education and the rise of individual over collective values. Finally, there have been social and political changes *vis-à-vis* the welfare state and the state's role in the economy. In practice states have lessened their intervention by reducing the public goods and services they provide. The deregulation of labour relations and the privatization process have weakened both the public sphere and collective values. These developments have set the groundwork for production changes that might be seen as a new industrial revolution.

Concurrent with the above, there has been a significant transformation of the postwar industrial relations system, which as Cappelli (2001) highlights, lasted little longer than a generation, despite the fact that its deeply rooted values and underlying institutions as well as the interests it served suggested that it would endure and bring progress along the lines prescribed by historical materialism.

### The first push: the market in the world of labour

In 1981, when France saw the difficulty of applying traditional Keynesian policies, it attempted to redress the imbalance in the labour market by reducing the part played by labour institutions, mainly through state regulation, unions and collective bargaining. Various shades of behaviour in terms of priorities set, insistence and tone could be observed in different national labour institutions. While few governments followed the ultraliberal response to the problem adopted by Thatcher in the United Kingdom (Hyman, 1994), this does not mean that antiliberal measures were accepted by unions, as evidenced in Spain in 1988, when a general strike paralyzed the country. Governments' political actions were certainly not a minor influence on the configuration of industrial relations. As Godard (1997, 2002) has stressed, institutional factors, particularly government policy, played a large part in configuring both company strategies and worker and union expectations, as well as their attitudes towards the changes taking place in companies.

At that time, 'Flexibility' seemed to offer the solution to many of the job market's problems. Blyton and Morris (1992) define this as a company's ability to adapt the size of their workforce, working time and skills base according to fluctuations in demand. Another definition of flexibility would highlight the role it can play in organizing work so that companies can respond quickly to changing consumer needs, while making improvements and thereby gaining competitive advantage. In the American literature, and in the context of a deregulated job market, flexibility is associated with what are known as 'high performance' organizational practices or innovations.

The solutions provided by flexibility both for the job market and for companies soon sparked the interest of European academics, managers and politicians. However, depending on the labour institutions concerned, flexibility was similar in certain ways and different in others. The differences involved the forms that flexibility can take, while the similarities involved the immediate consequences, that is, a shift of labour management power towards employers.

Flexibility basically consisted of the use of non-standard (atypical) employment contracts and the decentralization of production through sub-contracting or outsourcing. These two aspects of flexibility seemed to be leading to a single Post-Fordist system of industrial relations in Europe. However Hyman (1994) expressed doubt about this, and observed large distinctions and disparities as well as a high degree of ambiguity in terms of the direction in which things were moving. Ten or more years later these question marks remain. Although certain common traits can be identified, essentially the economic factors behind the changes, differences exist that can be attributed to institutional factors or the above-mentioned social changes. Before analyzing these common traits we shall briefly examine flexibility inside and outside companies.

### The macroeconomic dimension of flexibility

One measure of job market flexibility compares the sensitivity of job creation to growth in GDP. The combined figures for all the EU countries show little correlation between labour market regulation and unemployment. For example, according to Lasierra (2003) the labour regulations in Austria, the UK and Spain vary greatly but their GDP–employment figures are relatively similar. However national differences stand out clearly in the perception that entrepreneurs have of the rigidity of their own markets (European Commission, 1991). One must therefore conclude that different mechanisms exist to bring enough flexibility to reduce the institutional barriers to job creation.

## Job flexibility in companies

### Regulation and flexibility

Labour rigidity, as opposed to flexibility, is associated with job protection or security. A narrow view of this reduces job protection to mere legal regulation. However when there is no legal instrument or customary practice to enforce such laws, regulation loses its value (Bertola *et al.*, 1999). Thus laws may be very strict but their enforcement is very flexible.

As noted by Morgan *et al.* (2001) and Kalleberg (2001), there are measures that enhance job security and others that generate a great deal of labour instability, even though there may be varying degrees of protection built into the regulations. According to Morgan *et al.* (2001), other institutional factors have a bearing on certain aspects of employment relations, and specifically on job security. For instance unions, by handling individual and group conflicts and negotiating salaries, have an influence on working conditions, social improvements and job security. Hence a low rate of union membership makes flexibility easier to achieve.

The employment structure also has a bearing on job stability. The presence of atypical workers (self-employed, temporary workers, part-time workers, workers supplied by agencies) or subcontracted workers enables labour regulations to be overlooked and reduces the possibility for permanent employees to exert pressure. This contradicts the insider–outsider syndrome that, according to some academics, has had such a negative effect on the Spanish labour market (Revenga, 1994). However Morgan *et al.* (2001) acknowledge that when atypical workers are taken into account, interpretational doubts may arise. Are more atypical workers used because of a lack of flexibility in the regulations, or because there already is a great deal of flexibility? Whichever way this is seen, it seems that the final result for companies is greater flexibility.

The following hypothesis is also considered: the more training a company provides, the more interest it will have in retaining its employees. In other words, the greater the training the greater the job security. It is argued that the new types of employment contract, the increase in atypical workers, deregulation and the surrendering of industrial relations to a collective bargaining in which the playing field would be skewed in the favour of the employer, would all increase job flexibility for companies. Moreover, and this is something that other authors cited have not said, the corollary of flexibilization is a reduction in real salary costs. In this sense the functioning of the job market approaches the neoclassical auction model, in which the balance depends on whether the price of labour adapts to supply and demand, and whether it is able to overcome potential rigidities or disconnection from productivity.

Finally, Morgan *et al.* (2001) have found that of 10 EU countries, Spain is the fourth most flexible, behind the UK, Ireland and France. This figure stands in stark contrast to the widely held stereotype of the rigid job market in Spain (see for example Bertola, 1990).

## Organizational diversity as a paradigm

As mentioned at the beginning of this chapter, there are forces pushing for a real transformation of industrial relations in Europe. This has already manifest itself in a reduction in the number of permanent employees, in a broad spectrum of employment contracts linked to work being regulated by mercantile law, in the blurring of borders for companies, often hampering clear identification of which company an employee actually works for, and in the introduction of market mechanisms to manage work. What underpins these transformations are the notions of flexibility and decentralized production. These serve the same end – that is, they enable companies to act with as much leeway as possible and restrict labour relations to within the organization, ignoring any other commitment to workers beyond what occurs in the workplace, based on the characteristics and circumstances of the companies at any given time.

Once the job market is broken, which is what the first institutionists aimed to prevent, work is placed on the market and transformed into a productive factor that can be dealt with differentially and used to competitive advantage, not only in a downward sense by reducing costs, but also in an upward sense by affording it qualities that provide more opportunities for the company, as stated in the theory of resources and capabilities (Penrose, 1962; Fernández, 1993; Hamel and Prahalad, 1997).

Rubery (1999) notes that two contradictory trends are fragmenting the organization of labour in companies. While these are cited in reference to internal labour markets, they are also applicable to the dualization of the value of labour as a factor of production. On the one hand companies are prevented from organizing labour differentially, but at the same time labour has less and less autonomy and more and more factors are making its organization uniform.

With regard to the first of these trends, Rubery identifies a set of centrifugal forces that are giving companies a greater capacity to design their own employment structures and develop their own organizational practices. Two examples of this are the decentralization of collective bargaining and deregulation of the labour market. The result of deregulation is not a textbook fragmenting of the job market but greater power among organizations to set their own terms and conditions for employment. In this case, systematic resort to numerical flexibility weakens companies' future viability because it erodes their capacity to innovate (Kleinknecht, 1998).

The second trend is the tendency to make labour relations uniform. Rubery (1999) points to a series of centripetal forces that make organizations more fragmented and production more decentralized, thereby shortening employees' careers and indicating a lack of will or capacity to ensure job security. These centripetal forces are manifest in the widespread use of numerical flexibility in its various forms (Brunhes, 1989; Lasierra, 2001), not only in Spain but also in countries whose job markets differ in terms of their degree of regulation, such as Austria and the UK.

We could say that these trends are a logical response to Adam Smith's old adage that specialization in production is linked to the size of the market (see also Stigler, 1951). As long as demand is low, specialization of production takes place in individual units within a company, with each worker specializing in a particular area of production. When the size of the market increases the company grows and the specialist units become large enough to become companies in their own right. Fordist companies handled increased demand and growth of the company by pursuing economies of scale. Nowadays the variety of markets and product ranges, the need for greater market presence and other factors have led to a host of company models that must tackle a variety of different situations without losing the advantages gained in other periods, particularly the period of specialization in production.

In this regard we can identify a process that ranges from intracompany specialization to intercompany specialization. As Kern and Schumann

(1984) indicate, the division of labour is disappearing *within* the company but increasing *among* companies. One example of this is companies focusing on what they do best and outsourcing what they do not do well.

This leads us to the other prevalent trend (together with flexibility) in the reorganization of labour and production over the last two decades: the decentralization of production. This process has made intercompany specialization possible, and also enabled different levels of an organization to be coordinated, but in a centralized fashion, mainly by introducing market mechanisms in pursuit of efficient allocation of resources. Hence, the ironic outcomes of 'decentralized production' are centralized decision making and control processes (see the chapter by MacKenzie and Forde).

These developments suggest the need to analyze the situation on the basis of transaction cost theory and other business theories, such as the evolutionary theory, in respect of issues that affect the broker relationship or the separation of ownership and control. In short we need to open the 'black box' of neoclassical economics, but space constraints prevent us from doing so in this chapter. However organizational economics is essential to understanding labour relations and the functioning of the job market in general (for organisational theories see Putterman, 1996; Santos Redondo, 1997; Langlois and Robertson, 2000; García, 2001; Lasierra, 2001).

## The fragmentation of production

The result of the twofold process of decentralization and increased flexibility can also be observed in the proliferation of forms of production, including flexible specialization based on small production batches (as opposed to mass production – see Piore and Sabel, 1990) and Toyotaist or lean production (Womack *et al.*, 1992; Coriat, 1993). Flexible specialization, which gives small companies extraordinary possibilities, has been facilitated by revolutionary microcomputer developments that enable economies of scale to be achieved in small series production. In other words, economies of scale can be secured without incurring the transaction costs that would come from more brokers carrying out more transactions.

Some observers suggest that strategies focusing on the production of a variety of products will prevail over those which merely seek to optimize economies of scale. For example Piore and Sabel (1990) assume that eventually there will be no products whose demand increases enough and on a stable enough basis to warrant large volume production. This new organizational paradigm, which includes various types of ownership structure and capital allocation, represents a marked departure from the traditional management of operations by companies based on the Taylorist or Fordist model. The reality, however, is perhaps more complex.

First, mass production is not on the decline across the board. For instance it is not declining in the consumer electronics, automotive and chemical industries. Second, the fact that production is increasing in small companies does not mean that it is declining in large ones. Rather production is being restructured and large companies are decentralizing their production but not their control (Harrison, 1997). Third, some of the new sectors that are taking shape are clearly applying Fordist techniques. Franchises and the capital-intensive branches of the service sector have triggered a phenomenon known as the industrialization of services. Finally, there is a greater diversity of markets and consumer patterns. In many cases, market fragmentation cannot be attributed to Fordist production, but to product innovation, new producers coming on the scene and changes to consumer patterns, for instance the self-provision of services.

Hence there is now a large variety of organizational forms and different models for organizing work, ranging from typical Fordist labour relations, which give rise to traditional domestic job markets that are analogous to functional flexibility, to market relations via outsourcing, or total decentralization. The job relations that one can assume occur are those described by Becker and Huselid (1998) in the case of 'high performance' organizations. Based on functional flexibility, work is no longer considered a cost but an investment. Seen through the prism of resource and capacities theory, this investment is what provides companies with a competitive advantage. Meanwhile Bailey and Bernhardt (1997) find that the different measures adopted to achieve efficiency and productivity do not necessarily seem to require advanced human resource management practices.

### The fragmentation of labour

The diversity of business models is echoed by a wide range of employment models, allowing us to speak of different job markets. The American postwar job market, which can also be extrapolated to Europe, is characterized by Osterman (1988) as relating to a market with relatively stable products, a social structure in which the male head of the family provided a stable income that was sufficient to maintain an acceptable standard of living, clearly defined boundaries in companies and an implicit social contract between employers, workers and the state to ensure a certain degree of job stability and income.

As we already indicated, in this model labour was insulated from market forces, so companies did not use it as a competitive factor. Because the direct cost of labour – that is, salaries – and the indirect costs deriving from labour conditions were borne by the companies, they adjusted their staffing levels according to their market prospects. However employment was also guided by considerations of equity, defended and upheld by certain labour institutions, mainly trade unions, collective bargaining, labour regulations and public policy to sustain demand. This model broke down with the energy crisis of the mid 1970s, resulting in widespread unemployment in Western economies for no less than 20 years.

While the above model coexisted with other models (Kerr, 1985) the fragmentation of the job market was not as it is today, either in terms of the number of workers involved or in respect of their characteristics. To simplify the current situation, one could say there are two categories of workers: the old-style full-time workers with relative job stability, and very diverse atypical workers – temporary workers, self-employed workers, workers hired from temporary employment agencies and so on – all correlating with the plurality of organizational models mentioned earlier. One study that has become a classic on job market models is that by Osterman (1988), who names four job models: the salaried model, the industrial model, the craft model and the neoclassical unskilled labour model. More recently Carré *et al.* (2000) have identified two main job models: the standard (typical) model and the non-standard model, which in the service sector is in turn divided into four models: highly defined and delimited jobs, intensive, non-rationalized jobs, semi self-employment jobs, and highly specialized self-employment.

In addition to market and technical factors, the growth in atypical jobs is due to the fact that the industrial sector is undermining the labour institutions that once-promoted and upheld typical jobs, that is, trade unions and collective bargaining. In the service sector the higher proportion of salary costs in total costs, the difficulty of measuring and monitoring performance and the fact that the productive process is less predictable and harder to plan than in industry, favour the use of more typical workers. Although developed societies now consume more services, it should be remembered that the demand for labour is spawned by the need to produce.

## Organizational transformation and job fragmentation: an empirical analysis

Instead of delving deeply into all aspects of flexibility and its functions, we refer the reader to Boyer (1986), Lasierra (2001, 2003) and Ozaki (2000), among others, and concentrate here on the two most widely known types of flexibility: numerical flexibility, which involves the use of atypical workers, subcontracting or outsourcing; and the less accurately measurable functional flexibility, which is tied to organizational innovations and affects social characteristics such as job security, the chance of receiving in-house training and the likelihood of having a career path in the company. This section examines how flexibility materializes in companies, the immediate reasons for its existence and its impact on the job market.

Early studies indicated that numerical flexibility basically consisted of the use of different types of non-standard worker or the outsourcing of tasks or parts of production in order to match companies' work loads to their production needs (Atkinson, 1985). The first versions of flexibility in companies, associated with the core–periphery model, placed numerical flexibility in the protective periphery of the company. Traditional workers with traditional jobs were situated at the core. These workers provided the functional flexibility the company required to adapt to rapid technological and economic changes. According to MacInnes (1988), workers in the core enjoyed job stability and secure labour conditions.

Today the picture is much more nuanced. For instance Kalleberg (2001) suggests that numerical and functional flexibility have many different permutations that cannot easily be attributed to the core or the periphery. To begin with, demarcating the core and the periphery is a very imprecise business, and neither status nor salary differ very much between those in the company and those outside. To generalize, the only case in which there are significant labour differences is that between subcontracted workers and workers in the parent company.

Companies use various combinations of workers to obtain a high degree of flexibility. For example they may attain functional flexibility by hiring subcontract or atypical workers for specific, highly skilled tasks (in terms of job stability and relations with the company these workers are not part of the so-called core), while semi-skilled workers at the core of the company enable high levels of flexibility in both numerical and functional terms.

According to Ackroyd and Procter (1998), in British manufacturing the traits attributed to functional and numerical flexibility are not present in companies that attain high levels of productivity through the intensive use of capital coupled with medium-skilled workers. The workers in the core do not enjoy privileged status *vis-à-vis* other workers who have been subcontracted to perform certain functions. This stands in contrast to Atkinson's (1985) model of the flexible company. Nonetheless the former workers are in a better position than the subcontracted ones, although we must remember that this study relates to manufacturing industry. As the authors acknowledge, in this sector worker contribution to the final product is neither very high nor crucial.

If we wish to consider the reasons for change and the types of change that come about, we have to broaden our analysis to include the service sector, with all its diversity. In the service sector a job's relative status is more of a determining factor in estimating how, and how much, value is created.

Having considered the permutations of flexibility within companies and the specificities of different sectors, we shall now look at the two traditional categories of flexibility.

In the case of numerical flexibility, Table 3.1 shows the highly differentiated and quantitatively significant use of atypical workers in three EU countries with quite different labour institutions. This is a product of what Hyman (1994) calls national idiosyncrasies, historical legacy and institutional framework.

Before proceeding to analyze the reasons given by companies for using atypical workers and subcontracting (see Table 3.2), we draw attention to

Table 3.1  The use of atypical employees in three EU countries, 1985–99 (percentage of total workforce)

|  | 1985 | 1990 | 1994 | 1996 | 1997 | 1998 | 1999 |
|---|---|---|---|---|---|---|---|
| **Spain** | | | | | | | |
| Self-employed* | 22.6 | 20.9 | 22.1 | 21.5 | 20.9 | 20.2 | 19.3 |
| Part-timers | 5.8 | 4.9 | 6.9 | 8.0 | 8.2 | 8.0 | 8.3 |
| Temporary employees | 15.6 | 29.8 | 33.7 | 33.6 | 33.6 | 32.9 | 32.7 |
| Unemployment rate | 21.6 | 13.2 | 24.1 | 22.2 | 20.8 | 18.8 | 15.9 |
| **Austria** | | | | | | | |
| Self-employed | 11.3 | 11.3 | 10.8 | 10.8 | 10.8 | 11.0 | 10.9 |
| Part-timers | 11.1 | 13.3 | 13.9 | 14.9 | 14.7 | 15.8 | 16.8 |
| Temporary employees | n.a. | n.a. | 6.0 | 8.0 | 7.8 | 7.8 | 7.5 |
| Unemployment rate | 3.6 | 3.2 | 4.0 | 4.3 | 4.4 | 4.5 | 3.7 |
| **United Kingdom** | | | | | | | |
| Self-employed | 11.6 | 13.5 | 12.9 | 12.6 | 12.4 | 12.1 | 11.7 |
| Part-timers | 21.2 | 21.7 | 23.8 | 24.6 | 24.9 | 24.9 | 24.8 |
| Temporary employees | 7.0 | 5.2 | 6.5 | 7.1 | 7.4 | 7.1 | 6.8 |
| Unemployment rate | 11.5 | 7.0 | 9.6 | 8.2 | 7.0 | 6.3 | 6.1 |

\* The relative weight of agriculture and services connected to the restaurant and hotel industry and tourism, which are all comparatively higher in Spain, would have to be adjusted in the Spanish survey.

the fact that carrying out a comparative analysis is rendered difficult by the heterogeneity of surveys in both content and procedure, as pointed out by Gramm and Schnell (2001). Here we shall compare two studies. The first, Cully et al. (1999), is based on the 1998 Workplace Employment Relations Survey (WERS); the second is a survey of 430 companies in an industrial region in Spain, from which 126 valid responses were obtained. Taking into account the sampling and data-gathering techniques used, one cannot conclude that the Spanish survey is a statistically representative sample, but it has been verified that there are no biases and therefore we can attribute a non-negligible value to the results. Also, in this survey the questionnaire was an adaptation of the 1990 WERS questionnaire, and is therefore comparable due to the similarity of the questions (for a summary of the WERS results see Cully et al., 1999, pp. 36–7).

Turning now to functional flexibility, this is more difficult to define. Corderi et al. (1993) associate it with the broadening of tasks or multi-faceted work, rotation and the development of independent teams – in short, a response to the narrow Taylorist model. An extrapolation of this characterization associates functional flexibility with the use of 'high-performance' practices, as noted earlier.

La Sierra (2003) has conducted a study that included the OECD (2001) analysis of the adoption of new working methods in various countries, and

Table 3.2 Reasons for the use of subcontracting and atypical workers (percentage of positive answers in each survey)

| Cully et al. (1999) | | Lasierra (2001) | |
|---|---|---|---|
| Subcontracting | | Subcontracting | |
| Cost savings | 48 | Cost savings | 56 |
| Focus on core business | 27 | Flexibility, given technical or market uncertainties | 46 |
| Improve the quality of the service | 21 | Quality improvement | 42 |
| Atypical workers | | Atypical workers | |
| Short-term cover (peaks in demand) | 59 | Short-term cover | 78 |
| Adjust the workforce in line with demand | 40 | Flexibility, given technical or market uncertainties | 68 |
| Obtain specialist skills | 21 | Rigidity of labour legislation | 53 |
| Cover maternity leave | 22 | | |

compared the results of this with those of his previous survey (La Sierra, 2001). Functional flexibility is defined in terms of certain practices, along the lines suggested by MacInnes (1988), that is, job rotation, multifaceted work and certain high-performance innovations or practices. Company characteristics such as sector, age, size, type of production and technology used are also included in the analysis, as is a variable that is fundamental to determining the way in which labour is organized: the company's competitive advantage or strategy. A distinction is made between competition in terms of costs, quality and flexibility.

The findings of the study coincide with a great many of the conclusions reached by the OECD (2001), despite their technical and methodological differences. It appears that the type of competition (in this case quality) and the sector are particularly important considerations when making organizational innovations. There also seems to be a close link between functional flexibility and these innovations. In general, flexible methods are used when production is complex, for example when there is differentiated production and greater use of technology.

## Consequences for labour relations and the job market

The fragmentation of organizations and the consequent fragmentation of the job market has resulted in inequalities in the parameters that define labour as a factor of production. Table 3.3 details five of these parameters.

*Table 3.3* Employment systems and their effects on job characteristics

| | *Requisite qualifications* | *Qualification to carry out tasks* | *Salaries* | *Development of skills and qualifications* | *Job stability and time spent on the job* |
|---|---|---|---|---|---|
| Outsourcing | Decrease | Unchanged or decreases | Decrease | Decreases | Decrease |
| Temporary work | Decrease | Unchanged or decreases | Decrease | Decreases | Decrease |
| Functional flexibility | Increase | Increases | Unchanged or increase | Increases | Unchanged or increase |

*Source*: Adapted from Moss *et al.* (2000, p. 117).

The various types of flexibility that we have discussed do not have an equal impact on these parameters, although whether or not they have the same impact in all types of organization has yet to be empirically studied. Traditional employment is being replaced by outsourcing and contingent work, with an accompanying reduction of the implicit guarantees associated with permanent work. This move also involves a broadening of tasks, the flattening of hierarchical structures and disruptions in the career ladder as many high-level jobs are being delegated to workers from the external market.

It appears that changes to the types of work give rise to modifications in areas such as qualifications, professional requirements, salaries and job security. The broadening of tasks associated with functional flexibility generally improves the first two of these, while salaries and job security generally worsen. It would seem that there is dualism with companies introducing numerical and functional flexibility (see Table 3.2).

The application of these employment systems in different types of organization, as we have attempted to indicate, does not have an even impact on job characteristics as these do not mechanically fit into core–periphery company models.

As Table 3.3 also shows, virtually all the job characteristics worsen for outsourced or temporary workers. The neoclassical orientation in employment policy means that workers themselves are deemed responsible for not having good enough jobs or sufficient work. This is based on the theory of human capital and the notion that being employable is an individual's responsibility, that is, it is up to individuals to accumulate human capital. In a certain sense, companies are seen in such views as exempt from designing and applying their own employment policies, and their capacity to do so has been reduced. According to Lasierra (2001), this is not the case and the shift in power has left companies with considerable room for manoeuvre in this regard. Government authorities could, however, counter certain types of inertia or vicious circles that lead companies to comfortably settle into enviornments or sectors that do not require workers from the primary sector.

## Conclusions

The fragmentation of the job market is the result of a fundamental reorganization of production for technical, economic, social and even political and ideological reasons. The reorganization of production has taken on a host of forms, based on the fact that companies are able to make freer use of their productive resources. This is true in both legal and technical terms. At the same time this reorganization has been strongly driven by market pressure, perhaps more prevalent now than in the past, to attain high levels of efficiency. The imperatives guiding reorganization – flexibility and the decentralization of production – seem to underpin different types of organization. In this sense, institutions are important in influencing how individual companies apply employment flexibility and the decentralization of their production,

The results of this fragmentation call into question the way in which orthodox economics views companies and the job market. Specifically, what occurs within companies is not taken into consideration, and jobs are reduced to a type of commodity thereby making it difficult to interpret how the job market and related policies function. In this regard the policies that materialize tend to be *laissez faire*, the short-term implications being an increase in un-employment and poor or precarious jobs. There is also a possibility that companies do not take full advantage of labour's potential since they consider labour a mere production cost. In the long term this weakening of companies could affect employment.

An alternative course, without ruling out the possibility of flexibility and decentralization, would be to highlight the role of labour as an important tool for modernizing companies and generating value.

## References

Ackroyd, S. and S. Procter (1998) 'British manufacturing organization and workplace industrial relations: some attributes of the new flexible firm', *British Journal of Industrial Relations*, June, pp.163–83.
Atkinson, J. (1985) 'Flexibility, uncertainty and manpower management', IMS Report, University of Sussex.
Bailey, T. R. and A. D. Bernhardt (1997) 'In search of the high road in low-wage industry', *Politics & Society*, 25 (2), pp. 179–201.
Becker, B. E. and M. A. Huselid (1998) 'High performance work systems and firm performance: A synthesis of research and managerial implications', *Research in Personnel and Human Resources Management*, 16, pp. 53–101.
Bertola, G. (1990) 'Job security, employment and wages', *European Economic Review*, 34 (4), pp. 851–79.
Bertola, G., T. Boeri and S. Cazes (1999) 'Employment protection and labour market adjustment in some OECD countries: Evolving institutions and variable enforcement', mimeo, Instituto Europeo de Florencia.
Blyton, P. and J. Morris (1992) 'HRM and the limits of flexibility', in P. Blyton and J. Turnbull (eds), *Reassessing Human Resource Management* (London: Sage), pp. 116–30.
Boyer, R. (1986) *La flexibilidad del trabajo en Europa: un estudio comparativo* (Madrid: Ministerio de Trabajo y Seguridad Social).
Brunhes, B. (1989) 'La flexibilidad de la mano de obra en las empresas: estudio comparativo de cuatro países europeo', in *OCDE (1991) Perspectivas del empleo* (Madrid: MTSS).
Campbell, D. (1996) 'La empresa globalizadora y las instituciones laborales', in Bailey *Las multinacionales y el empleo: la economía global* (Madrid: Ministerio de Trabajo y Seguridad Social).
Cappelli, P. (2001) *El nuevo pacto en el trabajo* (Barcelona: Ediciones Granica).

Carré, F., M. Ferber, L. Golden and S. A. Herzenberg (eds) (2000) *Non Standard Work. The Nature and Challenges of Changing Employment Arrangements* (IRRA, University of Illinois).
Corderi, J. P. Sevastos, W. Mueller and S. Parker (1993) 'Correlates of employee attitudes toward functional flexibility', *Human Relations*, 46 (6), pp. 705–23.
Coriat, B. (1993) *Pensar al revés: Trabajo y organización en la empresa japonesa* (Madrid: Ed. Siglo XXI).
Cully, M., S. Woodland, A. O'Reilly and G. Dix (1999) *Britain at Work* (London: Routledge).
European Commission (1991) 'Developments in the labour markets in the Community: results of a survey covering employers and employees', *European Economy*, 3, pp. 7–50.
Fernández, Z. (1993) 'La organización interna como ventaja competitiva para la empresa', *Papeles de Economía Española*, 56, pp. 178–93.
García, C. E. (2001) *Análisis económico de las organizaciones* (Madrid: Alianza Editorial).
Godard, J. (1997) 'Managerial strategies, labour and employment relations and the state: the Canadian case and beyond', *British Journal of Industrial Relations*, 35 (3), pp. 399–426.
Godard, J. (2002) 'Institutional environments, employer practices, and states in liberal market economies', *Industrial Relations*, 41 (2), pp. 249–86.
Gramm, C. L. and J. F. Schnell (2001) 'The use of flexible staffing arrangements in core production jobs', *Industrial and Labor Relations Review*, 54 (2), pp. 245–58.
Grimshaw, D., K. G. Ward, J. Rubery and H. Beynon (2001) 'Organisations and transformation of the internal labour market', *Work, Employment and Society*, 15 (1), pp. 25–54.
Hamel, G. and C. Prahalad (1997) *Compitiendo por el futuro* (Barcelona: Ariel Economía).
Harrison, B. (1997) *La empresa que viene. La evolución del poder empresarial en la era de la flexibilidad* (Barcelona: Paidós Empresa).
Hyman, R. (1994) 'Industrial relations in Western Europe: An era of ambiguity?', *Industrial Relations*, 33 (1), pp.1–24.
Kalleberg, A. L. (2001) 'Organizing flexibility: The flexible firm in a new century', *British Journal of Industrial Relations*, 39 (4), pp. 479–504.
Kern, H and M. Schumann (1989) *El fin de la división del trabajo* (Madrid: Ministerio de Trabajo y Seguridad Social).
Kerr, C. (1985) *Mercados de trabajo y determinación de los salarios: la balkanización de los mercados de trabajo* (Madrid: Ministerio de Trabajo y Seguridad Social).
Kleinknecht, A. (1998) 'Is labour market flexibility harmful to innovation?', *Cambridge Journal of Economics*, 22, pp. 387–96.
Langlois, R. N. and P. L. Robertson (2000) *Empresas, mercados y cambio económico* (Barcelona: Biblioteca Episteme).
Lasierra, J. M. (1994) 'Análisis económico de la reforma laboral 1993–1994', *Cuadernos Aragoneses de Economía, Facultad de Ciencias Económicas*, 4 (2), pp. 419–33.
Lasierra, J. M. (1995) 'Notas sobre flexibilidad y participación en la relación laboral', *Acciones e Investigaciones Sociales*, 3, pp. 53–68.
Lasierra, J. M. (2001) *Mercado de trabajo y estrategias empresariales* (Madrid: Consejo Económico y Social).
Lasierra, J. M. (2003) 'La flexibilidad como el nuevo eje del mundo del trabajo', *Revista Andaluza de Relaciones Laborales*, 12, pp. 139–57.
Leisink, P. (ed.) (1999) *Globalization and Labour Relations* (Aldershot: Edward Elgar).

MacInnes, J. (1988) 'The question of flexibility', *Personnel Review*, 17 (3), pp. 12–15.
Morgan, J., V. Genre and C. Wilson (2001) 'Measuring employment security in Europe using surveys of employers', *Industrial Relations*, 40 (1), pp.
Moss, Ph., H. Salzman and Ch. Tilly (2000) 'Limits to market-mediated employment: from deconstruction to reconstruction of internal labor markets', in F. Carré, M. Ferber, L. Golden and A. Herzenberg (eds), *Non Standard Work. The Nature and Challenges of Changing Employment Arrangements* (Cornell: IRRA, University of Cornell).
OECD (2001) *Perspectivas del empleo* (Paris: OECD).
Osterman, P. (1988) *Employment futures* (Oxford: Oxford University Press).
Ozaki, M. (2000) *Negociar la flexibilidad. Función de los interlocutores sociales y del estado* (Geneva: International Labour Organisation).
Penrose, E. T. (1962) *Teoría del crecimiento de la empresa* (Madrid: Aguilar).
Piore. M. and C. Sabel (1990) *La Segunda ruptura industrial* (Madrid: Alianza Universidad).
Putterman, L. (ed.) (1994) *La naturaleza económica de la empresa* (Madrid: Alianza).
Revenga, A. (1994) 'Aspectos microeconómicos del mercado de trabajo español', in *El paro en España: ¿Tiene solución?* (Madrid: Consejo Superior de Cámaras de Comercio, Industria y Navegación).
Rubery, J. (1999) 'Fragmenting the internal labour market', in P. Leisink (ed.), *Globalization and Labour Relations* (Aldershot: Edward Elgar).
Ruesga, S., J. M. La Sierra and C. Murayama (2002) *Economía del trabajo y politica laboral* (Madrid: Pirámide).
Santos Redondo, M. (1997) *Los economistas y la empresa* (Madrid: Alianza economía).
Stigler, G. (1951) 'The division of labor is limited by the extent of the market', *Journal of Political Economy*, 59, (3), pp. 185–93.
Womack, P. J., D. T. Jones and D. Roos (1995) *La máquina que cambió el mundo* (Madrid: McGraw-Hill).

# 4
# The Degradation of Employment in Spain: From the Salaried Employment Norm to the Entrepreneurial Employment Norm[1]

*Carlos Prieto*

## Employment: economic activity and social norms

Economists, sociologists, political scientists and statisticians all seem to agree upon the definition of employment, and it is a very simple one. Employment is work done in exchange for monetary remuneration. Whatever the content and context of work, it is considered to be employment if it is remunerated. If it is not remunerated it is not employment.[2] This definition has been criticized by feminists. What is called into question is not so much the express formulation of employment in reference to an implicit definition of 'work', as 'the habitual use of a definition of work that excludes all forms of unremunerated productive activity, especially that done by women in the home'.[3]

Here the employment crisis in Spain will be examined will the help of a somewhat different definition of employment. For the purposes of this chapter, employment is interpreted as a social norm deployed in a host of dimensions. This way of interpreting employment opens up new horizons for analysis and an understanding not only of employment but also of society as a whole.

The notion that employment should be understood as a social norm can be argued in at least two ways. The first consists of showing how since the end of the nineteenth century in industrialized countries employment has been constructed as a social category, and how this categorization has been affected by social and political regulations (Salais *et al.*, 1990; Topalov, 1994, 2000). The second argument is based on the assumption that all social and cognitive categories 'are the crystallized trace ... of plural, continuous and evolutionary processes in the characterization of the [social] world' (Demazière, 2003, p. 213). The purpose is to deconstruct the meaning that people commonly attach to the social category of employment. For the author the notion of employment has a clear regulatory component, but brief reference will be made to the second line of argument.

As noted at the start of this section, there is considerable unanimity among experts in defining employment as work that is remunerated monetarily. However in the social and collective awareness there does not seem to be such a strict assimilation between remunerated work and employment, although the significance attributed by the population to the social category of employment does partially coincide with that of the experts. Employment is always remunerated work, but the contrary is not true. This is where the common social awareness differs from economic science. The cases in which remunerated work is not considered employment are vast and varied, ranging from drug trafficking to selling flowers at traffic lights, and generally all jobs done in the submerged economy. If we apply the experts' definition of employment in strict terms – that is, work in exchange for remuneration – to all these cases there is no doubt that they should be included in the category of employment. Nevertheless no one, not even the persons engaged in these activities, or those in their immediate environment, would say that the people carrying out these activities are employed.

Thus in the social conscience of the population, not all remunerated work is put into the social and cognitive category of employment. The remunerated work of civil servants, long-term workers in large companies and all those who effectively fall under the rules of a collective bargaining agreement stand in contrast to remunerated jobs that are not considered employment. In order for remunerated work to be considered employment it must meet certain minimum requirements, and the more it meets these requirements the more it is considered to be employment.

The social category of employment that appears in the collective consciousness therefore has all the traits of a social norm: employment is remunerated work, but it is only recognized as such if it meets certain criteria that define social norms. For example it must meet minimum criteria under the heading of justice: a remuneration that is considered to be fair, working hours that are viewed as just, satisfactory health and safety measures, a certain degree of social protection and so on. Otherwise it will be merely seen as work or a job. If this is the meaning of employment as a social category and all categories of this type are the expression of their social and historical construction, then it must be concluded that the social category of employment in any of its formulations involves a regulatory component. In any event, analyzing employment from this perspective can contribute to our understanding of it and its dynamics of change.[4]

The minimum criteria for justice referred to above relate to work as an activity. However work is also to do with persons. In Western societies, not everyone who wants to be a worker is one. There are classes of persons that can and must work in the social area of the market, and classes that cannot or must not. For example, in general adult males must work, but in no event should children or adolescents be made to work. Some individuals consider that women should not work either, particularly if they have young children.

All social norms, whether they classify, value and establish hierarchies of individuals or classify, value and establish hierarchies of activities, only acquire meaning if they are an integral part of the social order. But all social orders – understood not in their legal but in their sociological sense – consist of a hierarchical array of activities and individuals that are only able to progress without turmoil if a certain threshold of ideological legitimacy and justification is attained. In this context any social norm is both shared and disputed at the same time. The disputability of any norm is inscribed in an ongoing dynamic of change triggered by the relations between social classes. Thus norms are socially constructed social facts that undergo constant change throughout history. Whatever the traits of their social regulation may be, their existence and concretion are no more than the contingent, unstable, transitory result of the relations between social classes (Prieto, 2003).

Given this theoretical background, the objective of this chapter is to compare the social employment norms that prevailed in two recent periods of Spanish history with clearly different traits. The first period, the 'constitution years' (1976–82), coincided with the decline of Keynesianism in European countries.[5] The second period (from 1982 to the present) we shall call the 'globalization years'. During the constitution years the existence of secure, stable, full-time, salaried employment with rights (although only for males) was used as a yardstick to judge the employment situation. Certain authors, particularly Castel (1995), with whom we substantially agree, have characterized the type of society in which that employment norm prevailed as *société salariale* (wage-earning society).[6] However we prefer to call it 'the social norm of salaried employment' or the 'salaried employment norm'. During the globalization years the norm has become flexible employment – that is, employment and employment conditions must continuously adapt to the requirements of business and competition while job security and social and labour rights take a back seat.[7] Given that market competition now plays a key role in configuring the new social norm, we could also speak of an 'entrepreneurial employment norm'.[8]

## The salaried employment norm during the constitution years

Experts in Spain and elsewhere in Europe all agree on one thing when comparing the employment situation in the Keynesian years (the 1960s and 1970s) with the years since: the contrast between the current mass unemployment and the previous 'full employment'. Spain is paradigmatic in this regard. During the former period the unemployment rate did not exceed 2.5 per cent until the second half of the 1970s. During the latter period it has fluctuated between 25 per cent in 1994 and 11.1 per cent in 2002. Although statistically speaking the constitution years were not actually ones of full employment, as we will shall see shortly, they were in terms of the employment norm in Spain and the rest of Europe: the salaried employment norm.

Thus full employment is the trait that best characterizes the period. Full employment is often understood as simply a lack of unemployment, but in the salaried employment norm this trait is just one of many, including fair employment.[9]

Both the 1980 Employment Act (*Ley Básica del Empleo*) and the Spanish constitution explicitly proclaimed full employment as a principal goal of public policy. According to the constitution, the public authorities 'shall carry out policy oriented towards full employment' (Article 40, paragraph 1) while the Employment Act referred to 'bringing about and maintaining the full employment level'. In order to glean the full meaning and relevance of this political objective in the constitution years one must take into account the following: (1) the notion of full employment in that period can only be understood as part of the Keynesian convention; (2) that to aim for full employment in 1980 when the unemployment rate had already risen to 8.7 per cent was to accept a major political challenge, although it was not understood as anything but an absence of unemployment; and (3) that the objective of full employment would gradually vanish from the political horizon. In this context there seems to be just one rationale for striving for full employment: the rising unemployment rate was seen as jeopardizing the cohesive democratic society desired by the major social and political forces of the time.

As noted above, among the basic components of the salaried employment norm of the constitution years the notion of fair employment was as important as the objective of full employment. The Employment Act gave an inkling of this when it stated that, as well as full employment, public employment policy should have the objective of 'fostering the improvement of living and working conditions' (LBE/80, Article 1, paragraph two). The two objectives were inseparable: there could be no full employment without fair employment and no fair employment without full employment.[10] In Spain, most of the facets of fair employment were roughly the same as those found in other European countries during the 1970s as part of the salaried employment norm.[11]

Fair employment was stable employment. Labour stability (a term expressly used in legislation) is a phenomenon that can be empirically observed. At the beginning of the 1980s, 88 per cent of workers had been with their companies for more than five years and 64 per cent for more than ten (Pries, 1988). The legal and labour rules expressly promoted this stability and there was only one standard employment contract: the indefinite contract. The only exceptions were in cases where there was a valid reason for setting a fixed term. Indefinite contracts promoted job security as relatively high compensation had to be paid for wrongful or unfair dismissal.[12] A long negotiation process (with workers' representatives) and subsequent processing was added to this when dismissal came in groups.

With fair employment the amount of time spent on the job was subject to regulation. Working time was both limited in quantity (there was a distinction here between an ordinary and an extraordinary working day) and chronologically ordered, particularly by the day or week. The definition of an ordinary working day only applied to full-time jobs – that is, jobs that required a set number of working hours to be put in, with the possible addition of overtime, which was paid at a rate that was 75 per cent higher than the ordinary rate.

Fair employment also included differentiated remuneration in the form of salaries, whose level was mostly determined by collective bargaining between union representatives and representatives of companies. No salary, negotiated or otherwise, could fall below the minimum guaranteed professional wages (*Salario Minimo Interprofesional*), which were set annually and guaranteed by the central government. The 1976 Industrial Relations Act (Article 28, paragraph 1) refers to this in the following terms: 'The State shall ensure minimum guaranteed interprofessional wages that are sufficient, as related to the levels of national economic development attained, to enable ... a worker and his family to lead a moral, dignified life.' During the constitution years there were four salient trends in salaries: (1) their increase in real terms, even in years with a clear containment of increases through collective bargaining; (2) 'a strong trend – through claims for linear increases – to narrow the gaps between wages' (Serrano and Malo de Molina, 1979, p. 315), which was also bolstered by the tax rules on personal and family income; (3) a significant difference between the wages actually received and those in the agreement, 'reducing the excessive significance of marginal wage benefits by absorbing them in the basic wage' (ibid.); and (4) a substantial increase in the coverage of collective bargaining, which rose from 60 per cent of all workers in 1977 to 86 per cent in 1984.

Moreover fair employment rules significantly limited the extent to which employers could exercise decision-making power regarding the tasks assigned to employees, and after the repressive decades of the Franco regime, salaried workers were given the right to organize, be represented and act as a class with its own interests.

Finally, fair employment was associated with ongoing improvement of workers' working and living conditions in terms of job and economic security, social protection and social recognition.[13] The benefits of this were felt not only by the workers but also by their families and the entire social class. Undoubtedly some of the aspects of the salaried employment norm played a crucial part in the acceptance by the salaried class of Spain's reformed capitalism.

The result of all this was a true, politically constructed social order in which the notions of salaried work and salaried workers took on a central role.[14] Moreover social and legal regulations did respond to the demands made by workers, through their collective organizations, in esuring that the order was 'just'. This gave rise to the decommodification[15] of work (job security and stability, strict entitlement to social and economic services) and rules on their entrepreneurial use (limitations on working time and content, and the right for workers to organize and act collectively), making 'a moral and dignified life' possible for all workers.

The importance attached to the salaried employment norm of the constitution years became particularly evident when temporary contracts not linked to any specific cause and part-time hiring first came on the scene. Legislators seem to have been cautious about incorporating these employment practices into the social norm of employment. They were legislated for, but on an exceptional and transitory basis: 'as long as the current employment conditions exist' (third transitory provision of the 1980 Workers' Statute).[16] Temporary and part-time hiring were considered so atypical and so politically and socially irrelevant that the regular Survey of the Working Population[17] did not offer any statistics on these categories during those years.

Thus far we have only taken two characteristics of workers into account: their situation as salaried workers and their age. This reflects the system of social categorizations of the time. Later the feminist movement and studies of wage relations from a gender perspective drew attention to a concealed dimension of the salaried employment norm. Fair employment was not geared to all adult citizens without distinction. Rather it only applied to males, as 'workers' in the accepted sense could only be male workers. In a context in which the social services did not provide day care for children or the elderly and families did not have the means to employ carers, the result was an unequal division of labour and social positions between men and women. The market and work were geared to males, while females were expected to stay at home and take care of their family and household. This is illustrated by the average female employment rate in 1980: a paltry 26.5 per cent compared with 97.5 per cent for males.

On the face of it there was nothing particularly atypical about this division of tasks between the sexes. As Esping-Andersen (1999, p. 44) writes, in the political economy of the decades following the Second World War, when the first welfare states were being established:

> it was assumed that women . . . were housewives and men were 'standard production workers' . . . the only ones to provide income for the family and to be entitled to social rights. And this was also based on a prototype of paths in life: women left work when they married and had children. They were therefore available to take care of their children, and later of their aging parents.

The only difference was that by the constitution years the situation in other countries had changed.

## The globalization years and the entrepreneurial employment norm

As the constitution years gave way to the globalization years, especially during the 1990s, the employment situation and the accompanying social norm changed radically in terms of job security, the properties defining (salaried) work and those defining its subjects. In most EU countries the unemployment rate during the 1990s stagnated at around 10 per cent, but in Spain the figure was closer to 20 per cent. In 1994 it rose as high as 25 per cent. Thus Spain went from nearly full employment to very high unemployment. This situation was considered potentially dangerous in terms of sparking social conflict. However this failed to materialize. Moreover in general labour conflict during the 1990s was far lower than it had been than during the 1960s and 1970s.

As unemployment rose the ideal of full employment vanished from the political horizon and was replaced by 'the fight against unemployment and the bolstering of our capacity to generate employment' (amendment to the Workers' Statute in 1994). After the Lisbon 2000 Intergovernmental Conference, full employment in the European Union, including Spain, was once again spoken of, but as we shall see this did not have the same significance as the ideal of the past as changes were made to the employment norm. As Bouffartigue (1999, p. 25) puts it, unemployment was 'the main destabilisation vector of the employment norm, and beyond it, salaried society as such'.[18]

When in 2000 full employment was once again touted it had nothing to do with the full employment of the past since the principle of fair employment was replaced by flexible employment.[19] Here flexible employment is understood as the set of social norms and practices that facilitate workers meeting the requirements of business and the economy.[20] Thus the flexible employment norm can also be called the entrepreneurial employment norm. Whatever name is given to it, it stands in stark contrast to the salaried employment norm.

Flexible employment is rather insecure and unstable, particularly in the case of workers with fixed-term contracts. By 2002, 31.2 per cent of all salaried workers had fixed-term contracts, a third of them for less than six months. The signifance of this is illustrated by the fact that at the beginning of the 1980s, 88 per cent of workers had been with their company for more than five years, but in 2002 the figure was just 50 per cent.[21] This change also has a regulatory aspect in that indefinite employment contracts are no longer favoured by law.

With flexible employment, working time tends to be strictly geared to employer production interests (Prieto and Ramos, 1999). The historical trend towards a reduction of working hours has been contained and sometimes reversed. This can be observed in collective bargaining and, even more so, in workplaces. The average annual number of working hours agreed in collective bargaining went down by 232.9 hours (10.3 per cent) between 1978 and 1993. Thereafter the average number held steady or slightly increased. Another new development is attention to how working time is structured.[22] Since 1994, 'by default' working hours have been calculated on a yearly basis, although distributions by the day or week are possible, with companies being free to decide how the hours are distributed. In the past this could only have come from a collective bargaining agreement. Nowadays it is rarely necessary to resort to overtime and workers are not paid at the previous marked-up rate unless it is expressly provided for in a collective agreement. Lastly, legislation on full-time employment currently coexists with legislation on part-time employment. In Spain the proportion of part-time workers is only 8.3 per cent, much lower than in other European countries, but at least part time work is now regulated.

Under flexible employment, salaries tend to vary according to each company's situation and the profitability of each worker. This has considerable social effects in that it increases inequality and widens the gaps in income distribution. This trend is increasingly apparent within collective bargaining since at least 1994 (Miguélez and Rebollo, 1999). Another factor in the increase in income inequality is the reduction of taxation in the highest income bracket. Thus the meaning of the minimum guaranteed professional wage has changed greatly.

The current situation of trade unionism is somewhat paradoxical. If we were to consider things from a formal and institutionalized standpoint, it could be asserted that trade union activity in labour relations has withstood the neoliberalizing gale in Spain. The high rate of coverage of collective bargaining agreements is proof of this, as is union participation in social dialogue during the first term of office of the conservative Popular Party (1996–99). However if we examine the issue through the lens of labour relations in the workplace, things look very different. Behind closed doors, many companies pay very little attention to collective bargaining agreements that should apply across the board to an entire sector (Martínez Lucio, 1998). The gap between what is written into an agreement, or even into general law, and what actually occurs is wide and is particularly significant in the case of salaries and working hours (Prieto and Roquero, 2001). In practice labour relations are handled directly between companies and workers, and there is very little mediation, if any, by trade unions (Miguélez and Rebollo, 1999).

Another major change is that social and economic protection is increasingly being based on individual private insurance rather than public insurance. The implementation of flexible employment aims activate workers *vis-à-vis* their responsibilities.[23] This explains the succession of reforms in the pension system and unemployment benefits, with a stiffening of the conditions for obtaining these benefits. Along the same lines, unemployment is no longer considered to be the result of the functioning of the economic system and something for the government to tackle through comprehensive economic policy measures. Rather each unemployed individual is now increasingly viewed as responsible for his or her employability.

Three very different types of change can be observed in the shift from the regulation of (salaried) work to the regulation of work subjects. First, with new entrants to the labour market beginning their working lives much later and the reduction of the average retirement age the length of the working life has shortened. The later entry of new workers to the job market can be explained by the increase in further and higher education (27 per cent of those aged 25–9 have university degrees) and a certain reluctance to start their working lives in precarious conditions (the employment rate of males aged 16–19 has dropped from 47.5 per cent to 29.5 per cent, while 64 per cent of those aged 16–24 have temporary employment contracts). Meanwhile the reduction of the average retirement age is primarily due to companies reducing their labour costs by bringing forward the retirement of those who are most expensive, that is, the oldest workers.

Second, there has been a feminization of the workforce. A substantial increase in the female employment rate (52.7 per cent of women between the ages of 16 and 64 in 2002 compared with 28.9 per cent in 1980)[24] has brought a marked change in the composition of the working population. In 1980 women comprised only 29.1 per cent of the total workforce, by 2002 they comprised 39.3 per cent. Thus women are gradually leaving their role as housewives and are joining men in the world of work.[25]

Third, immigrant workers from countries outside the EU have joined the Spanish job market, overwhelmingly for economic reasons and often illegally. In 1980 immigration was an unknown phenomenon in Spain, but in 2004 immigrants are estimated to account for 6–8 per cent of the total workforce.[26]

When taken together, the developments described above show that the situation of work and workers is of a very different order from that provided by the salaried employment norm, under which work and workers had a central place in the structure of the social system and the definition of individual and group identities. This centrality was expressed in a set of norms ensuring that all employment involved adequate material and social conditions, and that workers obtained sufficient remuneration from their jobs to lead a dignified life. Although that work and those workers belonged to a capitalist system, based on the political power of capital and the state,[27] capital accepted this centrality in exchange for being able to maintain and reproduce the logic and practice of maximizing the benefits of private enterprise. Now the tables have turned.

Ostensibly employment still holds a priority position, and there is no political, social or economic measure to indicate the contrary. After meticulously studying all the social and labour legislation passed during the 1980s and 1990s, Bilbao (1999a, p. 313) concluded that 'Employment is the central motif behind all labour market reforms. Job creation is the central argument in all legislative changes.' But this only seems to pertain when the conditions for economic growth are favourable, and in the current scenario of economic globalization, different measures are required to improve the competitiveness of Spanish companies and the Spanish economy as a whole. Hence flexible employment and growing job insecurity (Bilbao, 1999b).

A basic feature of flexibilization is that the overall employment system has has to incorporate flexibility. The door has been opened for the national economy, every company has to match the quantity, quality and cost of the workforce to its production needs. The most visible manifestation of this is the use of permanent and temporary workers by companies to varying degrees. Since the Spanish survey of the working population began to provide figures on the subject the regulation of temporary and part-time contracts the percentage of temporary salaried workers has hovered in the range of 30–35 per cent. Hence this type of work has become a structural part of the Spanish labour market. While the job security of workers with indefinite contracts has diminished (dismissal procedures have been steadily streamlined and redundancy costs are lower than they were during the constitution years), there is no doubt that fixed-term workers are in a far more precarious position. Indeed same contracts are for a matter of days. To the increase in fixed-term contracts must be added the decentralization of production by means of outsourcing (Valdés Dal-Re, 2002). Companies' contractual commitment to many of their workers is now so limited that 27.7 per cent of workers no longer know how many employees there are in the companies where they work (Labour Force Survey, 2002).

This constitutes a radical change from the previous norm. In the current formulation of the social system, employment has been demoted several rungs down the hierarchical ladder of priorities. In effect it has been degraded.[28] Moreover the border has been blurred between standard employment with unstable contracts (especially part-time contracts) and abnormal salaried work in the submerged economy.

## The salaried employment norm versus the contested entrepreneurial norm

Although the salaried employment norm (Fordist or Keynesian) was formerly widely accepted by social and political players in labour relations and grass roots workers, this was not the case in all industrialized countries or during the 1930s, when the norm was implemented. Later, at the end of the 1960s, there was such turmoil that some saw it as a revolution (Crouch and Pizzorno, 1989). What does seem to be true is that acceptance of the rules on which the capitalist economy and the demands of the salaried class were articulated through the political sphere were much greater than they currently are. This manifested itself in a general acceptance (not only among social democrats) of Keynesianism as a social and economic theory and as a model of social and economic policy. This acceptance has led many researchers to interpret the welfare state, whose best expression is the salaried employment norm, as the result of an implicit political and economic pact, albeit asymmetrical, between corporate representatives of industrial capitalism and the salaried class, represented by trade unions and backed by the institutions of a democratic state. Alonso (2000, p. 118) sums up the basic points of this pact as follows:

> [This] pact . . . meant that labour accepted the logic of private benefit and the pre-eminence of the market as a central tool for growth as long as capital acknowledged the need to internalise, through public goods such as social and economic rights, the externalities of economic growth in processes of arbitration, negotiation and social pacts made in a corporatist manner by organisations representing interests within the state itself.[29]

Using the 'Keynesian' pact to explain the meaning of the salaried employment norm enables us to understand some of its basic aspects – that is, those included in the ideas of the economist John Maynard Keynes. Yet at the same time it can hinder our understanding of other concepts. Limiting and structuring working time, and developing measures for health and safety at work, social insurance, trade unions as the monitors of national labour regulations, employment contracts and so on are all social and labour institutions belonging to the salaried employment norm. These began to take shape in the last decades of the nineteenth century and were consolidated during the first decades of the twentieth century. What made them possible was the successful political challenge posed by the organized workers' movement to the first liberal order, coupled with the size of reformist thought (Prieto, 2003). Thus the 'Keynesian pact' came into use long before Keynes published his ideas.[30] Such a long history enables us to understand how this phenomenon was consolidated and accepted in Western European countries over the decades following the Second World War. It also enables us to understand the full scope of the crisis of the 1980s.

As discussed earlier, from the beginning of the 1980s unemployment rose far higher in Spain than elsewhere in Europe. This automatically increased the perceived value of work. In order to obtain and keep a job, the working population has had to be more flexible than it would in a situation of full employment. However flexibility is far from absolute. Given the high degree of legitimacy accorded to the salaried employment norm by workers, this cannot happen. Also, to varying extents a good number of the earlier social and labour protection guarantees (within the terrain of regular employment) have been maintained despite the 'deprotecting regulations' that have appeared since the 1980s.[31]

One of the pillars of the flexible employment norm is that priority is attached to individuals as opposed to groups (hence the full meaning of the so-called employability policy and the more recent European 'activation' policy).[32] In this regard some workers, particularly the better educated and well-connected, have been advantaged by the new system and enjoy greater (relative) autonomy at work (Bouffartigue and Bouteiller, 2002). This differentiation of winners and losers tends to coincide with the general social ordering. Ordinary native males predominate in jobs where many aspects of the salaried norm are still maintained; better educated and well-connected Spanish males prevail in the segment where labour flexibility primarily takes the form of autonomy[33] in managing one's (ever increasing and intense) workload; and women, immigrants and young people predominate in jobs with the greatest insecurity.[34] The degree of subordination in these three social categories is linked to scant social power and to patterns of individual orientation towards employment.[35]

While the flexible employment norm has become commonplace in Spain, this does not mean that it has been passively accepted. The various government proposals to make the labour market more flexible between 1985 and 2002 sparked no fewer than five general strikes, two of which (in 1988 and 2002) received mass support from workers. The trade union slogan of the time was 'Secure and stable employment with rights' (*Por un empleo seguro, estable y con derechos*).[36] Nonetheless this collective resistance did not prevent flexible employment from being implemented, and one wonders whether workers eventually took it on as a legitimate norm or endured it as an inevitable evil. There appears to have been no research on this issue.

It would, however, be incorrect to assume that resigned acceptance of the new employment norm makes it unmovable. As stated at the beginning of the chapter, unmodifiable social norms do not exist because all social norms are the result of tensions between social classes, and these tensions always lead to change. Just as with the economic crisis of the 1970s, the acceleration of unemployment and the 'corporate forces of capitalism' (Alonso, 2000) put an end to the salaried norm and implanted a very different one, there is always the possibility that a new social norm will replace the current one.

A full return to the salaried employment norm is unlikely, but the time has come to develop a new, more integrating employment norm, for two reasons. First, since the liberalization of labour markets during the 1980s and 1990s in all European countries the employment situation has not improved or has only improved marginally (in Spain, during 2002, despite the strong increase in employment over the last few years, there was still an 11 per cent unemployment rate, the highest of all, while 30.1 per cent of all temporary workers complained of poor-quality employment), so an increasing number of experts, including those in the OECD, and politicians have lost faith in 'deprotecting' labour regulation as a means of increasing employment and improving the plight of the most negatively affected social strata. Second, the majority of the working population is opposed to an increase in flexibility, and this opposition is increasing (even among the immigrant population).[37]

The history of how employment norms are developed shows that two prerequisites will have to be met in order to eliminate the flexible employment norm. The first is a social force that is large and widespread enough to justify the ending of the norm and its replacement by another that takes working-class interests more fully into account. This can only be coordinated by the trade union movement. The second prerequisite, which must be combined with the first in the interest of political efficiency, is the development, as was done during the long process of developing the salaried employment norm,[38] of reformist thought that is not only suited to the times but also imaginative and innovative. In practical terms it must include a reworked form of labour flexibility that is beneficial both to the functioning of the economy and to people's working and living conditions, and also returns the security relinquished during the current period.[39]

In any event, it seems there is a clear consensus in favour of dynamic reform. From a per capita income standpoint our societies are much richer than they were in the 1970s, so there is no reason for any citizen-worker to have worse working and living conditions than in the past.

## Notes

1. This chapter is a shorter and revised version of an article published in the magazine *Sistema* (July 2002) under the title 'La degradación del empleo o la norma social del empleo flexibilizado'.
2. 'Persons who take care of their homes *without remuneration,* as well as persons providing social or beneficent services that are *not remunerated* and generally all persons carrying out *non-profit activities*' are not employed. Spanish Survey of the Working Population (emphasis added).
3. The social literature on this point is extensive. Durán (1997) and Carrasco (1999) are representative examples.
4. In a different way Miguélez (2003b), in an excellent article published in the magazine *Sistema*, defends this same idea. Miguélez defines employment as 'the social conditions in which [salaried] work is performed' (ibid., p. 151).
5. Important legislation during these years included the Industrial Relations Act of 1976, the Workers' Statute (*Estatuto de los Trabajadores*) and the Basic Employment Act of 1980. The current Spanish constitution was passed in 1978.
6. The type of society and model of social regulation that we are referring to with the concept of 'salaried society' coincide with those attached to the much better known and wider used concept of Fordism. The reason we prefer 'salaried society' is that it better conveys the political dimension of the social order that both terms aim to define.
7. See Bilbao (1999a).

8. This term comes from Santos (1994).
9. The concept 'fair employment' can also be found in Miguélez (2003a).
10. This is notion of full employment draws from Keynes and Beveridge (1988).
11. See Bouffartigue (1999).
12. For Miguélez (2003a), stability and security are the most important attributes of fair employment. Miguélez writes: 'Stability and security in employment were conditions that were so far removed from discussion during that period . . . that they were virtually absent from the subjective balance regarding work and collective bargaining demands' (ibid., p. 152).
13. Proof of the fact that this ongoing improvement was conceived as a true social norm and not as the mere result of economic growth is that the 1980 Workers' Statute included salary increases based on 'seniority'.
14. The 1978 Spanish constitution only required Spanish citizens to fulfil two duties; the 'duty to work' (Article 35) and the duty to serve Spain militarily.
15. The concept of decommodification goes back to Polanandi. Some sociologists have returned to this concept to explain the transformations in labour relations in welfare states (see for instance Esping-Andersen, 1993). However the concept conceals that fact that the state may also intervene, according to its own logic, to commodify the workforce. One example of this is its involvement in training (see Alonso, 1999).
16. On this topic see Royal Decree 1445/82 in which, two years after the major reform of the Workers' Statute, temporary and part-time hiring were accepted and regulated.
17. The *Encuesta de Población Activa*.
18. See also Alaluf and Martínez (1999), who also speak of destabilization.
19. As Alonso (2000, p. 71) rightly points out, the notion of flexibility 'is the fundamental cognitive (and ideological) device' of Post-Fordist regulation.
20. This a rather simple definition, but we feel that it adequately expresses the common use of the term. For a more detailed definition see Recio (1997).
21. Unless stated otherwise, all the figures on flexible employment come from the 2002 Survey of the Working Population in Spain.
22. Seen numbers 15–16 of *Economia and Sociología del Trabajo* (1992), which is a special issue on the reduction and reordering of working time. Although it is somewhat outdated owing to changes over the last few years, it is a good source of information.
23. Interestingly, this is the same reasoning used by Mandeville to justify the need not only for there to be poor people, but also to pay miserable wages, thereby condemning the poor to eternal work.
24. Even so, this is still one of the lowest rates in Europe.
25. The transformation of women from housewives into workers has not made gender inequalities disappear. Inequalities have merely shifted their terrain into the area of employment. See Maruani *et al.* (2000).
26. Given the high proportion of immigrants without work permits it is impossible to ascertain the exact figure.
27. 'European nation-states developed a capacity to govern "their" economies and apply public power to control economic activity and the results of the market as a function of the "public interest" ' (Boander and Drache, 1996, p. 300). 'The two imperatives of the benefactor State that it was able relatively successfully to harmonise were the imperative of maintaining and sustaining private accumulation and the imperative of bringing about cohesion and reducing conflict in society

through public policies of consumption and social legitimisation' (Alonso, 2000, p. 121).
28. A more detailed development of this idea can be found in Prieto (2003, section 3).
29. Miguélez (2003, p. 157) develops this same line of reasoning to explain the fundaments of fair employment: 'The guarantee', of fair employment 'therefore exists and has a social-collective nature. It is not a mere concession. It does not solely respond to the momentary economic situation. Nor is it the result of any laws. It is the result of relations between the social partners.'
30. For the importance of the period between the First and Second World Wars for the building of Welfare states, see Ashford (1989) and Monereo Pérez (1996).
31. We use the term 'deprotecting regulations' rather than 'deregulation' because flexibilization has involved not less regulation but different regulation.
32. 'Employability' is the correlate on the individual level of 'competitiveness' on the entrepreneurial level. Just as it is up to companies to be competitive, workers are responsible for their own employability. Serrano (2003) is worth consulting on 'activation' as a thread running across the European employment strategy.
33. Here we follow the distinction made by Bouffartigue and Bouteiller (2004).
34. Of the total number of unemployed or persons on temporary contracts, 75 per cent are women or persons under the age of 30.
35. For the concept of social negotiating power, see Villa (1990). According to Prieto (1999d, p. 146) the social power of the market is the condensed expression of economic, educational and social capital (in the sense that Bourdieu uses these concepts) that individuals have in the labour market.
36. This was also printed on the banner leading the united trade union march on May Day in 2001.
37. The following statement was made by an entrepreneur: 'The problem is that [immigrant workers] will accept anything, they'll work for tons of hours for a pittance and then, once they see what's going on and rub elbows with the rest, they don't want to be taken advantage of!' Colectivo IOÉ (2001, p.3).
38. Keynes was part of this.
39. This combination is taking shape under the concept known as 'flexi-security'. (Supiot, 1999; see also Gautié (2003).

## References

Alaluf, M. and E. Martínez (1999) 'Bélgica: el empleo desestabilizado por el desempleo. Empleo precario and desempleo activo', in C. Prieto (1999b), vol. 1.
Alaluf, M. and C. Prieto (eds) (2001) *Collective Bargaining and the Social Construction of Employment* (Brussels: European Trade Union Institute).
Alonso, L. E. (1999) *Trabajo v ciudadanía. Estudios sobre la crisis de la sociedad salarial* (Madrid: Trotta y Fundación).
Alonso, L. E. (2000) *Trabajo y posmodernidad: el empleo débil* (Madrid: Fundamentos).
Aragón Medina, J. (1998) *Euro y empleo* (Madrid: CES).
Ashford, D. E. (1989) *La aparición de los Estados de Bienestar* (Madrid: Ministerio de Trabajo y Seguridad Social).
Beveridge, W. H. (1988) *Pleno empleo en una sociedad libre* (Madrid: Ministerio de Trabajo y Seguridad Social).
Bilbao, A. (1999a) 'La posición del trabajo y la reforma del mercado de trabajo', in F. Miguélez and C. Prieto, *Las relaciones de empleo en España* (Madrid: Siglo XXI).

Bilbao, A. (1999b) *El empleo precario. Seguridad de la economía e inseguridad del trabajo* (Madrid: Libros de la Catarata).
Boander, R. and D. Drache (eds) (1996) *States against Markets: the Limits of Globalization* (London: Routledge).
Bouffartigue, P. (1999) *'Francia: la norma de empleo hecha trizas?'*, in C. Prieto, vol. 2.
Bouffartigue, P. and J. Bouteiller (2002) 'L'érosion de la norme du temps de travail', *Travail et Emploi*, 92. (Oct., pp. 43–59).
Bouffartigue, P. and J. Bouteiller (2004) 'A propos des normes du temps de travail. De l'érosion de la norme fordienne aux normes émergentes', *Revue de l'IRES*, 43, pp. 127–35.
Carnoy, M. (2001) *El trabajo flexibilizado en la era de la información* (Madrid: Alianza).
Carrasco, C. (ed.) (1999) *Mujeres y economía* (Madrid: Icaria and Antrazandt).
Castel, R. (1995) *Métamorphoses de la question sociale* (Paris: Fayard).
Colectivo IOÉ (2001) *No quierens ser menos! Exploración sobre la discriminación laboral de los inmigrantes en España* (Madrid: Unión General de Trabajadores).
Crouch, C. and A. Pizzorno (1989) *El resurgimiento del conflicto de clases en Europa Occidental a partir de 1968*, 2 vols (Madrid: Ministerio de Trabajo y Seguridad Social).
Demazière, D. (2003) *Le chômage. Comment peut-on être chômeur?* (Paris: Belin).
Durán, M. A. (ed.) (1997) *Bases sociales de la economía española* (Valencia: Alfons, G. (1993) *Tres mundos del Estado del Bienestar* (Valencia: Alfons el Magnànim).
Esping-Andersen, G. (1993) *Tres mundos del Estado del Bienestar* (Valencia: Alfons el Magnànim).
Esping-Andersen, G. (1999) *Fundamentos sociales de las economías postindustriales* (Barcelona: Ariel).
Gautié, J. (2003) *Quelle troisième voie? Entre marché du travail et protection sociale*, working paper no. 30 (www.cee-recherche.fr).
Martínez Lucio, M. (1998) 'Spain: Regulating Employment and Social Fragmentation', in A. Ferner and R. Hyman (eds), *Chenging Industried Relations in Europe* (Oxford: Blackwell).
Maruani, M., C. Rogerat and T. Torns, (2000) *Las nuevas fronteras de la desigualdad* (Madrid: Icaria and Antrazandt).
Miguélez, F. (2003a) 'Por qué empeora el empleo?', in R. Díaz Salazar (ed.), *Trabajadores precarios. El proletariado del siglo XXI* (Madrid: HOAC).
Miguélez, F. (2003b) 'Los veinte últimos años de las relaciones laborales', *Mientras Tanto*, 93, pp. 45–57.
Miguélez, F. and O. Rebollo (1999) 'Negociación colectiva en los noventa', in F. Miguélez and C. Prieto, *Las relaciones de empleo en España* (Madrid: Siglio XXI).
Monereo Pérez, J. L. (1996) *Derechos sociales de la ciudadanía y ordenamiento laboral* (Madrid: CES).
Offe, C. (1992) *La sociedad del trabajo. Problemas estructurales y perspectivas de futuro* (Madrid: Alianza).
Pérez Díaz, V. (1980) *Clase obrera, orden social y conciencia de clase* (Madrid: Fundación Nacional de Industria).
Pries, L. (1988) 'Calificación, relaciones laborales y mercado de trabajo: el concepto de estrechez del ámbito empresarial', *Revista Española de Investigaciones Sociológicas*, 41, pp. 81–115.
Prieto, C. (ed.) (1994) *Trabajadores and condiciones de trabajo* (Madrid: HOAC).
Prieto, C. (1996) 'Trabajo e identidad social femenina', unpublished report, Dirección General de la Mujer de la Communidad de Madrid, ERL.
Prieto, C. (1999a) 'Crisis del empleo, crisis del orden social?', in F. Miguélez and C. Prieto, *Las relacione s de empleo en. España* (Madrid: Siglo XXI).

Prieto, C. (ed.) (1999b) *La crisis del empleo en Europa*, 2 vols (Valencia: Germanía).
Prieto, C. (1999c) 'Globalización económica, relación de empleo y cohesión social', *Revista de Sociología*, 58, pp. 13–37.
Prieto, C. (1999d) 'Los estudios sobre mujer, trabajo y empleo: caminos recorridos, caminos por recorrer', *Política y Sociedad*, 32, Sept. Dec., pp. 141–51.
Prieto, C. (2000) 'Trabajo y orden social: de la nada a la sociedad de empleo (y su crisis)', *Política y Sociedad*, 34, pp. 19–32.
Prieto, C. (2002) 'La degradación del trabajo o la norma social del empleo flexibilizado', *Sistema*, 168–9 (July), pp. 89–106.
Prieto, C. (2003) 'Teoría social del trabajo', in S. Giner, *Teoría social moderna* (Barcelona: Ariel).
Prieto, C. and R. Ramos (1999) 'El tiempo de trabajo: entre la competitividad y los tiempos sociales', in F. Miguélez and C. Prieto, *Las relaciones de empleo en España* (Madrid: Siglio XXI).
Prieto, C. and E. Roquero (2001) 'The trade union movement and the regulation of the social norm of employment in Spain: from the institutional setting to the real world', in M. Alaluf and C. Prieto (eds), *Collective Bargaining and the Social Construction of Employment* (Brussels: European Trade Union Institute).
Recio, A. (1997) *Trabajo, personas, mercados. Manual de economía laboral* (Madrid and Icaria Fuhem).
Salais, R., N. Baverez and B. Reynaud (1990) *La invención del paro en Francia* (Madrid: Ministerio de Trabajo y Seguridad Social).
Santos, A. (1994) '*Trayectorias laborales de los parados de larga duración*', Faculty of Political Sciences and Sociology doctoral thesis (Universidad Complutense de Madrid).
Serrano Pascual, A. (2003) 'Towards convergence of European activation policies?', in D. Foden and L. Magnusson (eds), *Five Years' Experience of the Luxembourg Employment Strategy* (Brussels: ETUI and SALTSA).
Serrano, A. and J. L. Malo de Molina (1979) *Salarios y mercado de trabajo en España* (Madrid: Blume).
Supiot, A. (1999) *Au-delà de l'emploi* (Paris: Flammarion).
Topalov, C. (1996) *Naissance du chômeur. 1880–1910* (Paris: Albin Michel).
Topalov, C. (2000) 'La institucionalización del desempleo y la formación de las normas de empleo. Las experiencias francesa y británica (1911–1939)', *Política y Sociedad*, 34, pp. 133–59.
Torns, T. (2000) 'Paro y tolerancia social de la exclusión: el caso de España', in M. Maruani, C. Rogerat and T. Torns, *Las nuevas fronteras de la desigualdad. Hombres y mujeres en el mercado de trabajo* (Madrid: Icaria and Antrazandt).
Valdés Dal-Re, F. (2002) 'Descentralización productiva y desorganización del derecho del trabajo', *Sistema*, 168–9 (July), pp. 71–88.
Villa, P. (1990) *La estructuración de los mercados de trabajo* (Madrid: Ministerio de Trabajo y Seguridad Social).

# 5
# The Myth of Decentralization and the New Labour Market

*Robert MacKenzie and Chris Forde*

## Introduction

In recent decades the use of contingent forms of labour has been bound up in debates on organizational change and major disjunctures in the organization of production. From early debates on paradigmatic shifts towards more flexible approaches to production (Piore and Sabel, 1984; Atkinson and Meager, 1986) to more recent pronouncements on the shift to network organizations and post-bureaucratic forms (Miles and Snow, 1986; Heydebrand, 1989; Heckscher and Donnellon, 1994; Castells, 2000), the use of non-standard labour has been viewed as symptomatic of a radical transformation in the organization of production, and labour within production. The move away from full-time, permanent, direct employment contracts towards more contingent arrangements has taken various forms. This chapter concentrates on two key approaches to the use of contingent labour: subcontracting and recourse to temporary employment agencies.

Although there has been an undeniable increase in the use of subcontracting and agency workers (Cully *et al.*, 1999; Millward *et al.*, 2000), the extent to which such changes can be described as pervasive or representative of a sea change in the nature of employment in advanced capitalist economies is open to question (Taylor, 2003). This is not to deny that where such a shift has occurred it does represent a major redefinition of the nature of the employment relationship, but the danger of overstating the implications of this in terms of reflecting a paradigmatic shift in the organization of production must be recognized. The use of contingent employment forms have been interpreted as manifestations of a restructuring of production along the lines of decentralization and a dismantling of bureaucratic organizational forms. The broad-brush approach to analysis in much of this literature, however, obscures important nuances in the nature of these types of contingent labour. This chapter argues that the use of agency workers and subcontractors is not a given and constant phenomenon, rather it is based on social relations that develop over time and are shaped by a variety of contradictions and tensions. Consequently the reality of their use cannot be readily reconciled with notions of decentred post-bureaucratic forms.

Following a discussion of debates on the use of contingent labour as part of a new strategic approach to flexibility, the chapter examines the peculiarities associated with the use of agency workers and subcontracting arrangements. Whilst there are important qualitative differences between the two types of arrangement, recent trends in their use are consistent with centralization rather than decentralization. The themes of the chapter are pulled together in a general discussion of new organizational forms.

## The flexibility debate

Early debates on the use of contingent forms of employment focused on the extent to which this reflected a new strategic approach to flexibility. According to Atkinson and Meager (1986) The 'distancing strategies' adopted by firms allowed the core workers in the 'flexible firm' to concentrate on areas of comparative advantage. Numerical flexibility could be achieved by the use of 'peripheral' forms of employment to meet fluctuating demands for labour. Although the core–periphery rhetoric would prove seductive to management gurus and practitioners for some time, conceptual ambiguities (Pollert, 1988) and shaky empirical foundation (Marginson, 1989) seriously undermined its credibility. Rather than being a facet of new flexibility strategies, the use of contingent forms of labour represented a continuation of long-established practices (Wood and Smith, 1987; McGregor and Sproull, 1991; Legge, 1995), especially in the case of subcontractors (Bresnen et al., 1985), and contingent workers were mostly engaged for 'traditional reasons' (Hunter and MacInnes, 1991; Hunter et al., 1993).

Several observers questioned the notion that the decision to use flexible forms of labour is informed by a coherent labour (flexibility) strategy (Wood and Smith, 1987; Marginson, 1989; McGregor and Sproull, 1991; Hunter and MacInnes, 1991). Hunter and MacInnes (1991) conclude that such decisions were predominately pragmatic, rather than driven by a manpower strategy. Decisions are largely taken in response to changes in environmental factors such as the external labour market, competitive pressure and an awareness of business needs, which necessitate flexibility in the utilization of labour and the control of costs. However these are not quantitatively calculated decisions based on detailed cost comparisons, but rather are qualitative and based on perceptions of the behavioural characteristics of different types of labour (under different contracts) and how this fits in with broader business considerations. The extent to which contingent arrangements are a reflection of a coherent labour flexibility strategy is thus thrown into question – as indeed is the centrality of detailed labour policies to general commercial strategy.

More recently the use of contingent employment arrangements has been seen as a central component of a shift towards more fragmented relational forms (Clegg, 1990). Such fragmentation is said to be part of a paradigmatic shift in organizational form, a departure from the tradition of hierarchical bureaucratic organization that is variously depicted as a shift towards 'post-bureaucratic' (Heydebrand, 1989; Clegg, 1990; Heckscher and Donnellon, 1994), 'boundaryless' (Ashkenas et al., 1995) or 'network' (Miles and Snow, 1986; Thompson et al., 1991; Castells, 2000) forms of organization. Post-bureaucratic organizations are characterized by an increasingly decentralized structure (Heydebrand, 1989), complex and fragmented relational forms (Clegg, 1990) and reliance on the interaction of participants rather than their hierarchical organization (Heckscher and Donnellon, 1994). It is claimed that the competition and rivalry between contract partners associated with arms-length contracting is alleviated by a shift to relational contracting and a boundaryless association between the organizations (Ashkenas et al., 1995). This is associated with a reduction of power and control through hierarchical relations, which allows interorganizational capacity to flourish (Williams, 2002).

Such non-hierarchical environments, with dispersed configurations of power (ibid.), resemble the alternative organizational form of 'networks' (Miles and Snow, 1986; Thompson et al., 1991; Castells, 2000). Networks are located somewhere between markets and hierarchies – distinct from both, they provide the means to interconnect discrete organizations for the coordinated pursuit of a common purpose. Such relations are more structured than a market, less structured than a hierarchy and imply a more decentred approach. The notion of an increasingly decentred structure is a consistent theme in the various accounts of major shifts to new organizational forms.

Thus the use of contingent employment forms has been associated with the processes of decentralization, post-bureaucratic fragmentation and the emergence of network organizations. Given the broader explanatory aspirations of such approaches there is a tendency to treat the use of individual forms of contingent labour as unproblematic and consistent phenomena, however closer examination reveals that key aspects of their use are difficult to reconcile with such an analysis.

The remainder of this chapter focuses on two particular types of contingent arrangement – subcontracting and the use of temporary employment agencies – to explore these issues in more detail. In the UK, the 1998 Workplace Employee Relations Survey (WERS) revealed that subcontracting is the most common form of non-standard working arrangement, used in 90 per cent of organizations (Cully et al., 1999). It has a long history in the organization of production, and there is evidence that further growth in its use occured in the late 1990s. For example 26 per cent of the managers questioned in the 1998 WERS reported that their use of subcontractors had increased in the last five years, while just 3 per cent said it had gone down.

(At the time of writing we are awaiting the publication of equivalent figures from the 2004 WERS survey). This growth appears to have been partly driven by the desire of firms to make cost savings, as around half of those that had contracted out services previously conducted in-house cited cost savings as the main reason.

Similarly there has been a marked increase in the use of employment agencies over the last 20 years. In 1984 there were approximately 50000 agency workers in the UK. By 2000 the number had risen to 250000 and agency workers constituted 1 per cent of the employed workforce (Casey, 1987; Forde and Slater, 2003). First findings from the 2004 WERS reveal that 17 per cent of firms employed at least one agency temp (Kersley et al., 2005). This trend has not been confined to the UK. The temporary help industry has been characterized as one of the fastest growing sectors in the United States, whilst in Europe in the 1990s there was a general move towards the deregulation or legalization of the agency industry (OECD, 1999).

## Agency working

The intervention of the temporary employment agency between employer and employee creates a triangular employment relationship between the three parties, and this aspect of agency working has generated considerable interest (see Cordova, 1986; Bronstein, 1991; Sparke, 1994). However the intervention of a third party between employer and employee is not unique to agency working as intermediaries have been a central feature of both pre-capitalist and capitalist modes of production, taking on a variety of forms. What, then, is distinctive about the temporary employment agency relationship? Gottfried (1992) points to the altered 'spatial and temporal dimensions' that are created in temporary employment agency working. Agency working 'occupies an institutional space that spans multiple locations' (ibid., p. 447), with workers performing their tasks at numerous work sites and being subject to 'a double layer of management' (ibid., p. 449), that is, management by the agency and by the firm to which they are temporarily assigned. Agency work is also characterized by 'time discontinuities' and the 'intermittent deployment of temporary labour power' (ibid., p. 447). As such the temporary employment agency relationship involves the 'displacement of labor relations . . . that both spatially and institutionally separates out the buying of labor from its actual use' (Sparke, 1994, p. 294).

Partly as a result of these factors, it has been suggested that accounts that explain the use of agencies in terms of a move away from hierarchies towards 'spot markets' are at odds with the realities of agency working (Ward et al., 2001). Anomalies and contradictions that arise from the use of agency labour are perhaps 'representative of more wide-ranging sources of tension between the potential for adaption and co-operation offered by the traditional open-ended employment contract, and the potential for labour discipline and market responsiveness of the spot-market contract' (ibid., p. 4). Some of this tension arises from the impression of a growing decentralization (Marshall, 1999) that the use of arms-length relationships implies, which contrasts with the need for firms to retain control over the supply of labour, and the reality of increased hierarchical control and centralization that agency arrangements typically imply. Recent empirical research highlights some of these tensions, revealing the ways in which firms seek to retain or regain control over the supply of labour and the role played by agencies in mediating this process.

The use of the temporary employment agencies involves the transfer of responsibility from the firm to the agency for the supply of a number of workers. The division of responsibility between the client firm and the agency in respect of the payment of wages, the collection of national insurance and taxes, and employment conditions may be partially prescribed by law, although this varies considerably from country to country (see Blanpain, 1993). Beyond responsibilities set down in law, agencies may assume control (to varying degrees) of other aspects of the supply and management of labour. Indeed one of the most notable developments in agency working in recent years is that agencies have become involved in the management of labour within the client firm, that is, in the 'labour process practices . . . of induction and training, supervision, task allocation, performance monitoring and relations with other (temp and non-temp) workers' (Peck and Theodore, 1998, p. 665). Such responsibilities are increasingly contractually specified and are commonplace when agencies supply a large number of temps to firms on a quasipermanent basis, and agency managers typically spend some of their time on site (see Henson, 1996; Carnoy *et al.*, 1997; Forde, 1998).

However transferring some direct costs and uncertainty to an external agency results in firms losing control over the screening of workers, especially when supplying the requisite number of temps is given precedence over the quality of labour supplied. The primacy given to 'meeting the order' (Peck and Theodore, 1998) and pressures on agency consultants to sell labour are strengthened by the fact that consultants' commission is based on the number of 'sales' of temporary positions (Grimshaw *et al.*, 2003). Hence it is perhaps unsurprising that there is considerable dissatisfaction amongst firms with the quality of labour supplied (typically measured in terms of punctuality, reliability and ability to cope with the pace of assembly line work) (Parker, 1994; Henson, 1996; Peck and Theodore, 1998). Whilst this mainly relates to the supply of workers for low-skilled industrial work, the problem of quality is not limited to this area, as a study of agency supply teachers by Grimshaw *et al.* (2003) has revealed. Here the opportunistic behaviour exhibited by many agencies – sending supply teachers who were not perfectly matched to the requirements of the job in order to complete an order – was facilitated by a widespread shortage of permanent staff.

A number of emerging processes (both informal and formal) reveal the efforts of firms to retain or regain control of the supply and quality of labour. In firms that utilize large numbers of agency temps there have been moves to develop and formalize 'preferred' or 'single supplier' arrangements, whereby a single agency is contracted to supply all the temporary labour used by a firm (Carnoy et al., 1997; see also Forde, 2001). The supply of 'repeat workers' (Henson, 1996; Forde, 2001) – the re-engagement of temps who have previously worked for a company – has become a standard service offered by employment agencies with the ability of agencies to secure and retain lucrative quasipermanent single supplier contracts to supply large numbers of temps being dependent on their ability to provide a regular supply of repeat workers. This process has been formalized at many agencies through sophisticated systems to match experienced workers to assignments (Forde, 2001). Formal 'temp-to-perm' schemes – whereby workers are put on probation for a certain period of time, typically six to 13 weeks, after which the firm decides whether to take them on permanently – also reflects the desire of firms to regain control of the screening process.

Whilst agencies are heavily involved in the recruitment and selection process under such schemes, research has shown that firms use the schemes to increase their control of the supply of labour by specifying the skills requirements and personal characteristics of workers and making the agencies responsible for providing tailored training before workers are taken on by the firm (Purcell and Purcell, 1999; Ward et al., 2001). The power of employers in this regard has been revealed by studies of certain local labour markets in the UK, where the widespread use of agencies by firms as a means of screening and filtering workers has resulted in agency work 'becoming entrenched and institutionalised ... in a form which keeps entry wages low' (Elger and Smith, 1998, p. 324). Also apparent is the ability of both employers and agencies to shift elements of risk and uncertainty onto the worker through the processes described above. Forde (2001) has found that the costs and risks associated with providing repeat workers are largely borne by workers, whose flexibility and willingness to accept such assignments are closely monitored by agencies. The use of agencies as a screening device means that workers have 'to meet an often unspecified criterion in order to be eligible for permanent employment' (Ward et al., 2001, p. 8).

Yet far from being passive in these developments, it is important to recognize the active role played by agencies in facilitating the use of agency labour through the formalization and institutionalization of the processes outlined above. In the United States it has been argued that the rapid growth and development of the temporary help industry in the 1960s and 1970s was built on agencies' 'fragile legal foundation' as employers of temporary labour (Gonos, 1997, p. 88). This was due in no small part to the lobbying activities of agencies in the period and allowed US employers to use agency labour 'without obligation' (Gonos, 2001). Recent efforts by agencies to deepen their relations with clients through the development of agreements with other agencies to ensure that preferred supplier arrangements can be honoured (Carnoy *et al.*, 1997), plus the formalization of services such as the provision of repeat workers, have further consolidated the use of temporary labour. While such schemes have served to increase firms' control of their labour supply, they have also rendered agency work more insecure for the worker. This insecurity stems from the fact that agencies keep a surplus of workers on their books to ensure that clients' fluctuating requirements for reliable and flexible workers can be met.

It is important to point out some of the tensions and ironies that result from these strategies, and to highlight outcomes that run counter to those predicted in much of the flexibility literature. As noted in a number of studies, the use of temporary employees (rather than agency workers *per se*) can result in unanticipated rigidity rather than providing the firm with a flexible source of labour (Geary, 1992; Legge, 1995). Animosity between temporary and permanent workers, managers' ambivalence towards temporary staff and a sense of mistreatment amongst temporary workers have created a new type of rigidity, with the 'divide between permanent and temporary staff . . . acting to undo the advantages that might otherwise have been gained' (Geary, 1992, p. 267). Such tension is likely to be heightened as firms seek increased control over the agency labour supplied, and are guaranteed continuity by agencies in terms of the workers supplied, but the workers themselves are afforded little security in the assignments they are given. The implications of this were revealed in a study by Grimshaw *et al.* (2003), who found that the weak mutual sense of goodwill or trust' created by the use of supply teachers resulted in individuals bargaining with schools over non-contractual duties (such as marking and attendance at parents' evenings), in sharp contrast to the 'collegial "ethos" traditionally associated with the teaching profession' (ibid., p. 284). Finally, in many instances the use of agency workers reflects growing centralization within organizations. Head office pressure on departments to reduce their permanent workforce appears to be behind the signing of many large contracts between organizations and agencies (Purcell and Purcell, 1999) to disguise staffing levels or reduce labour costs (Ward *et al.*, 2001, p. 10).

## Subcontracting

Subcontracting is more than just one of a number of alternative sources of labour. This is reflected in the debate on the nature of contracts and the importance of interorganizational relationships. The growth of external contracting constitutes a significant development in the organization of production, with mediation of the firm's activities being conducted through a series of commerical contracts rather than via vertically integrated bureaucratic structures. This ostensibly means a move away from hierarchical relationships and towards market-based exchange. According to Deakin and Michie (1997), one of the key features of the deregulation of the economy over the past two decades has been the revival of the contract as the foremost mechanism of economic activity.

Much of the literature on subcontracting is concerned with the ways in which organizations alleviate the uncertainty associated with relocating elements of the production process beyond the boundaries of the organization. In terms of the contract between two commerical entities, as theexchange process impacts the operational requirements of the patron firm, the mechanisms for organizing that relationship are crucial. The increased use of subcontracted labour is often correlated with a rise in the administration, supervision and monitoring activities of the patron organization (Bresnen *et al.*, 1984; Deakin and Walsh, 1996; Hoggett, 1996; MacKenzie, 2002). Deakin and Walsh (1996) draw attention to the affect that the need to develop mechanisms for dealing with the complexity of performance specifications has upon the nature of the contract relationship. Contracts may be worded flexibly to allow details to be worked out at the time of delivery, but such contracts come to resemble organizations with incomplete and malleable employment agreements. Thus the paradox is created of a contract that works like an organization (Stinchcombe and Heimer, 1985, cited in Deakin and Walsh, 1996). What Stinchcombe (1990) refers to as 'contractual functional substitutes for hierarchy' – including relations of command, incentive systems, standard operating procedures, dispute resolution mechanisms and pricing variations that are partially insulated from market forces – make up an elaborate edifice that acts as a means of alleviating uncertainty about future events. Thus complex contractual arrangements become the functional equivalent of the hierarchy they have replaced. Contrary to the notion of a shift towards reliance on market relations or the dismantling of hierarchy, it can be argued that the creation of such complex structural underpinnings for subcontracting constitutes a reconfiguration of the bureaucratic organization of production (MacKenzie, 2002).

It is important to recognize that mediation of the contract relationship is more than the sum of the terms of an agreement and the bureaucratic structures erected to administer them. The ongoing mediation of the relationship depends on these structural features or administrative measures being combined with less tangible mechanisms to ensure the satisfactory operation of the subject function. As contracting activities become more important to the central production activity, however, the problem of supervision increases (Hunter and MacInnes, 1991). Although the need to ensure contract compliance and delivery mean that incomplete contracts contain elements of explicit monitoring, these are supplemented by other measures, notably the fostering of qualitatively different forms of relationship between the contracting parties. Deakin and Walsh (1996) note that such contracts require relations that go beyond the formal and necessitate the development of trust. Under such arrangements, fostered over time, the recourse to sanctions becomes less likely as this could damage the culture of sorting out problems informally. Trust acts as the basis of expectations of future performance (Deakin and Michie, 1997); it reflects a willingness to bear the risk of opportunistic behaviour by the contract partner, largely because such behaviour is unlikely to occur (Collins, 1997). Trust lessens uncertainty and complexity, and therefore reduces transaction costs (Deakin et al., 1997). Butler and Carney (1983) also point out the role of trust in 'oiling' the operation of the market through informal arrangements that grow out of long-term relationships. They note that the opportunism-reducing qualities associated with the development of long-term associations and informal relationships reduce the cost of gathering information for monitoring exchanges.[1] The benefits of such relationships have been observed at both the empirical and the theoretical levels, however these should not be reified to the extent that they obscure the more tangible structures and mechanisms that underpin them. Trust must be rooted in the institutional framework or the contractual environment (ibid.) in which it operates. Indeed contractual formality is thought to play an important role in building trust by setting limits on behaviour so as to avoid digression from expectations (ibid.)

At the empirical level, research on the so-called Japanese-style 'relational' (Oliver and Wilkinson, 1992) or 'obligational' (Morris and Imrie, 1993) contractual relationships in the 1980s and 1990s has provided insights into advanced subcontracting arrangements (Trevor and Christie, 1988; Turnbull, 1991; Oliver and Wilkinson, 1992; Morris and Imrie, 1993).[2] The Japanese model was contrasted with the British or Western tradition of subcontracting, which was characterized by a hands-off, transactions-based relationship in which price was of primary concern and quality a secondary consideration. The relationship was essentially market based, conducted via a series of spot contracts and relying on the threat of cessation to ensure delivery, and thus was adversarial in nature (Morris and Imrie, 1993). Conversely the obligational form of contracting (Turnbull, 1991; Morris and Imrie, 1993) associated with the Japanese system was based on the development of long-term relationships with suppliers. This close hierarchical relationship provided the benefits of a vertically integrated organization whilst incorporating the efficiency aspects of a market transaction (Turnbull, 1991). In other words firms found means of overcoming the uncertainty associated with externalization whilst maintaining the advantages.

Many of the features of the Japanese-style contracts could also be found in supplier partnerships and in partnership sourcing arrangements (Collins,

1997) between firms engaged in long-term relationships founded on loyalty and trust. Contracts were made with fewer suppliers and were based on 'requirements' rather than specified quantities. These relationships were characterized by 'supplier development', the patron firm's involvement in such areas as the establishment of management systems, and the improvement of quality (Collins, 1997; see also MacKenzie, 2002). Accommodating the demands of a large purchaser led to a great deal of internal restructuring by smaller firms (Ackroyd, 2002). This reflected a closer involvement between buyer and supplier in terms of the buyer influencing the internal practices of the supplier in such areas as R&D, investment and labour utilization (Turnbull, 1991; Oliver and Wilkinson, 1992; Morris and Imrie, 1993). By this means quality could be underwritten and, vitally, relocated to being the responsibility of the subcontractor.

Such migration of responsibility to the supply firm may lead to the relocation of the bureaucratic underpinnings of the organization of production (MacKenzie, 2002). This is informed by the need to ensure that appropriate mechanisms are in place in the supplier firm to manage the responsibilities bestowed by the terms of the contract, bureaucratic mechanisms commensurate with the organization of the element of the production for which it is responsible and for interfacing with the production function of the purchasing organisation (MacKenzie, 2002). It has been suggested that this form of contractual relationship seeks the advantages of vertical integration in terms of quality assurance, whilst competition between suppliers depresses the price (Collins, 1997).

'Quality' is a recurring theme in long-term contractual arrangements (Turnbull, 1991; Oliver and Wilkinson, 1992; Morris and Imrie, 1993; Collins, 1997, Deakin *et al.*, 1997). Assurance is associated with cooperation fostered by long association. Again, however, it must be noted that this may be underpinned by substantive regulatory mechanisms, such as TQM registration and BS5750 or ISO9000 accreditation (Deakin *et al.*, 1997; Collins, 1997). Collins (1997) suggests that large firms can compel suppliers to comply to such schemes, and points to the widespread incidence of large firms supplementing these awards with their own accreditation systems. Mechanisms for auditing, reporting and communicating information are therefore essential components of such relationships.

Such accreditation systems may extend beyond the firm as a whole to individual workers engaged in the production process (MacKenzie, 2000). This is a way of addressing potential quality problems arising from a lack of suitably skilled labour. In the absence of the transparency and guarantees associated with a direct employment relationship, accreditation of individual workers offers the patron firm some degree of assurance. When this is linked to a training programme, perhaps as part of the supplier development process, it can also be used to address the issue of labour supply in quantitative terms (ibid.). Underdeveloped mechanisms for skill reproduction, leading to shortages of suitably skilled labour, can be a problem in industries that rely heavily on subcontracting for the supply of labour (Forde and MacKenzie, 2004). Ensuring an adequate supply of appropriately qualified workers is one of the advantages associated with internal labour markets that is foregone when externalization takes place (see Doeringer and Piore, 1971; Williamson 1975). Problems with the quantity and quality of labour supply can affect performance and undermine the utility of subcontracting, therefore the actions taken by large organizations to regulate the supply of labour from external sources (MacKenzie, 2000) can again be seen as acting to reduce some of the uncertainty associated with reorganization of the production process and the use of external labour. The involvement of the purchaser in the development of managerial and quality-assurance systems in the supplier firm and the use of accreditation highlight the difference between such contractual arrangements and the anonymous exchange assumed in orthodox economic abstraction.

Moreover subcontracting is associated not only with an increase in bureaucracy in the patron firm but also, through the process of supplier development, the spread of bureaucracy to the supplier (MacKenzie, 2002). The creation of a bureaucratic edifice that straddles the organizational boundaries between patron and supplier reflects the desire of the former to gain some control over the process and reduce some of the uncertainty associated with externalization. The development of such structures is sometimes incremental, with additions being made when shortcomings or contradictions become evident (MacKenzie, 1998, 2000). Sako (1992) suggests that the 'obligational contractual relation' approach lies at one end of a continuum of potential trading patterns, with the spot-contracting, 'arms-length' approach lying at the other. This continuum could also be conceptualized as a path of development. Obligational contracting is not something that can be established overnight, and may require many interim measures and structures to help facilitate the development of the relationship (MacKenzie, 2002).

Ultimately, the development of such relations may depend on a degree of centralization, both in terms of the internal management of the contract function and through rationalization of the supply base, moving away from a network of local suppliers towards contracts with fewer, larger suppliers that are capable of accommodating such arrangements (MacKenzie, 1998, 2002). This casts some doubt on the assertion that subcontracting is associated with decentralization and a major paradigmatic shift towards decentred, post-bureaucratic organizational forms.

## Conclusion

The observations in this chapter suggest that the extent to which the use of agency workers and subcontractors can be reconciled with decentralization, post-bureaucratic fragmentation and the emergence of network organizations is questionable, as key aspects of their use are difficult to reconcile with such an analysis. A blurring of boundaries can be observed in the closer relations between firms and their subcontractors and agencies, the degree of involvement of firms in the development of organizational structures and processes in supplier firms (MacKenzie, 2000, 2002), and the redefining of the managerial responsibilities associated with longstanding agency agreements (Forde, 2001). However, associating the use of contingent labour with post-bureaucratic fragmentation (Heydebrand, 1989; Clegg, 1990) and thus decentralization (Hoggett, 1996) is problematic. First, it is wrong to suggest that this represents anything new and 'post-bureaucratic' given these practices have existed for a long time in many bureaucratic organizations (Pollert, 1988). Second, where the use of subcontractors or agency personnel is a long standing practice, the increased proceduralism associated with their utilization has often resulted in centralization rather than decentralization. The development of subcontracting arrangements has been accompanied by the rationalization of supplier bases and the centralization of contract management mechanisms (MacKenzie, 2000, 2002). Similarly the favouring of single supplier agreements with large employment agencies (Carnoy *et al.*, 1997) constitutes a process of centralization in the coordination of contingent labour. Furthermore the obsession with renouncing bureaucratic organization (Thompson and McHugh, 1990) ignores the considerable bureaucratic underpinnings associated with both subcontracting and agency use.

Arguably the key shortcoming of proponents of new organizational forms based on networks and boundaryless associations is their failure to address the issue of power adequately. Ackroyd (2002) is rightly critical of the tendency of network theories to omit issues of authority and control from the equation. Similarly proclamations of the advantages of boundaryless associations tend to side step the question of power, or assume that these arrangements render relations power-neutral (Grimshaw *et al.*, 2002). Despite assertions of the benefits of non-hierarchical environments (Williams, 2002) in reality most interfirm associations are characterized by hierarchical relations between dominant and subordinate actors (Ackroyd, 2002). Although reciprocity may exist (ibid.) it cannot be assumed that there is a balanced distribution of gains from the arrangement (Grimshaw *et al.*, 2002).

Relations between organizations and subcontractors or agencies may develop into long-term close associations, but even relational contracting cannot be assumed to be power-neutral (Dore, 1996). Because of the contractual incompleteness of longer-term relationships there is often ongoing negotiation over competing claims against unforeseen events (O'Connell Davidson, 1993), for which the inability to specify in advance is definitive to the nature of the contract form. These competing claims paradoxically demonstrate the existence of conflict in a process that inherently depends on cooperation, as well as indicating the presence of a power relationship (Bowles and Gintis, 1993; O'Connell Davidson, 1993; Deakin and Walsh, 1996). If power is taken as the ability of one agent to impose its will on another (Macneil, 1981) when the converse is not true (Bowles and Gintis, 1993) then this authority relation, regardless of its apparently voluntary nature, reflects a power relationship. The question is how this power is articulated when the parties come into contact with one another. Exchange is neither costless nor balanced. Bowles and Gintis (ibid.) posit the concept of a 'short-side power' relationship, where the burden of the cost of, for example, termination is borne disproportionately by one party. Macneil (1981) concurs that the process of contracting creates unilateral power based on dependencies of various kinds, such as sunk costs, which are only recoverable through prolonged relations. Deakin and Walsh (1996) suggest that the distribution of risk between two parties to a contract is a function of the power relationship, and that a powerful purchaser will make the provider bear more risk, regardless of the implications for technical efficiency. The transfer of risk is a central feature of both subcontracting and agency arrangements. A contractual relationship is in essence a social process and as such inherently involves power, irrespective of whether or not this is explicitly demonstrated. This power relationship must also be located in the balance of forces in the wider politicoeconomic environment, and a change in the latter has implications for the parties' ability to allocate risk or enforce claims (O'Connell Davidson, 1993). The failure to conceptualize power as a crucial factor in the interaction of parties to an exchange, whether mediated by the market or by bureaucratic, hierarchical structures is a serious omission.

The use of subcontracting and agency arrangements by firms must be viewed as part of the wider changes in the employment relationship, as reflected in the shifting boundary between the internal and external labour markets. They represent mechanisms that mediate the relationship between capital and labour, and regardless of the terms and specificities of the arrangement, they reflect alternative approaches to the same fundamental issues: ensuring that the production process is supplied with the requisite quantity and quality of labour; and within the production process, establishing the means to secure the contribution of that labour. It is important to recognize that the transaction for labour is different from the transaction for any other factor of production or process of exchange, due to the unique role played by labour in the production process. Nor should labour be regarded as passive in the organization of production, and by extension in the process of contracting for labour, a tendency that is apparent in studies that address contracting in abstraction from the production process and the relationship between capital and labour.

## Notes

1. Observers often assume that a high cost is associated with gathering the information needed to coordinate and monitor market transactions (Williamson, 1975; Butler, 1983; Butler and Carney, 1983; Riorden, 1990). This ignores the growth of outsourcing of functions previously, or indeed concurrently, performed in-house, under which the gathering of suitable knowledge has already occurred, thus reducing the costs associated with monitoring a market arrangement (MacKenzie, 1998).
2. Although these writers point out the irregular and problematical nature of these practices, there are certain conceptual consistencies that inform the study of Japanese-style contract arrangements.

## References

Ackroyd, S. (2002) *The Organization of Business: Applying Organizational Theory to Contemporary Change* (Oxford: Oxford University Press).

Ashkenas, R., D. Ulrich, T. Jick and S. Kerr (1995) *The Boundaryless Organisation* (San Francisco, CA: Jossey-Bass).

Atkinson, J. and N. Meager (1986) *New Forms of Work Organisation* (Brighton: Institute of Manpower Studies).

Blanpain, R. (ed.) (1993) *Temporary Work and Labor Law of the EC and Member States* (Deventer: Kluwer).

Bowles, S. and Gintis, H. (1993) 'The Revenge of *Homo Economicus*: Contested Exchange and the Revival of Political Economy', *Journal of Economic Perspectives*, 7 (1), pp. 83–102.

Bresnen, M. J., K. Wray, A. Bryman, A. D. Beardsworth, J. R. Ford and E. T. Keil (1985) 'Flexibility of Recruitment in the Construction Industry: Formalisation or Re-casualisation?', *Sociology*, 19 (1), pp. 108–24.

Bronstein, A. S. (1991) 'Temporary Work in Western Europe: threat or complement to permanent employment?', *International Labour Review*, 130 (3), pp. 291–311.

Butler, R. (1983) 'A Transactional Approach to Organizing Efficiency: Perspectives From Markets, Hierarchies, and Collectives', *Administration and Society*, 15 (3), pp. 323–62.

Butler, R. and M. G. Carney (1983) 'Managing Markets: Implications for the Make–Buy Decision', *Journal of Management Studies*, 20 (2), pp. 213–31.

Carnoy, M., M. Castells and C. Benner (1997) 'Labour Markets and Employment Practices in the Age of flexibility: a case study of the Silicon Valley', *International Labour Review*, 136 (1), pp. 27–50.

Casey, B. (1987) *Temporary Employment: Practice and Policy in Britain* (London: Policy Studies Institute).

Castells, M. (2000) *The Rise of the Network Society*, 2nd edn (Oxford: Blackwell).

Clegg, S. (1990) *Modern Organizations: Organization Studies in the Post-Modern World* (London: Sage).

Collins, H. (1997) 'Quality Assurance in Subcontracting', in S. Deakin and J. Michie (eds), *Contracts, Co-operation and Competition* (Oxford: Oxford University Press).

Cordova, E. (1986) 'From full-time wage employment to atypical employment: a major shift in the evolution of labour relations?', *International Labour Review*, 125 (6), pp. 641–58.

Cully, M., S. Woodland, A. O'Reilly and G. Dix (1999) *Britain at Work* (London: Routledge).

Deakin, N. and K. Walsh (1996) 'The Enabling State: The Role of Markets and Contracts', *Public Administration*, 74 (1), pp. 33–47.
Deakin, S. and J. Michie (1997) 'The Theory and Practice of Contracting', in S. Deakin and J. Michie (eds), *Contracts, Co-operation and Competition* (Oxford: Oxford University Press).
Deakin, S., C. Lane and F. Wilkinson (1997) 'Contract Law, Trust Relations and Incentives for Co-operation: A Comparative Study', in S. Deakin and J. Michie (eds), *Contracts, Co-operation and Competition* (Oxford: Oxford University Press).
Doeringer, P. and M. Piore (1971) *Internal Labour Markets and Manpower Analysis* (New York: M. E. Sharpe).
Dore, R. (1983) 'Goodwill and the Spirit of Market Capitalism', *British Journal of Sociology*, 34 (4), pp. 459–82.
Dore, R. (1996) 'Goodwill and the Spirit of Market Capitalism', in P. J. Buckley and J. Michie (eds), *Firms, Organizations and Contracts* (Oxford: Oxford University Press).
Elger, T. and C. Smith (1998) 'New Town, New Capital, New Workplace', *Economy and Society*, 27 (4), pp. 523–53.
Forde, C. (1998) 'Temporary Employment Agencies: Issues and Evidence', unpublished PhD thesis, University of Leeds.
Forde, C. (2001) 'Temporary Arrangements: The Activities of Employment Agencies in the UK', *Work, Employment and Society*, 15 (3), pp. 631–44.
Forde, C. and R. MacKenzie (2004) 'Cementing Skills: Training and Labour Utilisation in the UK Construction and Civil Engineering Sector', *Human Resource Management Journal*, 14 (3), pp. 74–88.
Forde, C. and G. Slater (2003) 'Continuing Cause for Concern: The Evolving Character and Regulation of Temporary Work', Discussion Papers in Political Economy, Nottingham Trent University, Department of Economics and Politics.
Geary, J. (1992) 'Employment Flexibility and Human Resource Management', *Work, Employment and Society*, 6 (2), pp. 251–70.
Gonos, G. (1997) 'The Contest over "Employer Status" in the Post-war United States: The Case of Temporary Help Firms', *Law and Society Review*, 31 (1), pp. 81–110.
Gonos, G. (2001) 'Fee-Splitting Revisited: Concealing Surplus Value in the Temporary Employment Relationship', *Politics and Society*, 29 (4), pp. 589–612.
Gottfried, H. (1992) 'In the Margins: Fiexibility as a Mode of Regulation in the Temporary Help Service Industry', *Work, Employment and Society*, 6 (3), pp. 443–60.
Grimshaw, D., J. Earnshaw and G. Hebson (2003) 'Private sector provision of supply teachers: a case of legal swings and professional roundabouts', *Journal of Education Policy*, 18 (3), pp. 267–88.
Grimshaw, D., S. Vincent and H. Willmott (2002) 'Going Privately: Partnership and Outsourcing in UK Public Services', *Public Administration*, 80 (3), pp. 475–502.
Heckscher, C. and A. Donnellon (eds) (1994) *The Post Bureaucratic Organisation: New Perspectives on Organisational Change* (London: Sage).
Henson, K. D. (1996) *Just A Temp* (Philadelphia, PA: Temple University Press).
Heydebrand, W. V. (1989) 'New Organizational Forms', *Work and Occupations*, 16 (3), pp. 323–57.
Hoggett, P. (1996) 'New Modes of Control in the Public Sector', *Public Administration*, 74 (1), pp. 9–32.
Hunter, L. C. and J. MacInnes (1991) *Employer Labour Use Strategies: Case Studies*, Department of Employment Research Paper no 87 (London: Department of Employment).

Legge, K. (1995) *Human Resource Management: Rhetoric and Realities* (London: Macmillan).
Kersley, B., C. Alpin, J. Forth, A. Bryson, H. Bewley, G. Dix and S. Oxenbridge (2005) *Inside the Workplace: First Findings from the 2004 Workplace Employment Relations Survey* (London: Routledge).
MacKenzie, R. (1998) *Deregulation and Employment: A Case Study of the Telecommunications Industry*, unpublished PhD thesis, University of Leeds.
MacKenzie, R. (2000) 'Subcontracting and the Reregulation of the Employment Relationship: A Case Study from the Telecommunications Industry', *Work, Employment and Society*, 14 (4), pp. 707–26.
MacKenzie, R. (2002) 'The Migration of Bureaucracy: Contracting and the Regulation of Labour in the Telecommunications Industry', *Work, Employment and Society*, 16 (4), pp. 599–616.
Macneil, I. R. (1981) 'Economic Analysis of Contractual Relations', in P. Burrows and C. G. Veljanovski (eds), *The Economic Approach to Law* (London: Butterworth).
Marginson, P. (1989) 'Employment Flexibility in Large Companies: Change or Continuity?', *Industrial Relations Journal*, 20, pp. 101–9.
Marshall, M. G. (1999) 'Flexible specialisation, supply-side institutionalism and the nature of work systems', *Review of Social Economy*, 57 (2), pp. 199–219.
McGregor, A. and A. Sproull (1991) *Employer Labour Use Strategies: Analysis of a National Survey*, Employment Department Research Series no 83 (London: Employment Department).
Miles, R. E. and C. C. Snow (1986) 'Organizations: New Concepts for New Forms', *California Management Review*, 28 (3), pp. 62–73.
Millward, N., A. Bryson and J. Forth (2000) *All Change at Work?: British Employment Relations 1980–98, as Portrayed by the Workplace Industrial Relations Survey Series* (London: Routledge).
Morris, J. and R. Imrie (1993) 'Japanese Style Subcontracting: Its Impact on European Industries', *Long Range Planning*, 26 (4), pp. 53–8.
O'Connell Davidson, J. (1993) *Privatization and Employment: The Case of the Water Industry* (London: Mansell).
OECD (1999) *Employment Outlook* (Paris: OECD).
Oliver, N. and B. Wilinson (1992) *Japanisation of British Industry: New Developments in the 1990s* (Oxford: Blackwell).
Parker, R. E. (1994) *Flesh Peddlers and Warm Bodies: The Temporary Help Industry and Its Workers* (New Jersey: Rutgers University Press).
Peck, J. and N. C. Theodore (1998) 'Trading Warm Bodies: Processing Contingent Labor in Chicago's Temp Industry', *Work, Employment and Society*, 12 (4), pp. 655–74.
Piore, M. and C. F. Sabel (1984) *The Second Industrial Divide; Possibilities of Prosperity* (New York: Basic Books).
Pollert, A. (1988) 'The Flexible Firm: Fixation or Fact?', *Work, Employment and Society*, 2 (3), pp. 281–316.
Purcell, K. and J. Purcell (1999) 'Insourcing, Outsourcing and the Growth of Contingent Labour as Evidence of Fiexible Employment Strategies', in R. Blanpain (ed.), *Non-Standard Work and Industrial Relations* (Kluwer Law International).
Riorden, M. H. (1990) 'What is Vertical Integration?', in M. Aoki, B. Gustafsson and O. E. Williamson (eds), *The Firm as a Nexus of Treaties* (London: Sage).
Rubery, J. and F. Wilkinson (eds) (1994) *Employer Policies and the Labour Market* (Oxford: Oxford University Press).
Sako, M. (1992) *Prices, Quality and Trust: Inter-firm Relations in Britain and Japan* (Cambridge: Cambridge University Press).

Sparke, M. (1994) 'A Prism for Contemporary Capitalism: Temporary Work as Displaced Labor as Value', *Antipode*, 26 (4), pp. 295–322.
Stinchcombe, A. L. (1990) *Information and Organizations* (Berkeley, CA: University of California Press).
Taylor, R. (2003) 'Britain's World of Work: Myths and Realities', *ESRC Future of Work Programme Report* (Swindon: ESRC).
Thompson, G., J. Frances, R. Levacic, and J. Mitchell (eds) (1991) *Markets, Hierarchies and Networks* (London: Sage).
Thompson, P. and D. McHugh (1990) *Work Organisations: A Critical Introduction* (London: MacMillan).
Trevor, M. and I. Christie (1988) *Manufacturers and Suppliers in Britain and Japan. Competitiveness and the Growth of Small Firms*, Policy Studies Institute Report 682 (London: Policy Studies Institute).
Turnbull, P. (1991) 'Buyer–Supplier Relations in the UK Automotive Industry', in P. Blyton and J. Morris (eds), *A Flexible Future? Prospects for Employment and Organisation* (Berlin: de Gruyter).
Ward, K., D. Grimshaw, J. Rubery and H. Beynon (2001) 'Dilemmas in the Management of Temporary Work Agency Staff', *Human Resource Management Journal*, 11, pp. 3–21.
Williams, P. (2002) 'The Competent Boundary Spanner', *Public Administration*, 80 (1), pp. 103–24.
Williamson, O. (1975) *Markets and Hierarchies* (New York: Free Press).
Wood, D. and P. Smith, (1987) *Employers' Labour Use Strategies: First Report on the 1987 Survey* (London: Department of Employment).

# Part III
# The State

# 6
# Are We Moving Towards a Post-Fordist State? Full Employment of the European Workforce

*Daniel Albarracín*

The liberal philosopher Ortega y Gasset put forward the idea of Europe as the sought after destiny of an 'invertebrate' Spain. The building of the European Union (EU) is currently at a phase of development where a new spatial and regional block is emerging to rival ASEAN, NAFTA, and Mercosur. The exhausting of national markets in the accumulation of capital requires a more contemporary form of development (Jessop, 2001) that broadens the EU's trade circuits on a supranational scale. The EU is an attempt to respond to this issue. And to be congruous, the EU must correspond to an analogous macroeconomic model of capital accumulation underpinned by a political, social and labour strategy that facilitates the conditions for dissipating the structural global crisis. This crisis has already persisted over time and its symptoms are acute (geo-political fragmentation into international blocks of adversaries, deterioration of social policy and working conditions, dramatic wars, and the rise of social protest movements, for example).

The European project is facing many problems, as demonstrated by the clashes over the EU constitution. While there is consensus on the social, economic and labour models among European governments and elites, national interests are still brought to bear, hampering supranational decision making and exacerbating disputes over market shares and institutional cohesion policies. The building of the regional market has involved negotiations and disagreements among disparate nation states against a backdrop of intensifying competition between world trading blocs.

The use of old Keynesian prescriptions to assuage recession in the short term has been discontinued for the time being and the EU member states, while the process of surrendering some of their national sovereignty, are determined to retain their patriotic underpinnings and are relinquishing no more than bits and pieces in the interest of macroeconomic coordination. In no case is there any true wish for political union, with full convergence of tax policy, labour regulations and social policy.[1]

This chapter will contribute to the analysis of this situation by investigating the social and labour transformations that have taken place in the EU and the roles played by states in modern capitalism. It will examine European social and labour policies from the standpoint of the relation over time between the bourgeois state and the capitalist market. It will then analyze the Spanish state's role in the social reproduction of the workforce. Finally, it will raise some questions about Europe as a regulatory process.

## Employment and wage relations

According to Gramsci (1992) the development of a stable civilization is only possible through the building of a series of legitimate institutions, and of cultural practices (as well as types of domination and exploitation). The EU is still in its construction phase, the legitimization that underpins it has not yet been forged. However, those who are leading the EU are aware that discourses to confer the project with substance must be developed and be consistent.

The new markets, made up of large regional blocks and backed by national government regulations to increase flexibility, have not yet been fully consolidated. Capitalist formations require a framework for stable accumulation, and therefore require institutions and political programmes to support and sustain markets at the transnational level. With saturated markets and institutions unable to govern markets in crisis, class struggle, adversarial international blocs and continuing wars the functioning of this framework is at a critical juncture (Fernández Duran, 2003). In this context, regulation of the labour market is crucial and wage relations take centre stage. The bourgeoisie strives to increase its rate of capital gains (Aglietta, 1979), thereby improving profit margins and growth rates.

From this standpoint, over the last 25 years the issue of employment has progressed from the back burner to becoming a priority in the building of Europe. The way in which employment is dealt with today differs from the postwar Keynesian–Fordist model (Alonso, 1999, 2000). The political, economic and social crisis of the 1970s resulted in lower economic growth rates, and in each new cycle it has become increasingly difficult to attain the growth rates of the previous cycle (Albarracín, 1994). While this has not been the only factor in job creation, given that national economic and employment policies differ, it has been a decisive conditioning factor over this period. At the same time unemployment has become a major concern.

Since the 1970s pressure has been brought to bear on social and economic development models. With the aim of finding a solution to the crisis of European capitalism, this bourgeois strategy has driven a restructuring of employment, the use of unemployment, deterioration of the social, political and labour rights of the dominated classes, and the pauperization of large segments of the population, despite the increase in the proportion of wage earners (for example women due to the entry of growing numbers to the labour market).

Over the course of this period the social-liberal left has chosen to view the problem through the single lens of unemployment, and therefore has concentrated on job creation, sometimes through measures to increase individual employability. But it has not considered all the factors on the employment supply side, nor has it considered the quality of employment. It has not called economic policy into question, nor salary relations in a capitalist framework, nor the structural crisis that late capitalism is undergoing (Albarracín and Montes, 1996).

The European Employment Strategy (EES) is attempting to tackle this problem from a traditional standpoint but using contemporary language, with the objective of overcoming the crisis in accumulation and unemployment. This strategy aims to reconcile the flexible movement of finance capital with the full mobilization of the workforce in order to bring about

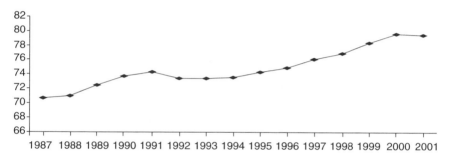

*Figure 6.1*   Employment rate, Spain, 1987–2001 (per cent)
*Source*: Labour Force Surveys National Statistical Bureau of Spain.

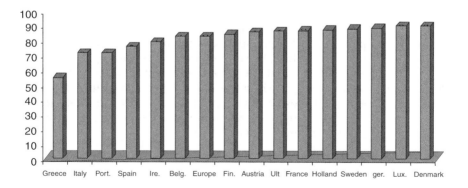

*Figure 6.2*   Employment rate, EU, 1997 (per cent)
*Source*: FeS-Union General de Trabajuobres (1998).

the maximum reproduction of capital. While those on the left have brought pressure to bear to achieve job creation, the bourgeoisie and defenders of capitalism have preferred an employment model that is rigid for workers but flexible for employers. So while jobs are being created, they are of poor quality and involve increasing subordination.

The rising employment rates in Spain and throughout the EU (Figures 6.1 and 6.2) have been generated by specific social conditions (the fragmentation of family groups, clientelism, consumer culture and so on). However over the years the aim of full employment has been replaced by 'progress towards the full employment of the potential workforce'.

## The rhetoric of the European Employment Strategy

The development of the EU has been dominated by the formation of the single market, with very specific requirements being imposed on the member states through the objectives set out in the Maastricht Treaty of 1992 and the Growth and Stability Pact under the Treaty of Amsterdam (1997). Meanwhile the euro and a single interest rate policy have been introduced in countries with divergent economies and needs, translating at the national level into fiscal adjustment policies, cutbacks in social spending, discouragement of investment, inflation control measures, the privatization of public enterprises, demands for moderation in wage rises and structural reforms in the job market. This has resulted in the degradation of waged work, measures to reduces direct and indirect costs, an increase in working hours, the intensification of work, the multiskilling of the workforce and a neo-Taylorist labour model. Many workers now have numerous suppored skills and can be moved from one production task to another as these arise or are extinguished by recession. Employment of a protected nature is steadily becoming 'jobs' in a more individualized manner (Alonso, 2000).

Employment is predicated solely on the free circulation of capital and liberalization of the flow of goods in conditions of monetary and inflationary stability, competitive market pressures and the privatization of economic initiative. There is job creation, but in precarious wage-earning conditions.[2]

The document that inspired the EU employment strategy was Delors' White Paper (Delors, 1993). In short the White Paper 'Europeanized' a compendium of neoliberal prescriptions (and a market with no safety nets)[3] that were moderated along neo-Keynesian lines. The resulting European Employment Strategy is based on four pillars:

- Improving workers' employability.
- Developing a business spirit and culture.
- Fostering adaptability among workers and companies.
- Bolstering equal opportunity policies for men and women.

These pillars are written into directives that legitimate the adoption of suitable measures. There are intermediate objectives establishing the basis for a convergence (Schumpeter, 1996).

Under the employment strategy the main players in economic innovation are business people as entrepreneurs.[4] It is they who make the investments that renew economic activity and boost production. The driver of production is technological innovation. In today's terms this refers to the scientific and technological revolution known as the *information society*.

The European Employment Strategy is framed in the spirit of sustainable development – that is, growth in production through technological innovation must be followed by new investment to ensure the renewal of the productive apparatus. Both job creation and ecologically sustainable development must result from growth in production.

Labour as a factor of production must be used to the utmost, and therefore as many working-aged people as possible must have access to employment. Hence training must be expanded (to increase existing workers' skills and to teach skills to people who are not yet in the labour force) and women's access to work must be promoted. Without abandoning the possibility of raising the retirement age, a new approach to labour must be put in place to respond to significant generational changes.

While major macroeconomic, agrarian, trade and diplomatic policies are defined in Brussels, national governments, guided by the Growth and Stability Pact, are free to set taxes and public spending,[5] and to regulate industrial relations. Therefore the strategy actively encourages local policies to salvage economically backward areas with weak links to the European market.[6] In a certain sense the strategy is the product of technocratic, centrally designed reengineering.[7]

The so-called third sector and the new employment possibilities it offers[8] are beginning to be promoted under the employment strategy. New possibilities are emerging from the privatization of public services,[9] as well as in areas such as private social security.

Thus the Amsterdam Treaty established a starting point for the coordination of EU-wide employment policies, or at least as far as the official discourse is concerned. However the major decisions will still be incumbent on the governments of each nation. Once these decisions have been 'self-imposed', a tautological justification will be made for these policies. Thus, national employment policies end up configuring what appears to be on paper a highly European policy'.

## The scope and limitations of the European Employment Strategy

The European Employment Strategy was approved at the Luxembourg Summit in 1997 in order to fight the growth of unemployment throughout Europe. Although unemployment has fallen since the strategy came into force (European Commission, 2002), people's fear of unemployment has certainly not, for the simple reason that job insecurity is increasingly being built into working conditions.

Almost everything has been left to the invisible hand of competition as the exclusive governing condition. The strategy is merely playing a new role in an old model: theoretically rationalizing social and labour policies in the framework of competition; and the modernization of companies within a European policy reflecting the aspiration to be the most competitive economy in the world. Nevertheless, the guidelines in the strategy do no more than promote a virtual neoliberal approach.

The strategies have been an imitation of a true convergence scheme on factors such as the homogenization of industrial relations, the harmonization of direct taxes, control of the flow of capital, interregional solidarity and so on. For several reasons the potential success of the strategy is limited. The social and labour policies came during a boom in the economy (1995–2000), and despite the austerity imposed by EU economic policy there was significant growth in employment. It would however be extremely difficult for the employment strategy to bring about a substantial improvement in the economy.

The member states have been required to draw up national employment action plans, which are designed to make the social and labour policies of each country visible and contrastable through reports with comparable headings. In practice, however, the plans have turned out to be no more than documents in which each government justifies its own social and labour policy, dressing up the initiatives it has already planned in EU jargon and artificially forcing them under the designated headings. All the member states have retained their sovereignty over employment and few are committed to true convergence. In short the strategy has merely synchronized flexible regulation within the European framework.

A few months after stock was first taken of the strategy in January 2003, amendments to it were announced. The strategy proposed by the Commission (Albarracín, 2003b) included the following objectives:

- To bring about full employment.
- To promote quality and productivity in work (better jobs), based on a knowledge-based economy.
- To promote cohesion through an inclusive job market.

In effect, this amounted to not addressing the 'natural' unemployment rate, to promoting the adaptability of the workforce, and to increasing the availability and employment of less productive segments of human resources. Three specific priorities were noted:

- The inclusion or reinclusion of women in the workforce.
- Helping older workers to remain in work.
- Making work more profitable.

The Commission also proposed a better 'governing' of the strategy through the participation of social partners and civil society, rationalizing the strategy with other EU policy coordination processes (economic policy), and greater efficiency by the services in charge of implementation.

Employment policy and the employability discourse gained ground over the 1990s and gradually replaced the Beveridge doctrine regarding the interwar years, a time of growing unemployment when many jobs lasted no longer than a few days and workers were paid piecemeal. This unemployment threatened social cohesion and productivity in an unstable economic system, but when national insurance schemes were introduced, unemployment was made bearable by public aid.

Under the Beveridge doctrine an individual's working life was conceived as alternating periods of employment and state-subsidized unemployment. During the depression of the 1930s this system served no other purpose than to temper conflict. However during the period of virtually full employment from the postwar years to the 1970s, the successor of this system, the welfare state, bore considerable fruit at low cost. Finally, despite growing unemployment from the 1970s, the system was gradually undermined because a lasting recession raised the prospect of long-term structural unemployment.

The first European Employment Strategy pledged that the unemployed would be provided with support, but this would be contingent on a commitment to work, exemplified by retraining and actively seeking employment. Workers' social protection costs were therefore made profitable by improving worker mobilization and the employability of individuals. The strategy contributed both to an increase in the employment rate and to making job markets more dynamic.

The emphasis in the revised strategy is on making new segments of the population, formerly outside the job market, available and employable. Based on the assumption that the most productive workers are already employed, what remains to be done is to promote the employment of those who are less productive or excluded from the job market for other reasons, thereby bringing about a more inclusive job market. Among those in question are low-productivity workers, older workers, immigrants, people at risk of social exclusion and women who have not yet joined the job market.

Meanwhile the term employability has been replaced by 'adaptability'. This is based on the premise of almost full employment, which means that it is no longer necessary to concentrate on improving unemployed workers' employability (their qualifications, skills, predisposition and so on), but rather on their ability to adapt to changes in their workplace by learning a variety of skills and increasing their functional capacities and interchangability. However this overlooks the fact that the EU is once again experiencing rising unemployment due to the recession that began in 2000. Moreover many jobs are of poor quality in terms of working conditions and workers' rights.

Another major limitation of the strategy is that it is dovetailed with economic policy, and the latter has barely changed because it still respects austerity criteria as determined by the dominating class in order to overcome its profitability crisis.

### The role of the state in employment in Spain: the real centext of EU strategy

In order to investigate the state's influence on the structure and orientation of employment in Spain, this section will draw on a study by Albarracín (2003a). During 1976–1995 the 'reproductive capital'[10] sector grew at an unprecedented rate. This was mostly due to the government's policy of providing greater public intervention, and of employing very high levels of labour. (The government took on more of an interventionist protagonist role in developing a flexible administration and regulation of the economy). A quantitative leap in state employment[11] was made between the 1970s and 1992,[12] but this gave way to slower growth until 1996, followed by a decisive tapering off until 2001. The key factor in this was the new 1996 government's orientation, which was midway between conservative and neoliberal.

There are various explanations of the state's action at least until 1996. First, the anticyclical measures taken by the state during periodic recessions in market accumulation are often cited, but its employment initiatives had come much earlier,[13] and the various public policies (macroeconomic, monetary, corporate price control and arbitrary, *ad hoc* industrial protection as opposed to a comprehensive, planned policy) exacerbated the recession, thereby causing even greater problems during the political transition.

The origins of this can be traced back to the 1920s and the Primo de Rivera dictatorship (the First World War was the equivalent turning point in the rest of Europe), which took steps to make trade unions, the state, companies and so on more corporatist in nature. The state grew in parallel to the market, and together they formed the cornerstone of wage-earning society in order to keep production and consumption in line with the accumulation pattern of that period. But when this model entered into crisis after the 1970s, the pressures of globalization itself required a deep rationalization of government. The state would only intervene to ensure production relations, to preserve the appropriation of surplus in different sectors, and to promote the accumulation of capital at a sufficient pace to prevent legitimacy-jeopardizing economic crises. Government 'metabolism' adjusted itself to international corporate and trading bloc capitalism.

Second, another explanation is that the increase in state intervention was due to a rearticulation of alliances that were previously underpinned by the small bourgeoisie and then partially integrated into the working class. This marked a new period of bourgeois hegemony, this time with a technocratic, modernizing bent. The state participated by distributing a portion of the surplus. In short, the portion of production managed by the state at different levels enabled the surplus to be redistributed,

However there are indications that the structural crisis shook the foundations of the wage-earning society. While the significant increase in wages, improved public services, the increase in public employment and the redistribution of the 1970s helped to offset the social and political opposition to the bourgeois regime, they did little to overcome the deep recession. On the contrary they actually made it worse by integrating a part of the subordinate class into the state sector and distributing the recession among the rest of the population. Only after great social restructuring was bourgeois hegemony restored under different principles (formal democracy, constitutional freedom, consumerism and so on) and the transformation of the state model, was reestablished. Yet this new development and approach can be considered to be ailing and increasingly contradictory in social and economic terms.

This restructuring, a profound restructuring of all aspects of the capitalist system (the introduction of regional markets, flexible regulations, decentralization, privatization, corporate policy aimed at flexible restructuring of the job market and labour relations, and so on), undermined wage-earning conditions (wages, working hours, professional categories, indirect wages, stability, and soon) in order to restore profits, but these were only recovered for short periods and inconsistently.

Amidst this restructuring the state implemented measures for the reproduction of the workforce and set rules for availability, employability and adaptability that were more stringent than in previous periods. The aim was to increase capital gains and the profitability of capitalist accumulation.

This leads us to the third explanation: the structural change in wage relations made working conditions flexible in the broadest sense of the term. This involved a succession of labour reforms and the use of subcontracting and outsourcing. Workers' contracts became less stable (temporary or part-time contracts, employment by the hour and so on), and many women worked in precarious conditions. This took place over two generations, with the younger generation bearing the brunt of the new situation. During this long transition the state oversaw education and vocational training, and established the conditions for access to social services, including unemployment benefit. The entire fabric of employment and social security was contingent on the availability of more family members (women and young people in addition to adult males), employability (possession of suitable skills and qualification) and adaptability.

In this transformation process of a 'superindustrial' service society (Albarracín, 2003a), the state greased the wheels for a neo-Taylorist recomposition (Castillo Mendoza and García López, 2001) within wage-earner relations. This was neo-Taylorist not only regarding job level (jobs versus equipment-machines) and of the workforce level (multi-task ability and substitutability), but also the relation between constant and variable capital (flexible job relations, volatile markets, changing sectors and branches in a process of constant saturation and depletion). Here, a re-composition was generated with a large gap between jobs and employment (explaining the decline of careers). The link between production and consumption was also neo-Taylorist (see Chapter 10). In addition, mass production was degraded (i.e. planned obsolescence), and markets were characterized by high speed and high status symbolics.

From this standpoint, we interpret neo-Taylorism as having an impact on relations between the production system, and consumption norms. Successive recompositions of the workforces and jobs in the framework of employment relations favoured the movement of the workforce from one sector to another or from one job market to another, and generated a flexible workforce (in terms of availability, employability and adaptability) as well as constant capital (based on automation, simplification, continuous supply, and so on.) Throughout all this, industrial policy was more or less absent, and the little policy that was introduced tended to be governed by international production criteria and markets.

It therefore seems that successive governments decided to extol a highly flexible strategy with which to manage a cheap and available workforce supported by an employer-class obsessed with the discourse of flexibility (Martínez Lucio and Blyton, 2001). This suited Spain's position as a producer of intermediate, standardized goods, i.e. an auxiliary to other centres of decision making. In short, all of these Spanish and highly capitalist policies were the clearest expression of what was viewed as a 'European' strategy. Since 1996, this process has done nothing but further a flexible regulation project based on neo-liberal values.

The arrival of a neoconservative government in 1996 to 2004 oriented Spain even more decisively towards this vision of a Europe of capital. Any type of significant social policy has been questioned, with the exception of policies contributing to enhancing the supply of the potential workforce and of channelling income to private capital (see Greenwood and Stuart, this volume). Hence, any discussion of the supranational level of regulation needs to be aware of changes in the national context.

### Europe, what Europe?

Europe, therefore, only exists in our collective imagination. Almost all governments invoke an imaginary Europe when implementing certain policies. The EU plays as much a symbolic role as a real one (the EU as a supranational entity only administers a marginal amount of Europe's GDP), promoting the implementation of monetary policy and the recommendation of policies put forward by certain dominant member states as policy for all the rest. This does not stand in the way of member states acquiring considerably complex forms of their own while they develop their regional bloc alliances in a world pulling in different directions. Nation-states, particularly at the local level, with varying degrees of dexterity, still develop employment policy and government-promoted social policy. *Thus Europe, by legitimating its common bourgeois design, has gone from being a distinct 'point of reference' to being an 'alibi'.*

In the context of Spain, aside from all the historical roots of the myths of Spanish identity (that so much anthropological and philosophical literature has generated), the tension between what is Spanish and what is European remains an ideological issue. From EEC membership to membership of NATO to legitimization of the nominal convergence criteria, the shortcomings of everything deemed Spanish are directly confronted within political discourse with the superiority of what is 'European' as the incarnation of a civilized international community. This perspective rules out any calling into question of a European political area, and ostensibly therefore also a social area. In this scenario, nothing but the yearned for materialists' 'harmonization' of living standards can fit.

Alongside the notion of progressiveness, other notions of European neocapitalism exist, presenting Europe as an economic bloc that aspires to become a global competitor to the United States but without offering an alternative model in any sense of the word. The building of the European Union, be it in the form of a *neo-Taylorist* state or a stateless macro-state, underpinned by an incomplete and imbalanced puzzle, a Meccano of complex nation states, cannot merely be understood as a design which is the fruit of the encounter of the bourgeoisie in various different European countries. The role of the players, both at the supra-and subordinate level, is always decisive. In this sense, the problematic design of the neo-Taylorist state seems to meet setbacks during popular consultations or referenda, such as the Nice Treaty (rejected by Ireland) or the joining of the euro (rejected by the UK and Denmark). In the end, even if merely to mediate their demands, political representatives must take into account protests and proposals made by social movements (regarding unemployment, precariousness in jobs, ecological unsustainability, and demands for democratization) when designing their various transnational projects.

We can also see the tremendous difficulty in reaching an agreement shared by all governments on a basic, minimum legal framework for this Europe of capital, as represented by the EU constitution. This neo-Taylorist state shows all of its fragility as a model since as a 'light' state it is unable to govern depleted, volatile, hyper-financialized markets. Yet this same neo-Taylorist state, solely aspiring to the flexible management of labour, capital flows, macroeconomic policy, and so forth, is firmly repressive of its most fragile subjects – that is, immigrants, subordinate classes, social movements, and stateless peoples. Neo-Taylorist regulation is therefore merely bureaucratic and linked to the bourgeois techno-structure and clientelism of major private corporations and public and semipublic corporations. In short the state and the market mirror each other's processes and means. Meanwhile, all of us are left to face an unsolved, irresolvable conflict, exacerbated by the mediocrity of this overall design.

These cracks in legitimacy trigger a certain setback in the system. When one considers that the member states confront the building of Europe on an asymmetrical basis, this holds true even more. While Germany has put forward a Europe of regions, France defends a Europe of nations, While Germany would like to extend its markets to the East, Spain would like to maintain its structural and cohesion funds. Meanwhile the new capitalist and pro-United States member states in Eastern Europe are anxious to mobilize their economies by joining the European market, particularly the highly Germanic sphere of influence, while following the United States in military and diplomatic terms. Failure and contradiction in economic policy may find themselves shored up by an EU that is as much military and surveillance based, denying alternative readings of the social identity of the region.

In short, Europe is going through a crisis while multilateral institutions such as the United Nations are weakening, while the mercantile tentacles of the strongest countries' transnational companies expand, and while global counter-capitalism movements are shaping new subjectivities and dynamics. Will international organizations supporting the development of homogenous standards remain intact (be they labour or economic standards for varying countries, regions, economies and peoples)? Are we not perhaps facing a future of international fragmentation threatening us with historical regression? Or perhaps we are faced with the need to transform a society based on myths of global capitalism and decisively set our sights on a design for international solidarity and on a democratic, anticlassist, popular, social and economic model.

## Notes

1. Here 'neo-Taylorist' refers to an updated model of the early twentieth century Taylorism enlarged to the European scale. This model is based on a liberal state that, without any capacity to intervene, correlates to a dual market and a mass labour organizational model with no integrating social protection or salary structure. We shun the term 'Post-Fordism' since what is known as the Fordist period was assumed to be characterised by a strong, interventionist state with a considerably organized social and labour model and a system integration through salaries and significant, albeit partial, public social policies. Post-Fordism tends to be referred to in a confusing way as a promising breakthrough. In our view, when diagnosing the contemporary development of capitalism, it is merely an empty shell.
2. 'Companies benefit from the resulting increase in productivity and workers benefit from having their jobs guaranteed . . . The changes in work within an

organisation or from one organisation to another will be more and more frequent. For many people, this phenomenon comes with increasing job insecurity. At the same time, new types of employment are becoming widespread, and in most cases these jobs are less protected, such as fixed term contracts, subcontracted jobs, pseudo self-employed workers etc. . . . This is why education, training, retraining and integration policies for the long term unemployed are necessary. There will be more obstacles to employment as it becomes increasing difficult or impossible for workers to adapt' (Economic and Social Committee, 2000, p. 10).

3. The European Economic and Social Committee (2000, p. 15) offered the following explanation: 'It will be necessary for politicians to take drastic action to eliminate and reverse the onslaught of regulations descending upon companies and society. . . . The market forces are continuously changing the rules and companies must innovate to survive.'

4. 'The citizens of the European Union have the ability to innovate and have enough entrepreneurial spirit to create all of the new, sustainable jobs we need . . . The elimination of jobs that are no longer competitive is easier the more new sustainable jobs are created in other sectors and the more often a job change leads to the perspective of better working conditions' (ibid., p. 7).

5. 'Public employment services (where 100,000 civil servants work in 5,000 local offices) carry out . . . information and placement services along with consultancy, professional counselling, training and the application of job market schemes. Most of the 65,000 million euros – 1% of GDP – spent annually by EU governments on active employment policies is therefore spent by these services. This amount is more than a third of the total allocation to employment policies (unemployment benefits and active policies)' (European Commission/Commission European; 2000b, p. 14).

6. 'The opening up of markets has accelerated the mobility of investment as well capital concentration. In parallel, the boom in the use of new technology in production, distribution and consumption has favoured the creation of a global market and the advent of the information society. These developments have stiffened competition even more. In order to face the new situation, local agents must now develop strategies based on specific qualities. Potential for endogenous development has been substantially bolstered by changes enabling technology to be put to use in production systems. This trend applies to microeconomic development and the creation of local production systems made up of small enterprises' (COM, 2000b, p. 5).

7. 'All policies carried out locally must be integrated into a single strategy in order to maximise their efficiency' (Comission European/European Commission, 2000b p. 23).

8. With regard to the third sector, 'currently, these organisations are far from being a negligible economic and social force in several countries, although they rarely have much recognition. In all, it is estimated that the sector provides 8,590,000 jobs, that is, 6.45% of total employment and 7.78% of remunerated employment. In addition, if the full time job equivalent of voluntary work were to be calculated, one could estimate that 10% of labour works in this third sector. . . . This growth can be explained in part by the subcontracting of certain functions that were formerly performed by the public sector and in part by the production of services to meet new needs' (Commission European/European Commission, 2000, p. 12).

9. 'This growth can be explained in part by the subcontracting of certain functions formerly performed by the public sector and in part by the production of services to meet new needs' (COM, 2000a, p. 12).
10. Where, aside from public employment, we can also include new private employment opportunities although they are difficult to estimate through official statistic.
11. A qualitative transformation had been made with the help of social policies introduced during the Franco regime from at the end of the 1960s. Growth ensued, but merely in quantitative terms, as did structural rationalization, whose effects became visible at the end of the 1990s.
12. Employment in the education, research, culture and health branches of the state rose from 723 971 jobs in 1976 to 1 489 968 in 1992, or a rise from 5 per cent to 12 per cent of total employment. There was also an increase in all other sectors, apart from the employment of domestic personnel. However this trend slowed and reversed from 1996.
13. The reforms were already underway when the recession hit Spain in 1975. 'In ... 1973 a new social security financing act came into force which, together with the 1967 act, enabled the progressive expansion of a public social and health care system, in certain cases with a marked clientelist nature, i.e. in agriculture, for the self-employed. Also, in 1974 unemployment benefits were extended to cover all workers. With the recession, this type of expenditure accounted for a high proportion of total expenditure on social protection. The expansion of other public services also began, as well as expenditure on subsidies for companies. Overall, from 1973 to 1977 public spending went from 23.3% of GDP to 27.6% and out of this spending, social services jumped from 8.5% to 10.4% of GDP' (González i Calvet, 1991, p. 142).

## References

Aglietta, M. (1979) *Regulación y crisis del capitalismo* (Madrid: Siglo XXI).
Albarracín, D. (2003a) *'De la utopía postindustrial a la crisis de las sociedades salariales de servicios'*, Unpublished doctoral thesis, UCM.
Albarracín, D. (2003b) 'La Comisión Europea pretende una estrategia europea del empleo más operativa', in *Herramientas de Formación y Empleo* (Madrid: Fundación CIREM).
Albarracín, D., R. Ibáñez and M. Ortí (2000) 'Las transformaciones históricas del Estado social como cuestión', *Cuadernos de Relaciones Laborales*, 16, pp. 135–76.
Albarracín, J. (1994) *La economía de mercado* (Madrid: Trotta).
Albarracín, J. and P. Montes (1996) 'El capitalismo tardío: La interpretación de Ernest Mandel del capitalismo contemporáneo', Paper presented to Centro de Estudios Ernest Mandel, Instituto Internacional de Investigacíion y Formación de Amsterdam.
Alonso, L. E. (1999) *Trabajo y ciudadanía. Estudios sobre la crisis de la sociedad salarial* (Madrid: Trotta).
Alonso, L. E. (2000) *Trabajo y postmodernidad: el empleo débil* (Madrid: Fundamentos).
Aragón, J. (2002) 'La estrategia europea del empleo: aportaciones y contradicciones', *Cuadernos de Relaciones Laborales*, 20 (1), pp. 15–57.
Castillo Mendoza, C. A. and J. García López (2001) 'Marx, entre el trabajo y el empleo', paper presented at the seventh National Sociological Congress, Salamanca, 20–22 September.
Delors, J. (1993) *Libro blanco: crecimiento, competitividad, empleo* Retos y pistas para entrar en el siglo XXI, Comisión de las Comunidades Europeas (París: CEE).

European Commission (1993) *Crecimiento, competitividad, empleo: retos y pistas para entrar en el siglo XXI* (Brussels: European Commission).

European Commission (2002) *Balance de cinco años de aplicación de la Estrategia Europea del Empleo*, COM (2002) 416 final (Brussels: European Commission).

European Commission (2003) *The future of the European Employment Strategy (EES). A strategy for full employment and better jobs for all*. (http://europa.eu.int/comm/ employment social/news/2003/jan/ees2003).

European Economic and Social Committee (2000) *Empleo, reforma económica y cohesión social: hacia una Europa de la innovación y del conocimiento*, 2000/C 117/13. 9–2–2000.

European and Social Committee (2000) http://europa.eu.int/scadplus/leg/es/cha/ c10241.htm

Fernández Duran, R. (2003) *Capitalismo (financiero) global y guerra permanente. El dólar, Wall Street y la guerra contra Irak* (Barcelona: Virus Editorial).

González i Calvet, J. (1991) 'Crisis, transición y estancamiento. La política económica española 1973–1982', in M. Etxezarreta, *La Reestructuración del capitalismo en España 1970–1990* (Barcelona: Icaria).

González Temprano, A. (1998) *La Política de Gasto Social (1984–1996). En la Administración del Estado y de las Comunidades Autónomas* (Madrid: CES).

Gramsci, A. (1992) *Antologia* (Madrid: Siglo XXI).

Jessop, B. (ed.) (2001) *Regulation Theory and the Crisis of Capitalism*, 5 vol (Cheltenham: Edward Elgar).

Martínez Lucio, M. and P. Blyton (2001) 'Constructing the Post-Fordist State? The Politics of Flexibility and Labour Markets in Contemporary Spain', B. Jessop (ed.), *Regulation Theory and the Crisis of Capitalism: Selected Writings* (Cheltenham: Edward Elgar).

Montes, Pedro (2001) *La historia inacabada del euro* (Madrid: Trotta).

Ortí, A. (1970) 'Política y sociedad en el umbral de los años setenta: Las bases sociales de la modernización política', in M. Martínez Cuadrad (ed.), *Cambio social y modernización política, anuario político español, 1969* (Madrid Edicusa).

Palloix, C. (1980) *Proceso de producción y crisis del capitalismo* (Madrid: H. Blume).

Rodríguez Cabrero, G. (1993a) 'La Politica Social en España: 1980–92', V Informe (Madrid: FOESSA).

Schumpeter, J. A. (1996) *Capitalismo, Socialismo y Democracia*, (Barcelona: Tomo I. Ediciones Folio).

# 7
# Employability and the Flexible Economy: Some Considerations of the Politics and Contradictions of the European Employment Strategy[1]

*Ian Greenwood and Mark Stuart*

## Introduction

Skills and learning are at the heart of the fixation with the Post-Fordist or new economy. The move to a new 'flexible' economy, it is often argued, requires constant updating and reforming of the skill base in response to the rhetoric and realities of organizational change. This places investment in training and development in a central political position. Training and the broader agendas of learning should not be seen merely as technical issues within the reproduction of labour as they have taken on a role of legitimating devices for many economies. Any shift to a learning culture needs to be discussed within the political and economic context of the state and new forms of intervention.

Against this backdrop, this chapter examines the politics of learning across Europe in the context of economic change and the institutional response of the European Union. The contemporary significance of learning, we are led to believe, is unquestionable. In an increasingly globalized world that is characterized by economic uncertainty, learning – or more typically lifelong learning – is often presented as a means of survival for individuals, companies and economies alike. This is certainly the case at the level of policy formation, where learning is seen as a necessary response to industrial and social exclusion. This agenda of 'employability' is, however, complex and costly and is best furthered, so the argument goes, through partnerships, such as those between employers and trades unions and between educational institutions, industry and the state. The themes of economic restructuring, lifelong learning and partnership are in reality connected. In the European Union (EU) the institutional medium through which employment, employability, lifelong learning and partnership are fused is the European Employment Strategy (EES).

This chapter examines the official policy language and texts of the EU and attempts to show how political understandings of learning have emerged that are closer to a neoliberal agenda than a social one. The chapter paper is divided into four main sections, the first of which outlines the economic and political context. This is followed by an account of the ways in which the EU has responded institutionally to global economic pressures. The discussion then turns to the themes of lifelong learning, partnership, employability and the underpinning discourse of flexibility. The concluding section positions the EES and lifelong learning within the contemporary economic and political context of the EU and the discussion on economic change.

## Globalization, economic restructuring and political ideology

At a simple level, the notion of globalization is frequently categorized as the rapid development of information and communication systems, increased economic competition, rapid technological change and accelerating flows of international finance capital (Ruigrok and Van Tulder, 1995). The concept of economic globalization as a theoretical construct is, however, problematic. According to Kassalow (1989) and Reich (1991) the world economy is undergoing a new industrial revolution, the corollary of which will be the dismantling of national economies. The consequences of this dynamic have, it is argued, been manifest at a variety of levels (Lash and Urry, 1987; Harvey, 1990; Purcell, 1993; Jessop, 1993).

At the political level, the forces of globalization are buttressed by the hegemonic tenets of neoliberalism, despite the recent obsession with the so-called 'third way' (Giddens, 1998). The emphasis of this political ideology on free-market competition and the removal of economic rigidities has had profound consequences for employment. Flexibility has been prioritized at the expense of employment security and welfare. In the realm of employment relations, collective bargaining has often been characterized as an undesirable feature of the modern economy, particularly in neoliberal economies such as the UK. In such countries, trade unions have been destabilized by legislation, their nationally based institutional safeguards have been assailed and they have witnessed social democratic political parties seeking to distance themselves from trade unionism (Clark, 1996; Waddington, 2000). At the level of production, it is often argued that Fordist production methods have been transcended by post-Fordist approaches, although this assertion remains contentious (Gilbert *et al.*, 1992). Nonetheless it is relatively uncontroversial to argue that shortened product lifecycles, the growth of niche markets, technological innovation and an increasingly global market have forced corporate and finance capital into a continuous state of restructuring and change. In extreme cases this has resulted in large-scale plant closure or extensive labour retrenchment.

### The European Union: economics and employment

The EU has been characterized as an economic space in which future economic growth is likely to slow and unemployment rise (Arestis and Sawyer, 2002). From 1973 until the late 1990s growth in employment resulted in 16 million jobs. However around eight million jobs disappeared during periods of economic downturn, and the net creation of jobs has been insufficient to keep pace with the growth of the working-age population to about 30 million (European Commission, 1997). In the EU there are currently in excess of 16 million people looking for work. In 2000 the unemployment rate for active young people was 16.3 per cent – 37.7 per cent for those aged 55–64 – and the overall unemployment rate of 8.2 per cent was twice that in the United States (European Commission, 2000a). The nature of new jobs has also changed. Many more jobs require higher and broader skills. Between 1995 and 2000 more than 60 per cent of total job creation across Europe was in the high-tech knowledge-intensive sector (ibid.).[2] Those who have lost their jobs are finding re-entry to employment hampered by a lack of appropriate skills. It is estimated that only 10 per cent of the unemployed currently receive training (ETUC, UNICE and CEEP, 1997).[3]

For the EU, the driving force for economic change and the organization of work is the competitive position of the EU in the global economy, particularly compared with the United States. Political, business and trade union leaders alike are promulgating the same message: increased competitiveness is the key to generating sustainable economic growth and jobs. However, the United States and the low-cost producers of the Far East are outperforming the EU in terms of both productivity and the development and utilization of new technologies (ERT, 2001). Knowledge and the development of a knowledge-based economy are increasingly seen (or at least at the rhetorical level) as the keys to heightened competitiveness and employability.

EU leaders and representatives of business view the reorganization and modernization of work as of central importance to this process. In the foreword to a UNICE policy statement on education and competitiveness, Dirk Hudig (the UNICE secretary general) comments that education and training are key in order to meet economic and social challenges and carry through a knowledge revolution (UNICE, 2000). Similarly, the influential European Round Table of Industrialists (ERT)[4] has stated that 'The competitive pressures of globalisation make the task of building the Knowledge Economy an urgent one' (ERT, 2001, p. 3). It is clear, however, that this is at the expense of life-long employment, as 'Lifelong learning . . . opens the door to allow people to move easily to another job and industry endorses this concept wholeheartedly' (ERT, 1994, p. 9).

The importance ascribed to the development of social dialogue, employability and lifelong learning is evident in a European Commission green paper, *Partnership for a New Organisation of Work* (1997). The green paper is clear that the modernization of work organization, through partnership, is not an option but a necessity. Furthermore acceptance of this is essential if the EU economy is to achieve greater productivity and competitiveness. Taylorist work organization based on mass production, it is argued, is no longer able to respond to the rapidly changing economic circumstances. The mantra of flexibility, both in the labour market and in work, is intoned throughout the document. Furthermore the rate of innovation and change is such that competitive advantage will increasingly depend on the ability of workers to create knowledge. For this to be achieved it is vital that employees acquire a wider range of competences and higher and broader skills.

## The institutional response

The EU has responded to intensified economic competition and its impact on employment levels in a number of ways. European Monetary Union (EMU) is the response at the macroeconomic level. The European Employment Strategy (EES) is the response to changes in the labour market, and it stresses the importance of social dialogue, employability and lifelong learning. The convergence criteria for EMU emanated from the Maastricht Treaty. These criteria, which apply to member states that participate in the single currency, the euro, require control of retail price inflation, the restriction of national debt to 60 per cent of gross domestic product (GDP) and the restriction of budget deficits to a maximum of 3 per cent of GDP.

The Stability and Growth Pact (SGP), which emerged from the Amsterdam Summit of 1997, and monetary policy by the European Central Bank (ECB) underpin the operation of EMU. The SGP governs the economic policies of those countries participating in the single currency. It also affects those countries in the EU that have not yet joined the single currency in that an annual convergence plan must be prepared. Under the requirements of the Maastricht Treaty, the SGP establishes four rules for economic policy that are designed to enable the ECB to achieve its central aim of price stability (Arestis *et al.*, 2002).

Commentators such as Hyman (2001) and Barnard and Deakin (1999) contend that EMU will hold down social costs and wage levels and that the overall effect will be deflationary. For example the economic guidelines in Article 99 of the EC Treaty, while calling for a high employment rate, also stipulate that increases in real wages must be kept below increases in productivity, and that reform of social protection systems is necessary. The same guidelines also point out that labour flexibility is central to the achievement of high employment. The SGP is designed to ensure that economic development is achieved through tight budgetary controls and price stability (Barnard and Deakin, 1999). In an analysis of the effect of EU monetary policy on employment levels, Arestis and Sawyer (2002) conclude that the current institutional and policy arrangements are inadequate for the creation of both full employment and low inflation. They also argue that the unrepresentative and undemocratic nature of the ECB is unhealthy and that its directors should be answerable to the European Parliament. Moreover the complete independence of the ECB from fiscal authorities makes a nexus between fiscal and monetary policy improbable. According to Arestis and Sawyer the policy objectives of the ECB should be extended to include not just price stability but also employment and growth.

### The European employment strategy

Attempts to find a European institutional response to the issue of unemployment and hence employability were sparked by the 1993 Delors White Paper (European Commission, 1993). In the introduction to the paper, Delors stated that the 'one and only reason' for the White Paper 'is unemployment'. Goetschy (1999) notes that the White Paper attempted to connect the deflationary effects of EMU with the creation of higher levels of employment. The White Paper also marked out education and training as key areas for policy action.

Following the publication of Delors' report, the delegates at the 1994 European Council meeting in Essen endorsed a multilateral employment monitoring procedure and a five-point plan of action for employment. The backdrop to the Essen plan was rapid growth in unemployment. Between 1990 and 1994 what is the current euro area lost around six million jobs. Between 1992 and 1997 the employment rate fell to below that in 1970, and below that in the United States and Japan (Goetschy, 1999). Member states were recommended to act and report on a number of key areas: the promotion of investment in vocational training and lifelong learning; increasing the employment dimensions of growth through increased flexibility in the organization of work and working time; wage restraint and job creation in local environmental and social services; improving the employment prospects of low-skilled workers by reducing non-wage labour costs; encouraging the mobility of workers; improving incentives for the unemployed to return to work; the reform of employment services; and focusing help on the disadvantaged and long-term unemployed.

In June 1997 the Treaty of Amsterdam made high employment a priority of the EU. It emphasized the importance of a skilled, trained and adaptable workforce and labour markets that were responsive to changing economic circumstances. Before the treaty implementation date of 1999, an extraordinary summit meeting on employment took place in Luxembourg in 1997 to launch the new employment policy. The policy was based on four pillars and included guidelines for action. At the 1998 Vienna summit the number of guidelines was extended from an initial 19 to 22, including a new target on lifelong learning. The first pillar was that of *employability*, defined as 'Making sure people can develop the right skills to take up job opportunities in a fast-changing world' to be achieved by investing in training systems, promoting active labour market policies and developing concrete targets for lifelong learning. The other pillars were *entrepreneurship*, *adaptability* and *equal opportunities*. Entrepreneurship was designed to make it easier to start and run a business and employ people. Adaptability referred to the development of new flexible ways of working and the reconciliation of flexibility and job security. Equal opportunities embodied equal access to jobs for all, equal treatment at work and reconciliation of work and family life (European Commission, 1999).

The EES is enacted in the form of an annual cycle of events. At the start of each year the European Council issues a set of employment guidelines, which each member state is obliged to transform into practice through the construction of a National Action Plan (NAP). In conjunction with the four pillars, member states are obliged to incorporate a number of horizontal objectives into their employment policies. At the time of writing these number six and embrace policy areas such as national targets for employment, quality in work, lifelong learning, monitoring and implementing the employment guidelines in a balance manner and the development of indicators for progress (European Council, 2001a).[5]

## Issues and connections

The overarching role of the EES is to support member states and social partners in their attempt to modernize work, which is necessary to respond to increasing international competition and create jobs (European Commission, 1999). Within the EES the impetus for modernization emanates from the pillar of adaptability. In this context, modernization is a call for increased flexibility, variation in working time and improvements in productivity. The pillar of entrepreneurship's emphasis on deregulation implies, however, that employability could well be synonymous with low-skilled, insecure forms of employment. The pillar of employability connects the notions of employability, lifelong learning and partnership. Similarly the pillar of adaptability advocates that the social partners should conclude agreements on lifelong learning in order to ensure the adaptability and flexibility of workers. This mirrors the requirements of the Maastricht Treaty, which also emphasizes labour market flexibility and the attainment of high employment. The tensions and potential contradictions between the internal strands of the EES, for example job creation and the precarious nature of such jobs, call for further examination of the nature of lifelong learning, employability and partnership within the processes of the EES.

Goetschy (1999) argues that the EES represents a change in priority in the EU agenda, in that unlike previous social policy initiatives, which were largely the exclusive prerogative of sovereign states, the EES provides a supra-European connecting mechanism for social policy. However the context in which these issues are being driven forward is the dynamic between the social policies contained the EES and the macroeconomic policy requirements of EMU. The objective of full employment, although still part of the lexicon of debate, has been replaced by the notion of high employment. This is made clear in the text of the Employment Title of the Treaty of Amsterdam. Barnard and Deakin (1999) view the substance of the Employment Title as constituting a defeat for centralized macroeconomic, reflationary, demand-side responses to the deflationary, monetary strictures of EMU. Sweden, for example, argued that the commitment should be to full rather than high employment.

While the stresses and contradictions in the juxtaposition of social and monetary goals will continue to unfold dialectically, what is clear is the primacy of monetary over fiscal policy and the needs of business over those of organized labour. The policy agenda of the EU and the requirements of business have illuminated the concepts of lifelong learning and employability in a precise way. Both are embedded in the necessity for flexibility, both outside work through the workings of the labour market, and inside work thorough functional flexibility and the polyvalent worker. Partnership is offered as the mechanism by which this particular formulation is to be delivered. Similarly a change in the rationale of lifelong learning has occurred through a shift in emphasis from the social benefits of lifelong learning to the primacy of economic factors – that is, from formal educational processes to a focus on the employer and the workplace. Finally, in recognition of the fact that learning in a very much wider setting than formal education is now a central feature of working life; the term learning has replaced that of education.

Coffield (1999) argues that irrespective of the nature of debates on lifelong learning or the learning society, the socioeconomic context is provided by capitalism, or in Coffield's words, 'capitalism is the only show in town' (ibid., p. 15). For Coffield, the role of the social partners, business, trade unions, the state and education is crucial in curtailing the power of corporate interests and developing a discourse on lifelong learning and the learning society. Just as lifelong learning is increasingly conceptualized as a necessary response to changing economic conditions, so the responsibility for learning is passed to individuals, who are exhorted to update their skills regularly in order to retain their employability. This resonates with the notion of the 'risk society' and the tendency of the modern state to offload certain risks onto the individual (Beck, 1992). In this context policy makers increasingly see lifelong learning as an essential prerequisite for facing up to economic uncertainty. This is exemplified in a European Commission White Paper, which states that 'the move to the learning society must be centred on the individual' (European Commission, 1996a, p. 51). Tight (1998) and Darmon *et al.* (1999) suggest that throughout Europe conceptions of lifelong learning and a learning society are being used as polemics for mechanisms of social control (see also Coffield, 1999). Individuals are increasingly socially constrained to accept employers' demands for increased flexibility, with the promise of employability being used as a cover for political retreat from a commitment to full employment to a future based on uncertainty and insecure employment.

**Pressure for change**

The capitalist economy is characterized by a number of features. It is essentially oriented towards capital accumulation, with crisis being the consequence of a lack of accumulation. It is technologically and organizationally dynamic and continuously innovates its regulatory systems in order to control its source of value and profit: labour (Harvey, 1990). These conditions are contradictory and inherently crisis prone. Furthermore, crisis periods of overaccumulation – the situation in which idle capital and labour exist simultaneously but remain unassociated – are endemic in the capitalist mode of production (Marx, 1963). Capitalism is therefore constantly engaged in attempting to contain this tendency. Harvey (1990) argues that the long postwar boom was primarily due to the resolution of the accumulation problem. This resolution was achieved in two ways: by spatial absorption, or the displacement of excess capital and labour through the geographical expansion of capitalism; and by temporal displacement, which involved either switching resources from current to future needs – for example from current consumption to long-term investment in physical or social infrastructures – or increasing efficiency in order to absorb overcapacity.

From the mid 1970s the capacity to resolve the problem of overaccumulation came to an end. The contemporary relationship between the large trading blocs and the low-cost production centres in the developing world is one of competition to extract surplus value more efficiently. To this scenario is added the conundrum of the comparative costs of welfare systems, particularly the amount of economic output returned to the economically inactive. Hence reform of the social security and welfare systems features prominently in the Delors White Paper (European Commission, 1993) and the European Council's Guidelines for member states' employment policies (European Council, 2001a). The task for the EU, then, is to increase its aggregate level of surplus value. How can this be done? In order to answer this question it is useful first to look at the nature of employability and its relation to employment.

## Employability

The EES defines employability as 'Making sure people can develop the right skills to take up job opportunities in a fast changing world' (European Commission, 1999). UNICE (2000) holds the view that lifelong learning empowers individuals in terms of their employability. It notes that 'Employability is a multifaceted concept . . . Different aspects of employability include . . . individual worker adaptability' (ibid., p. 5). UNICE also argues that in order to increase employability it is vital to improve the quality of education and training. Here quality is defined as 'the ability to respond to the needs of *companies*, of flexibility and adaptability' (ibid., emphasis added). UNICE adds, however, that education and training should not be viewed as a substitute for the reforms needed to address the structural causes of unemployment (ibid.) One such cause is inflexible labour markets. Others are the relatively high cost of unskilled labour and inflexible employment and wage systems. Similarly the European Council (2001a,) invites the social partners to negotiate . . . agreements to modernise work, including flexible working, and the European Round Table of Industrialists (2001) is clear that increased flexibility is required to improve competitiveness. The latter adds that the attitude of workers must change: individuals must develop an attitude of entrepreneurship but primarily an acceptance that they themselves are 'responsible for their own employment destiny . . . and . . . training requirements' (ibid., p. 4). The themes of individual responsibility, flexibility and adaptability seemingly everywhere frame the notions of employability and lifelong learning.

Attempts have been made to define employability, but as Lefresne (1999) notes, any understanding is tied intimately at the conceptual level to notions of the labour market, and at the practical level to the perceived needs of business and the expedients of national politics and the polity of the EU. The Scandinavian notion of employability, in the form of policies for the management of both employment and unemployment, is based on the concept of social responsibility. This could be extended to encompass socially constructed employability coordinated by multiple actors at the local level (ibid.) It is argued here, however, that the neoliberal, supply side view of employability and unemployment has pervaded the discourses of both European policy makers and the business community at large. This suggestion is based on the assumption that firms employ individuals largely on the basis of their qualities, for example their level of skill, and with an eye to the cost of employment. Individuals are unemployed either because they choose to be or because they do not possess sufficient human capital to offset the cost of employment. Thus unemployment in this sense is the fault of the individual, and the discourse on employability is in effect a mechanism with which to persuade the unemployed that this is indeed the case.

In the EU employment policy is increasingly directed at inducing individuals to increase their human capital, for example through training. In this regard UNICE (2000) asserts that business needs must drive this. In a similar vein, the European Commission (2001, p. 5) emphasizes that 'the key to strengthening Europe's competitiveness is improving the employability and adaptability of the workforce'. Lifelong learning has, it seems, become merely an adjunct to employability, a process designed to address the problems of the ageing population and the obligations of the economy. There is no sense of lifelong learning as a life-enhancing, creative force for all-round development. Moreover, it is difficult to find anywhere a representation of the view that unemployment might just as well be caused by the inability of the economy to create a sufficient number of jobs.

## Social partnership

The mechanics and potential influence of the EES indicate a central role for social partnership. This is an explicit requirement in the EES concerns with employability and adaptability (Barnard and Deakin, 1999). Contemporary economic, political and demographic forces for change will inevitably have an impact on the European pluralist model of partnership and the prominence of employee participation and voice. It remains to be seen whether this model will be able to withstand such pressures. For Hyman (2001) the power of international finance capital, multinational companies and Anglo-American shareholder value constitutes an irresistible force for change to the European social model. 'Rhineland capitalism' and employment relationships based on codetermination and partnership are, according to Hyman, in an increasingly precarious state, a view that is shared by Streeck (1997). Meanwhile, Goetschy (1999) argues that the EU and the EES are vehicles for the creation of a disposable workforce based on flexible labour markets. This may ultimately lead to the normalization of precarious forms of work. If this analysis is correct, the validity of social partnership, as observed through the eyes of trade union members, might well be called into question. However, Goetschy also notes that the trade union side of the social partner relationship often supports EU texts with a somewhat uncritical approach to EMU and the objective of price stability.

## Real politics and flexibility (again)

However much EU policy statements are dissected, or developments within social dialogue are nuanced, the March 2002 EU summit meeting on economic reform perhaps provides a lens through which to observe the political reality of the EU and the potential direction of economic policy. The coalition of Tony Blair, Jose Maria Aznar and Silvio Berlusconi on the issues of workers' rights and labour market flexibility presented a challenge to those who saw 'social' Europe and the EES as sentinels of labour standards. These political leaders were united in their belief that increased workers' rights were not in the interests of European business and that more, not less, flexibility was needed in the labour market.

In 1996, as a lead in to the discussion on his proposal for a confidence pact on action for employment in Europe, the then president of the Commission, Jacques Santer, organized a meeting of the social partners to discuss, among other things, labour market flexibility and labour costs. Both sides supported 'positive' forms of flexibility such as teamworking, multiskilling and new patterns of work, but disagreed over major areas of policy. The employers wanted to address the high social and labour costs and argued for reductions in wage costs. They also blamed unemployment on deficient education and training systems, while the unions contended that a lack of jobs was the ultimate cause of unemployment. The meeting failed to result in a joint declaration, ultimately weakening the terms of the confidence pact when it was eventually adopted (European Commission, 1996b). At the levels of the state, the EU and business, the exhortation for increased flexibility has been unceasing.

For Pollert (1988), debates on flexibility are fundamentally ideological in nature. Business interests, she contends, maintain that the primary solution to changes in market conditions is better management of labour flexibility. She argues that other features of production – such as organization and design, marketing, the structure of capital, capital investment, and investment in R&D, exchange rates and trade relations – all have been 'swept off the table' (ibid., p. 43). She further contends that concern with flexibility, in all its manifestations, is not new. Capital has always struggled for labour flexibility, which is central to the potential of labour (that is, labour power) being extended and intensified as part of the process of extracting increased surplus value.

## Discussion: the EES and the cult of learning – catalyst or chimera?

When describing the development of the Amsterdam Treaty, Goetschy (1999) observes that employment was not originally scheduled for discussion. Two factors contributed to its eventual debate. First, progress in other key policy areas was stalled. Therefore employment, and its socially unifying appeal became an important political goal. Second, public perception of the deflationary effects of EMU had created problems for those politicians and business leaders who saw monetary union as of crucial importance to the defence of the European economy. Hence movement on the employment agenda was viewed as a means of rallying public opinion behind the project of monetary union.

According to Pierson *et al.* (1999), the prospect of the EES's success is limited by the fact that none of the key political actors involved in its conception actually favour all its components. The British, for example, give importance to increased market dynamism, whilst the Dutch emphasize macroeconomic stability. For the German and French governments it is the creation of a level European playing field that is of central importance.

Pierson *et al.* further suggest that the EES works well as a policy agenda but does not 'provide a sense of broader coherence' (ibid., p. 284).

Whatever the politics of the game, the fundamental driving force for developments within EU employment policy are the economic imperatives of twenty-first century capitalism. The EU and its member states are attempting to ameliorate the effects of these economic pressures by means of institutional devices: EMU at the macroeconomic level and the EES in the social world of work. The agenda of business is clear: flexibility in the labour market and the organization of work are of central importance. These goals are reflected in the politics of the EU.

For the EU, the ability to increase productivity, to increase the rate at which surplus value is extracted, is an immediate imperative. The cost of welfare provision in the context of high unemployment makes this task doubly urgent. Fundamental political issues of wealth redistribution need to be addressed here. Through partnership, the trade unions are being courted by businesses to deliver the goals of flexibility, modernization and higher levels of profit to their shareholders. The ability to increase the absolute rate of surplus value is ever more difficult. The restrictions on working time introduced by the Working Time Directive have had an impact here. The main means of increasing surplus value is to increase the relative rate. Through an increase in skill levels the socially necessary labour time is effectively reduced and productivity is potentially increased. This is the real purpose of lifelong learning, or perhaps what might be more correctly termed lifetime flexibility.

Arestis *et al.* (2002) point to the contradictory nature of EU monetary policy. Through the mechanism of EMU, attempts to control inflation will lead to a reduction in investment and productive capacity. This will negatively affect the ability of the economy to expand employment without inflationary pressures. The ability of the EES to create jobs must therefore be questioned. In institutional terms the Luxembourg process is probably a positive development in social policy. However the primacy of monetary policy must inevitably cage the EES and impair its ability to function in any other than a perfunctory way. As a mechanism for reducing unemployment it is therefore in all probability fatally flawed.

The *Memorandum on Lifelong Learning* (European Commission, 2000b) and the consultation exercise on its contents have provided a significant input to the EU debate on lifelong learning. The European Commission's (2001) response to the consultation exercise offers a definition of lifelong learning that is centred on the four objectives of personal fulfilment, active citizenship, social inclusion, and employability and adaptability. Lifelong learning is defined as 'all learning activity undertaken throughout life, with the aim of improving knowledge, skills and competencies within a personal, civic, social and or, employment related perspective' (ibid., p. 9). This conceptualization of lifelong learning is one that most citizens, workers and educationalists would probably countenance. However in the context of current economic policy and the requirements of business, evidence suggests that such an outlook is chimerical. Current notions of lifelong learning are contained within a cloying economic discourse directed at the production of the 'flexible worker'. Coffield (1999) bemoans the fact that the sentiments and vision attached to lifelong learning and the learning society by the Faure report (1972), with its emphasis on a democratic coalition between education and industry and the development of human potential, have, or at least in the UK, been subverted by the 'master' concept of flexibility. For Coffield (1999, p. 15), this concept has produced not a learning society but 'a flexible society fit for globalisation'.

Undoubtedly, training for and at work is crucially important, however individuals are more than workers. Current official discourse provides little room for the manifold, life-enhancing potential offered by learning. In many ways the choices afforded are those presented by Nyberg,[6] who describes lifelong learning as 'a few decades of rushing between temporary employments and re-training, ending in unemployment and premature retirement from working life'. Or lifelong learning could be as envisioned by Delors et al. (1996, p. 21):

> There is a need to rethink and broaden the notion of lifelong education. Not only must it adapt to changes in the nature of work but it must also constitute a continuous process of forming whole human beings – their knowledge and aptitudes as well as the critical faculty and ability to act. It should enable people to develop awareness of themselves and their environment and encourage them to play their social role at work and in the community.

Perhaps even more powerful is the vision of Faure et al. (1972) that lifelong education is the key to complete fulfilment and the process of democracy. Policy makers need to move away from the prevailing, one-dimensional notion of lifelong learning and offer to the citizens of the EU the 'learning for life' described by Delors and Faure. The ability of the EES to contribute to such a future seems to be very limited.

The question of lifelong learning will become the basis for alternative characterizations and engagements as social movements and trade unions begin to challenge both market-based and individualized notions of it. The fact that the EU learning agenda has been enveloped in such an approach shows an awareness of its potential to be otherwise. Learning, ironically, has its origins in deeper social and rights-driven understandings of work and society. Throughout Europe, active dialogues are emerging beyond EU institutions in an attempt to articulate a more inclusive and participative approach to learning. Indeed, the linking of workplace needs to broader social needs is common in certain Scandinavian contexts, as shown in part above. More importantly, by focusing attention on learning the future may give rise to countermeanings and new, more mobilization-based agendas. In this respect the ideological and political dimensions of learning may prove to be a new form of contestation within the evolving economy and society of Europe.

## Notes

1. The research for this article was funded by the European Commission grant HPSE-CT2001-00049.
2. It is important not to conflate the growth in jobs in the high-tech knowledge intensive sector with growth in high-skill occupations. As Keep (2000, p. 2) notes, 'the production of high technology goods, does not always require a high knowledge input from the bulk of the employees'. There is also evidence of significant growth in relatively low-skilled and low-paid areas of work.
3. ETUC = European Trade Union Confederation; UNICE = Union of Industrial and Employers Confederations of Europe; CEEP = European Centre of Enterprises with Public Participation.
4. The ERT is a grouping of major European companies that has substantial involvement with the decision-making machinery of the EU. Its website is www.ert.be.
5. Since writing the article the EES has been reviewed and some of its key priorities changed. See European Commission (2003, 2005).
6. www.cpiml.org/pgs/organs/liberation/2001/2001annualNo/europe.htm.

## References

Arestis, P., K. McCauley and M. Sawyer (2002) 'The Future of the Euro: Is there an Alternative to the Stability and Growth Pact?' (p.arestis@sbu.ac.uk).
Arestis, P. and M. Sawyer (2002) 'Monetary Policies in the Eurosystem and Alternatives for Full Employment' (p.arestis@sbu.ac.uk).
Barnard, C. and S. Deakin (1999) 'A year of living dangerously? EC social rights, employment policy and EMU', *Industrial Relations Journal*, 30 (4), pp. 355–72.
Beck, U. (1992) *Risk Society: Towards a New Modernity* (London: Sage).
Clark, I. (1996) 'The State and New Industrial Relations', in I. J. Beardswell (ed.), *Contemporary Industrial Relations* (New York: Oxford University Press).
Coffield, F. (1998) 'A Tale of Three Little Pigs: Building the Learning Society with Straw', *Evaluation and Research in Education*, 12 (1), pp. 44–58.
Coffield, F. (1999) 'Breaking the Consensus: Lifelong Learning as Social Control', inaugural professorial lecture, University of Newcastle, UK, February.
Darmon, I., C. Frade and K. Hadjivassiliou (1999) 'The Comparative Dimension in Continuous Vocational Training: a Preliminary Framework', in F. Coffield (ed.), *Why's the Beer up North Always Stronger? Studies of Lifelong Learning in Europe* (Bristol: Policy Press).
Delors, J., I. A. Mufti, I. Amagi, R. Carneiro, F. Chung, B. Geremek, W. Gorham, A. Kornhauser, M. Manley, M. Padrón Quero, M.A. Savané, K. Singh, R. Stavenhagen, M. W. Suhr, Z. Nanzhao (1996) *Learning: The Treasure Within*, Report to UNESCO of the International Commission on Education for the Twenty-First Century (London and Paris).
European Trade Union Congress, Union des Industries de la Communauté Europeénne and CEEP (1997) *Social Partners' Contribution to the Employment Summit*.

European Commission (1993) *Growth Competitiveness and Employment* (Delors' White Paper) (Luxembourg: OOPEC).
European Commission (1996a) *Teaching and Learning: Towards the Learning Society*, White Paper on education and training (Luxembourg: Official Publications of the EC).
European Commission (1996b) *Action for Employment in Europe: A Confidence Pact*, CSE (96) 1 final (Brussels: European Commission).
European Commission (1997) *Green Paper: Partnership for a New Organisation of Work*, COM (97) 128 (Brussels: European Commission).
European Commission (1999) *The European Employment Strategy. Investing in People* (Luxembourg: Office for Official Publications of the European Communities).
European Commission (2000a) *Joint Employment Report 2001*, COM (2001) 438 final (Brussels: European Commission).
European Commission (2000b) *A Memorandum on Lifelong Learning*, Commission Staff Working Paper SEC(2000) 1832 (Brussels: European Commission) also available at http://europa.eu.int/comm/education/life/memoen.pdf).
European Commission (2001) *Making a European Area of Lifelong Learning*, COM (2001) 678 final (Brussels: European Commission).
European Commission (2003) *The Future of the European Employment Strategy* (Brussels: EC).
European Commission (2005) *Draft Joint Employment Report 2004/5*, COM yyy final 1 (Brussels: EC).
European Council (2001a) *Proposal for a Council Decision on Guidelines for Member States' Employment Policies for the Year 2002*, COM (2001) 511 final (Brussels: Official Journal of the European Communities).
European Council (2001b) *Council Decision on Guidelines for Member States' employment policies for the year 2001*, (2001/63/EC) (Brussels: Official Journal of the European Communities).
European Round Table of Industrialists (ERT) (1994) *Education for Europeans. Towards the Learning Society* (Brussels: ERT).
European Round Table of Industrialists (ERT) (2001) *Actions for Competitiveness through the Knowledge Economy in Europe* (Brussels: ERT).
Faure, E., (1972) *Learning to be: The world of education today and tomorrow* (Paris: UNESCO/Harrap).
Giddens, A. (1998) *The Third Way* (Oxford: Polity Press).
Gilbert, N., R. Burrows and A. Pollert (1992) *Fordism and Flexibility: Divisions and Change* (Basingstoke: Macmillan).
Goetschy, J. (1999) 'The European Employment Strategy: Genesis and Development', *European Journal of Industrial Relations*, 5 (2), pp. 117–37.
Harvey, D. (1990) *The Condition of Postmodernity* (Oxford: Blackwell).
Hyman, R. (2001) 'The Europeanisation – or the erosion – of industrial relations?' *Industrial Relations Journal*, 32 (4), pp. 280–94.
Jessop, B. (1993) 'Towards a Schumpeterian workfare state? Preliminary remarks on post-Fordist political economy', *Studies in Political Economy*, 40, pp. 7–39.
Kassalow, E. M. (1989) 'Technological change in the US; unions and employers in a new era', in A. Gladstone (eds), *Current Issues in Labour Relations: an International Perspective* (Berlin: Walter de Gruyter), pp. 43–56.
Keep, E. (2000) 'Creating a Knowledge Driven Economy – Definitions, Challenges and Opportunities', SKOPE Policy Paper No. 2 (Oxford).
Lash, S. and J. Urry (1987) *The End of Organised Capitalism* (Cambridge: Polity Press).

Lefresne, F. (1999) 'Employability at the Heart of the European Employment Strategy', *Transfer*, 5 (4), pp. 460–80.

Marx, K. (1963) *Capital: Volume 1* (Moscow: Progress).

Pierson, P., A. Forster and E. Jones (1999) 'Politics of Europe 99 changing the guard in the European Union: in with the new, out with the old?', *Industrial Relations Journal*, 30 (4), pp. 277–90.

Pollert, A. (1988) 'Dismantling Flexibility', *Capital and Class*, 34, pp. 42–75.

Przeworski, A. (2001) 'How Many Ways Can Be Third?', in A. Glyn (ed.), *Social Democracy in Neoliberal Times* (Oxford: Oxford University Press).

Purcell, J. (1993) 'The End of Institutional Industrial Relations', *Political Quartlerly*, 64 (1), pp. 6–23.

Reich, R. (1991) *The Work of Nations: Preparing Ourselves for 21st Century Capitalism* (New York: Alfred Knopf).

Ruigrok, W. and R. Van Tulder (1995) *The Logic of International Restructuring* (London: Routledge).

Sennett, R. (1998) *The Corrosion of Character: The Personal Consequences of Work in the New Capitalism* (New York: W. W. Norton).

Streeck, Wolfgang (1997) *Citizenship under Regime Competition: The Case of the European Works Councils*, Jean Monnet Chair Paper 97/42, Robert Schuman Centre, (Florence: European University Institute).

Tight, M. (1998) 'Lifelong Learning: Opportunity or Compulsion?', *British Journal of Educational Studies*, 46 (3), pp. 251–63.

UNICE (2000) *For Education and Training Policies which Foster Competitiveness and Employment* (Brussels: UNICE).

Waddington, J. (2000) 'Towards a reform agenda? European trade unions in transition', *Industrial Relations Journal*, 31 (4), pp. 317–30.

# 8
# Post-Fordism and Organizational Change in State Administration
*Ian Kirkpatrick*

Few would dispute the fact that radical changes have taken place in the funding and organization of public services in developed countries. Demands for administrative reform have been 'continual, often intense, and sometimes harsh' (Pollitt and Boukaert, 2000, p. 274). For some these developments represent a global shift away from traditional modes of public administration and towards the paradigm of new public management (Osborne and Gaebler, 1992; OECD, 1995). Others take an even broader view. It has been argued that attempts to reorganize public services are part of a wider process of state restructuring that can be explained by general transformations in the global economy (Palan and Abbott, 1996; Burnham, 1999; Whitfield, 2001). From this perspective the changes taking place in state administration represent nothing less than a shift from Fordism to Post-Fordism (Burrows and Loader, 1994).

As we shall see, there are many advantages of describing change in this way. The notion of regime transformation helps to convey a sense of the radical nature of management reforms and draws links between these developments and wider shifts in the economic domain. However at the same time it is important to recognize that this approach is not problem free. A number of scholars have raised questions about the high level of theoretical abstraction involved and the risk of oversimplifying transitions in structures and policies. The attempt to periodize change in terms of 'old' and 'new' is also said to downplay continuity, uneven development and resistance to change (Pollert, 1991; Bagguley, 1994). Finally there is a risk of adopting an overly deterministic stance, of assuming a preordained direction of change towards more effective or functional modes of organizing (Amin, 1994).

This chapter reviews debates on the usefulness of the Post-Fordist state literature for understanding change in public services. After setting out the broad ideas and propositions of the approach, some of the main criticisms of it are considered. The final section addresses some of the implications of this critique. It is argued that the approach might be usefully developed by incorporating certain concepts and ideas taken from mainstream institutional theory. In this way one might better account for the diversity of welfare state forms and outcomes of restructuring while retaining the idea of a broad shift in accumulation regimes.

Before we begin it should be noted that considerable reference will be made here to developments in the UK. In large part this is due to the radical nature of restructuring in the UK compared with other developed countries (Hood, 1995; Kickert, 1997; Flynn, 2000). As Bach (1999, p. 14) suggests, 'public service reforms in Britain have the greatest claim to the epithet "transformation" '. However, while this will be my focus, examples will also be drawn from other European states.

## The Post-Fordist state thesis

In recent literature the terms Fordism and Post-Fordism are widely used, sometimes from quite distinct theoretical standpoints (see Amin, 1994, for a comprehensive review). In relation to debates on change in public services, perhaps the most influential approach is that derived from regulation theory (Aglietta, 1979; Jessop, 1992). Here the emphasis is firmly on seeking to understand and periodize macro-socioeconomic changes in capitalist regimes of accumulation. It is argued that capitalism developed in a series of distinct phases, each characterized by internal contradictions and sources of instability. Most recently this process has involved a transition from Fordism (lasting until the mid 1970s) to a qualitatively new accumulation regime of Post- or neo-Fordism.

The term Fordism in this context has a number of connotations. Most obviously it refers to a distinct mode of organization based on mass production, scientific management, hierarchical control and economies of scale. But the notion of a Fordist regime takes in much more than this. Also important are the broader institutions that support the system of production, such as those linked to mass consumption, mass employment and the nation state. Fordism therefore refers to the whole social organization of a regime, including production processes, wage regulations, consumption patterns, corporate management and structures, and state activities (Wallace, 1998).

### Fordism and the state

In much of the literature the nation state is depicted as playing a pivotal role in supporting and promoting Fordist mass production and consumption. For example Jessop (1994, p. 256) notes that 'the Keynesian welfare state helped to secure the conditions for Fordist economic expansion'. An important aspect of this was macroeconomic policy. Here the emphasis on Keynesian demand management, steady growth and full employment are all viewed as crucial. The nation state is also seen as directly implicated in the development of mass consumption. Not only did the state provide and maintain the necessary infrastructure (such as transportation), it promoted norms of consumption through intervention in the labour market and the regulation of collective bargaining. Finally, it is suggested that welfare policies played a key part in the legitimation of the regime and in managing some of the social problems generated by it (Offe, 1984). Public services helped to 'ensure an educated, housed and healthy workforce', thus providing a 'base on which mass production and consumption could flourish' (Stoker, 1989, p. 151). In the UK this was partly realized through the development of a centralized system of welfare state provision in the late 1940s (Ackroyd, 1995). Funded out of general and local taxation, this system was founded on the principle of universal entitlement to services (including health, social care and education), regardless of ability to pay (Klein, 1989). Models of universal welfare based on state monopoly of service delivery were also developed in other European countries, most notably in Scandinavia (Ferrera, 1998).

Many argue that the welfare state was Fordist in terms of its mode of organization. For example Geddes (1988, p. 87) claims that in the UK the state was quite deliberately organized 'according to methods and by labour processes derived from Fordist capital'. Others suggest that management reforms in local government and the National Health Service during the 1960s and 1970s drew explicitly on models of organization adopted by large private firms (Dent, 1993; Ackroyd, 1995).

Three aspects of welfare state organization are said to be Fordist. The first is the vertically integrated nature of public services. In the UK, central and local government administrations took responsibility for the strategic planning and funding of services and for the management of provision. Second, and closely related to the above, was the centralized nature of decision making. Just as in large corporate firms, in areas such as health care and central and local government administration there were a large number of tiers and upward accountability to policy makers. Finally, it is argued that the welfare state was Fordist because the various social services were standardized or mass produced (Stoker, 1989, p. 152). Much emphasis was placed on ensuring uniformity of provision, with minimal scope for flexible responses to the needs of diverse groups of users. According to Geddes (1988, p. 87) service production was 'organised on an assembly line "principle" with professional and semi professional "people processors" replacing the material processing lines of mechanical factories'.

## Towards a Post-Fordist state

A central claim made in the literature is that from the mid 1970s intensified competition, globalization and technological change served to undermine the effectiveness of Fordist modes of state regulation. The rising cost of social welfare was also an important factor (Flynn, 2000). In some countries (such as the UK) this cost rose in line with the demand for public services, initiating a state fiscal crisis and political demands for reform (Foster and Plowden, 1996).

There has been considerable debate on the exact nature and timing of this crisis (Burrows and Loader, 1994; Clarke, 1995). However most observers agree that in the developed countries some kind of restructuring did take place. This is believed to have had radical implications both for the regulatory functions of nation states and for their organizational form (Hoggett, 1994). These two issues will be discussed in turn below.

### The changing role of the welfare state

According to Jessop (1994, p. 263) the restructuring of global capitalism has led to the development of a 'hollowed-out Schumpeterian workfare state'. By this he refers to a state that is increasingly less concerned with Keynesian macroeconomic policy goals (such as full domestic employment and redistributive rights) and more with a 'productivist reordering of social policy' (ibid.). The role of the state has therefore shifted radically to one of promoting:

> product, process, organisational and market innovation in open economies in order to strengthen as far as possible the structural competitiveness of the national economy by intervening on the supply side; and to subordinate social policy to the needs of labour market flexibility and/or the constraints of international competition. (Ibid.)

This change, it is argued, also involves the weakening or hollowing out of the nation state. Central government powers and capacities are increasingly being lost to institutions at the supranational level (to regulate globalization processes) and at the regional or subnational level.

These general changes in the nature of state regulation are thought to have important implications for the types of welfare service provided, and to whom (Burnham, 1999; Whitfield, 2001). It is argued that the focus on international competitiveness has forced governments to introduce measures aimed at cost containment and retrenchment (Flynn, 2000), especially in countries where the political elites subscribe to a neoliberal reform agenda (Hutton, 2003). In the UK, for example, tight cash limits were first introduced by the 1974–79 Labour government and then greatly extended and refined by the subsequent Conservative governments. Moves were also made to reduce the size and scope of the public sector (rolling back the frontiers of the state), through privatization and compulsory competitive tendering (Shaoul, 1999–1).

A further consequence of state restructuring is that governments have made changes to the provision of and entitlement to public services. In the UK, the trend has been towards 'a more "lean and mean" approach to public services and benefits' (Clarke, 1995, p. 50). This is reflected in attempts to develop a dual welfare system, with greater emphasis on home ownership, private pensions, private medical insurance and private education, all underwritten by tax relief and other related measures (Gamble, 1988). Also significant are moves to target or means test services (like social care and health care) according to criteria such as ability to pay or the level of risk involved. In the UK this process has been marked and, it might be argued, represents a clear departure from the postwar commitment to universal welfare provision based on citizenship rights (Rhodes, 2000). Elsewhere in Europe such change has been less dramatic. However in most countries, including those with highly developed welfare systems (such as Sweden and Denmark), some downsizing or 'recalibration' of services and entitlements has occurred (Ferrera and Hemerijck, 2003).[1]

### The changing organization of the welfare state

As noted above, considerable attention has been given in the literature to changes to the organization of the welfare state. Just as large corporate firms have been required to restructure their operations – moving towards more decentralized and flexible systems – so too, it is argued, have public services. In both the public and the private sector the trend is supposedly towards a distinctly Post-Fordist mode of organizing.

Helping to drive this change have been ideas and concepts associated with new public management (NPM) (McLaughlin *et al.*, 2002). Central to NPM is the goal of bringing the public and private sectors closer together in terms of practices and goals. Emphasis is placed on empowering public service managers and reducing the level of bureaucratic regulation and oversight (Hood, 1995). Interest in these ideas was (and continues to be) strongest in the Anglo-Saxon countries, especially the United States, the UK and New Zealand (Kickert, 1997). However during the 1990s moves to reform public management spread more widely, including to most European states (Bach and Della Rocca, 2000). This has led many to predict convergence on a new managerialist (or Post-Fordist) mode of state organization (Osborne and Gaebler, 1992; OECD, 1995)

Three main elements of this new organizational regime can be identified. The first is a departure from the principle of vertical integration, whereby government takes responsibility for planning, funding and delivering services. In the UK, from the early 1990s a number of policies were introduced to separate purchaser and provider roles and to delegate the latter to voluntary and private sector organizations. This kind of restructuring was most apparent in local government, with a growing portfolio of services being made subject to compulsory competitive tendering. The separation of purchaser and provider roles was also marked in health and social care. In the former an internal market was constructed in 1993, with general practitioners and health authorities acting as major purchasers from hospitals, which were redesignated as quasi-commercial self-governing trusts. This trend towards the marketization of services was not reversed when a Labour government replaced the conservatives in 1997 (Colling, 2001). The current government, it appears, is strongly committed to the principle of a mixed economy of service provision and has sought to extend it through such initiatives as public–private partnerships (Bach, 2002).

The second key change is the move to fragment and decentralize the management of public services. In the UK and elsewhere, policy makers have invoked the model of the multidivisional company and sought to replace large, integrated and unified service providers with a multiplicity of smaller and more focused 'business units'. This process has involved some delegation of management responsibilities to operational levels in schools, hospitals and social care agencies (Kessler *et al.*, 2000). Hence, just as in the private sector, a more fragmented and decentralized mode of organizing has been established in public services (Dent, 1995). Bureaucratic principles no longer 'constitute the essential mode of organisational control' in public services. The traditional approach of 'control by hierarchy', which focused on the monitoring of process, has been replaced by 'control by contract', where the focus is on output decisions (Hoggett, 1991, p. 45).

The final change that is indicative of a Post-Fordist mode of organizing is a more flexible approach to service delivery and employment. According to Stoker (1989, p. 162–3) 'The "Fordist" approach of providing a standard product for a captive user is no longer viable in an era of choice and competition.' Believing this, governments have experimented with more flexible modes of service provision and professional organization. One example in the UK was the attempt during the 1990s to establish a system of care management in social services (Harris, 1998). Under this system the role of the professional social worker shifted to assessing individual clients' needs and putting together flexible care packages that would be delivered by internal or (increasingly) external service providers. Likewise a key goal of the internal market in health care was (in theory at least) to tailor or customize services to individual patients' needs and demands (Dent, 1995).

The goal of flexibility also had implications for employment and personnel policies. In the UK there have been moves to decentralize collective bargaining and introduce variable or performance-related pay in the public services (White, 1999). A further shift away from Fordist personnel practices is the weakening of the traditional commitment to standardized and secure employment. In the UK there is now a far greater emphasis on 'numerical flexibility' and the use of temporary and part-time contracts for a wide range of employees. Indeed the incidence of contingent work is now more common in the public services than in private firms, especially in areas such as education and health care (Winchester and Bach, 1999).

## Critique

So far this chapter has outlined arguments in favour of the Post-Fordist state thesis, drawing mainly on examples from UK public services. However as noted earlier this approach to theorizing change has not been without its critics. Questions have been raised about the assumed relationship between state forms and accumulation regimes and how these should be understood (Peck and Tickell, 1994). Critics also draw attention to the limitations of the approach for analyzing organizational change. Here attention has focussed on the extent to which it is accurate to describe the preformed state as Fordist, and whether the current restructuring is leading unambiguously to Post-Fordist organizational forms.

### Public services and Fordism

The notion that all welfare state systems converged on a Fordist mode of organizing is problematic for two reasons. First, a growing body of comparative research points to the existence of a large variety of welfare state policies and structures (Esping-Anderson, 1990; Pollitt and Boukaert, 2000). In Europe it was not always the case that central and local governments took direct responsibility for running public services (Ferrera, 1998). For example in the Netherlands the management of many services (including health, social security, education and justice) was effectively delegated to non-profit-making paragovernmental agencies with semi-independent legal status (Flynn and Strehl, 1996). Even in Anglo-Saxon countries such as the UK and Australia, there were considerable differences in the way services were organized (Harris and MacDonald, 2000). While in the UK the government had a virtual monopoly over service provision (especially in health and education), in Australia the focus was on regulating employment to create a 'wage earners welfare state'. Because of this a large, vertically integrated state bureaucracy to control social services never emerged in Australia. From the start much greater emphasis was placed on the establishment of a fragmented, mixed economy of social care.

The second problem arises from the fact that in all countries some public organizations were more Fordist than others (Hoggett, 1994). This was especially true of labour-intensive services such as health, education and social care. These services were never truly Fordist, but were instead characterized by a mixture of bureaucratic and professional modes of organizing (Clarke and Newman, 1997). This is not to deny that in social services, education and to a lesser extent health, many trappings of Fordist organization were (and still are) apparent. Professional groups did operate within a framework of hierarchical controls, budgetary constraints and formal procedures, but these controls were never fully established (Ackroyd et al., 1989). To a greater or lesser extent producer groups such as teachers and social workers were able to exercise autonomy over the means (and sometimes ends) of service provision. Given this, it is hard to talk about these services as being subject to tight hierarchical controls or as being standardized. Even in the most 'managed' contexts, such as social work, there was considerable variation in the way in which front line practitioners defined clients' needs and entitlements, and consequently in the nature and levels of services provided (Hugman, 1994).

These observations cast doubt on the idea that the welfare state organizations were exclusively Fordist. They also tend to reinforce the point made elsewhere about the risk of 'historical amnesia' (Clarke, 1995, p. 43) in this approach. The desire to find a common benchmark against which change could be assessed may have led to an oversimplification of the past against which the new (or Post-Fordist) could be defined.

**Current restructuring**

It is of course possible to argue that even if all welfare systems did not conform to a Fordist model of organization the current process of restructuring can still be described as Post-Fordist in its general direction. As noted earlier, there is some evidence for this in the UK and elsewhere. However it is questionable whether these developments amount to a radical or fundamental break with the past (Lash and Urry, 1994). A key problem is that while many countries have attempted to restructure their public services they have done so for different reasons and with markedly different results (Flynn and Strehl, 1996; Kickert *et al.*, 1997; Lynn, 1998; Bach, 1999; Pollitt and Boukaert, 2000). For example, Hood (1995, p. 99) notes a wide gap between a 'high NPM group' of countries (including Sweden and the UK) that have implemented change and a 'low NPM group' (including Germany). The findings of this study and others suggest that it may be 'premature to predict a public services version of the "End of History" ' (Bach and Della Rocca, 2000, p. 95).

A further problem is that where restructuring has occurred there have been some unintended consequences. For example, in the UK, while there has been some movement towards more decentralized and flexible modes of organizing there is also evidence of a trend in the opposite direction, towards greater central control and standardization. The following subsections will discuss these tendencies in more detail.

*Centralizing tendencies*

Moves by the UK government to centralize control over budgets and policy decisions during the 1990s took place in a number of areas, but they were especially marked in employment relations. According to White (1999), in most services pay determination continued to be 'largely based on national grades and annual increases in grade rates'. In sectors such as local government and the National Health Service there was only limited movement away from national agreements (Colling, 2001). Even in the case of the

Civil Service, where the national structure of collective bargaining was abolished, the central government (and above all the Treasury) continued to intervene in the process of pay determination (Corby, 1998). There and elsewhere, tight cost control imperatives worked against decentralization and 'acted to compromise the integrity and workability of many performance pay schemes' (Duncan, 2001, p. 30).

A further sign of the growing centralization of public services in the UK was that both Conservative and Labour governments sought to define and regulate the professions (Newman, 2000; Foster and Wilding, 2000). This manifested itself in a number of ways. First, there was growing use of tightly drawn legislation, departmental guidance and other mechanisms to prescribe practice at the local level (Hoggett, 1996; Broadbent and Laughlin, 2002). In secondary education, for example, the introduction of a national curriculum in 1988 represented a significant break with the past by greatly limiting the scope of professional teachers to define the nature and content of education delivery (Fergusson, 2000).

The drive to control practice also had implications for the style and frequency of external evaluation (Hood *et al.*, 1999). In the past the central government had taken an interactive, advisory and essentially non-judgemental approach (Henkel, 1991). But the late 1980s this had largely been abandoned. In its place was established a mode of formal inspection aimed at ensuring conformity with centrally defined policy, holding 'the inspected for account for what they had done, and how' (Day and Klein, 1990, p. 4). During the 1990s this led to increased attention to measuring the performance of public services and to more confrontational styles of inspection (symbolized most vividly by the practices of Ofstead) (Hoggett, 1996; Power, 1997). More recently, under New Labour there has been a further proliferation of performance targets in areas such as health, social care and education (Cutler and Waine, 2000). Indeed the government now makes far greater use of comparative performance statistics to highlight and reward success (assigning 'beacon' status) and to 'name and shame' so-called 'failing' service providers (Webb, 1999).

Public sector restructuring in the UK has therefore been associated with some powerful centralizing tendencies. This is not to deny that responsibilities have been devolved to local managers and professionals. Rather the point is that such devolution has occurred within a framework of new policy controls, financial controls and inspection practices that are far more tightly drawn than in the past. Elsewhere in Europe, as noted earlier, NPM reforms have been less extensive. However in some countries, including France, Sweden and the Netherlands, there has been growing emphasis on performance measurement. As in the UK, this is producing a tension between the desire to regulate services centrally and trying to devolve control to managers and local politicians (Pollitt and Boukaert, 2000).

*Towards the standardization of decision making*

Earlier we saw how there has been some experimentation with flexible modes of service organization and employment practices in the UK and elsewhere. However once again there have been some contradictory developments. According to Flynn (1999, p. 35) a key thrust of Conservative and than Labour government policy in the UK has been to close off 'indeterminate and open-ended features of professional practice'. The trend, many argue, is towards increased proceduralization of decision making in many areas – one might say, towards a deepening of Fordist controls rather than a departure from them.

Examples of this tendency can be found throughout UK public services. In social care, for instance, a number of factors – new legislation (see above), central government directives (prescribing such practices as client assessment and care planning procedures) and explicit rationing procedures – have combined to reduce greatly the autonomy of social work professionals (Harris, 1998). Similarly in secondary education the national curriculum has led to 'more concentrated and explicit control over the teacher labour process' (Sinclair *et al.*, 1996, p. 642). Even in healthcare, an area in which the state has been least willing to intrude upon professional freedom, there have been moves in this direction. In recent years, the Department of health and the National Institute for Clinical Excellence (established in 1999) has played a growing part in the specification of models for clinical practice. These models, derived from 'evidence-based' appraisals of clinical interventions, represent an attempt to achieve a more standardized scientific–bureaucratic approach to decision making (Harrison, 2002).

For some these tendencies indicate a shift towards a neo-Taylorist style of management in UK public services (for example Pollitt, 1993; Broadbent and Laughlin, 2002). Others have questioned this view, pointing to the continuing power of the professions to negotiate and mediate management rules (for example Kirkpatrick *et al.*, 2004). But what is largely beyond dispute is that the overall level of bureaucratic regulation has increased rather than decreased. Throughout the public services this has resulted in greater work intensification and conflict between management and labour (Green, 2001).

## Discussion

The preceding section highlighted a number of difficulties with the notions of Fordism and Post-Fordism in relation to public service restructuring. Not only is it difficult to generalize about past organizational forms, but one is also hard pressed to explain current trends using these models. Indeed the search for clearly delineated breaks in regimes may lead one to downplay the complexity of the past and to understate the forces for continuity. Linked to this is also a risk of overdeterminism (Pollert, 1991). Implicit in many accounts is the idea that Post-Fordist organizational forms are functional or necessary given the changing conditions. While there may be contestation and uneven development, in the long term it is assumed that a particular model of devolved, flexible organization will ultimately prevail. As such the literature considered in this chapter has much in common with more mainstream descriptions of NPM (Osborne and Gaebler, 1992). Here too the emphasis is on describing change in terms of a 'clear-cut movement . . . away from outmoded traditional ways of organising and conducting public business towards up-to-date, state-of-the-art methods and styles' (Hood, 1998, p. 196).

These problems are clearly very serious. However recognition of this does not mean that all attempts to theorize change in terms of a broad shift in regimes should be abandoned. As noted earlier, the regulationist approach does have some important merits. For one thing it helps to convey a sense of the scale, pace and radical nature of change taking place in some OECD countries. The notion of a Fordist state also encourages us to look beyond the specific nature of particular administrative reforms and to understand these in relation to more general processes of economic restructuring. As Ackroyd (2002, p. 214) suggests, 'changes in the provision of welfare services, are not random events . . . but part of a wider process of change promoted from within the capitalist economy'. Given this, rather than abandon the concept of regime transition a preferable course may be to look for ways in which this kind of explanation can be revised or developed.

It is of course beyond the scope of this chapter to deal fully with these issues. However it is possible to outline a few lines of enquiry that might be useful in developing our understanding. The first comes from regulation theory itself. Within this approach there has been much debate on the paradigmatic status of Fordist regimes, with some scholars pointing to national paths or variations in development (Peck and Tickell, 1994; Boyer and Hollingsworth, 1997). Consideration is also given to the possibility that the outcomes of restructuring may be mixed, involving both change and continuity. To describe this, many invoke the notion of a neo-rather than a Post-Fordist regime. Neo-Fordism implies a mode of organizing production that builds on Fordist principles – through more flexible working practices and technology – but adapts them to suit changing circumstances (Lane, 1995).

These concepts may be of some help in explaining the current processes of public sector restructuring. Indeed one might argue that what has emerged in the UK and elsewhere in Europe is a kind of 'neobureaucratic' mode of organizing, or a state that is 'simultaneously centralised and decentralised' (Farrell and Morris, 2003, p. 130; see also Laffin, 1998). From this perspective the current trend towards greater bureaucratic regulation is perfectly understandable. As governments fragment public services and devolve responsibilities, they must simultaneously find new ways to maintain overall control and coordination (Clarke and Newman, 1997). The notion of a neo-Fordist state does therefore have some explanatory value. However one should not overexaggerate this. The approach is still overly schematic and, with some exceptions (notably the work of Jessop, 1994), largely fails to account for the diversity and unevenness of restructuring both within and between states.

A second line of enquiry comes from mainstream institutional theory. Here the focus is on the historical development of welfare regimes and the emergence of particular social, political and economic institutions that have shaped how these operate. One of the best known example of this is Esping-Andersen's (1990, 1999) classification of three 'worlds' of welfare capitalism. According to this model it is useful to differentiate between welfare regimes (previously 'states') in terms of their sociopolitical origins and degree of decommodification, or detachment of social rights from market forces. Three dominant regimes or 'worlds' are identified – 'liberal', 'conservative' and 'social democratic' (Ferrera, 1998, suggest a fourth: 'southern European').

Other institutional approaches focus more on the political and administrative structures of nation states. Pollitt and Boukaert (2000), for example, identify a number of dimensions along which politico-administrative systems might be compared. Here attention is drawn to the structure of the state (the level of decentralization), the nature of executive government, relationships between ministers and civil servants and the dominant administrative cultures that shape policy making and practice.

This kind of institutional analysis can advance our understanding of restructuring in a number of ways. First, it enables us to look at the way in which general pressures for change work themselves out in different institutional and political contexts and how this may lead to variable, path dependent outcomes. As Zeltin (2003, pp. 7–8) puts it:

> although developed capitalist countries may all face broad common challenges such as globalisation, deindustrialisation, or population aging ... these manifest themselves in very different forms and intensities deepening on pre-existing economic profiles, institutional configurations, and policy legacies.

The emphasis is therefore on how regime-specific institutions and political dynamics will, to some extent, determine the content, pace and timing of public sector restructuring (Pollitt and Boukaert, 2000). In some countries, such as the UK, the characteristics of government and political elites have produced a particular brand of market-driven reform that focuses on downsizing the public sector and improving efficiency (Flynn, 2000). By contrast in Nordic countries such as Sweden a primary goal of NPM reform has been to enhance the quality of public services and (in the early stages at least) 'to ward off the New Right agenda for privatisation' (Hood, 1995, p. 107).

The second, related, advantage of institutional analysis is that it can help us to understand some of the contradictory outcomes of restructuring, for example, the simultaneous occurrence of centralization and decentralization. Important here is the way in which policy choices are shaped by political dynamics and particular constellations of interests and ideologies. In the UK, it has been noted how successive Conservative governments sought to reconcile competing ideas in their drive for reform (Clarke and Newman, 1997). At one extreme, and linked to public choice theory, was the need to re-establish the primacy of representative government over bureaucracy (Aucoin, 1990). On the other was a 'managerialist school of thought' that was more concerned with the 'need to re-establish the primacy of managerial principles over bureaucracy' (ibid., p. 115). These two ideas, it is argued, pushed in opposite directions in terms of the kind of organizational change required. Public choice theory suggested far greater central control by politically accountable executives operating with tight budgetary constraints to curb the power of budget-maximizing officials. By contrast managerialists pointed to the necessity of greater decentralization, deregulation and freedom to manage.

It is partly because of these competing political objectives in the reform process, some argue, that in the UK there was such a marked tension between moves both to centralize and to decentralize control over public services (Hoggett, 1996). Even under New Labour this has remained the case. While the post-1997 period has witnessed important shifts in policy (for example 'best value' and the wider modernization agenda) there has been a great deal of continuity. Not only has New Labour accepted the logic of a decentralized, market-driven public sector, it also shares with the previous administration a (neoliberal) desire to reign in and regulate provider power (Clarke et al., 2000). The result, according to Colling (2001, p. 607), is that 'service managers are offered greater flexibility, but control and accountability are ensured through organizational change, performance review, and continuing financial constraint'.

There are, then, a number of ways in which one might develop and enrich the regulationist account of change. The notion of a neo-Fordist state is helpful in drawing attention to the way in which devolved organization can be combined with attempts to centralize control. This kind of analysis can be extended even further if reference is made to institutional theories. What these facilitate is an appreciation of the diversity of welfare regimes and the different ways in which nation states have responded to global pressures for change. They also point to how 'processes of transformation' can be 'more partial, more uneven, more contradictory and less finished' than is sometimes implied in the post-Fordist state literature

(Clarke, 1995, p. 44). Of course this is not to ignore problems that could arise from overstating path dependency and national political dynamics (Zeltin, 2003). Rather the point is to develop a more nuanced account of how the broad forces that drive restructuring work themselves out in particular contexts, and to recognize the uneven, unintended and sometimes contradictory nature of organizational change.

### Note

1. This process may have been intensified by the Maastricht convergence criteria for membership of the European Monetary Union and by the provisions of the 1997 Growth and Stability Pact.

### References

Ackroyd, S. (1995) 'From public administration to public sector management: understanding contemporary change in British public services', *International Journal of Public Sector Management*, 8 (2), pp. 19–32.

Ackroyd, S. (2002) *The Organisation of Business* (Oxford: Oxford University Press).

Ackroyd, S., J. Hughes and K. Soothill (1989) 'Public sector services and their management', *Journal of Management Studies*, 26 (6), pp. 603–19.

Aglietta, M. (1979) *A Theory of Capitalist Regulation* (London: New Left Books).

Amin, A. (1994) 'Post-Fordism: models, fantasies and phantoms of transition', in A. Amin, *Post Fordism: A Reader* (Oxford: Blackwell).

Aucoin, P. (1990) 'Administrative reform in public management: paradigm, principles, paradoxes and pendulums', *Governance*, 3, pp. 115–57.

Bach, S. (1999) 'Europe: changing public service employment relations', in S. Bach, L. Bordogna, G. Della Rocca and D. Winchester (eds), *Public Service Employment Relations in Europe: Transformation, Modernisation or Inertia?* (London: Routledge).

Bach, S. (2002) 'Public-sector employment relations reform under Labour: muddling through or modernisation?', *British Journal of Industrial Relations*, 40 (2), pp. 319–39.

Bach, S. and G. Della Rocca (2000). 'The management strategies of public sector employers in Europe', *Industrial Relations Journal*, 31, pp. 82–96.

Bagguley, P. (1994) 'Prisoners of the Beveridge dream? The political mobilisation of the poor against contemporary welfare regimes', in R. Burrows and B. Loader (eds), *Towards a Post Fordist Welfare State* (London: Routledge).

Boyer, R. and J. R. Hollingsworth (1997) 'The variety of institutional arrangements and their complementarity in modern economies', in J. R. Hollingsworth and R. Boyer (eds), *Contemporary Capitalism* (Cambridge: Cambridge University Press).

Broadbent, J. and R. Laughlin (2002) 'Public service professionals and the new public management: control of the professions in the public services', in K. McLaughlin, S. P. Osborne and E. Ferlie (eds), *New Public Management: Current Trends and Future Prospects* (London: Routledge).

Burnham, P. (1999) 'The politics of economic management in the 1990s', *New Political Economy*, 4 (1), pp. 37–54.

Burrows, R. and B. Loader (eds) (1994) *Towards a Post Fordist Welfare State* (London: Routledge).

Clarke, J. (1995) 'After social work?', in N. Parton (ed.), *Social Theory, Social Change and Social Work* (London, Routledge).

Clarke, J., S. Gerwitz and E. McLaughlin (2000) 'Reinventing the welfare state', in J. Clarke, S. Gerwitz and E. McLaughlin (eds), *New Managerialism New Welfare?* (London: Sage).
Clarke, J. and J. Newman (1997) *The Managerial State* (London: Sage).
Colling, T. (2001) 'Human Resources in the Public Sector', in I. Beardwell and L. Holden (eds), *Human Resource Management: A Contemporary Perspective*, 4th edn (London: Pitman).
Corby, S. (1998). 'Industrial relations in Civil Service agencies: transition or transformation?', *Industrial Relations Journal*, 29, pp. 194–206.
Cutler, T. and B. Waine (2000) 'Managerialism reformed? New Labour and public sector management', *Social Policy and Administration*, 34 (3), pp. 318–32.
Day, P. and R. Klein (1990) *Inspecting the Inspectorates* (London: Joseph Rowntree Foundation).
Dent, M. (1993) 'Professionalism, educated labour and the state: hospital medicine and the new managerialism', *Sociological Review*, 41, pp. 244–73.
Dent, M. (1995) 'The new National Health Service – a case of post-modernism', *Organization Studies*, 16 (5), pp. 875–99.
Duncan, C. (2001) 'The impact of two decades of reform of British public sector industrial relations', *Public Money and Management*, Jan.-March, pp. 27–34.
Esping-Andersen, G. (1990) *The Three Worlds of Welfare Capitalism* (Cambridge: Polity Press).
Esping-Andersen, G. (1999) *Social Foundations of Post Industrial Economies* (Oxford: Oxford University Press).
Farrel, C. and J. Morris (2003) 'The "neo-bureaucratic" state: Professionals, managers and professional managers in schools, general practices and social work', *Organization*, 10 (1), pp. 129–56.
Fergusson, R. (2000) 'Modernising managerialism in education', in J. Clarke, S. Gerwitz and E. McLaughlin (eds), *New Managerialism New Welfare?* (London: Sage).
Ferrera, M. (1998) 'The four "social Europes": between universalism and selectivity', in M. Rhodes and Y. Meny (eds), *The Future of European Welfare: A New Social Contract?* (Basingstoke: Macmillan).
Ferrera, M. and A. Hemerijck (2003) 'Recalibrating Europe's welfare regimes', in J. Zeltin and D. M. Trubek (eds), *Governing Work and Welfare in a New Economy* (Oxford: Oxford University Press).
Flynn, N. (2000) 'Managerialism in the public services: some international trends', in J. Clarke, S. Gerwitz and E. McLaughlin (eds), *New Managerialism New Welfare?* (London: Sage).
Flynn, N. and F. Strehl (eds) (1996) *Public Sector Management in Europe* (London: Prentice Hall, Harvester Wheatsheaf).
Flynn, R. (1999) 'Managerialism, professionalism and quasi markets', in M. Exworthy and S. Halford (eds), *Professionals and the New Managerialism in the Public Sector* (Buckingham: Open University Press).
Forde, C. and G. Slater (2001) 'Just a temporary phenomenon? The rise and fall of temporary work in the UK', paper presented at the European Work and Employment Research Centre, Manchester School of Management, March.
Foster, C. and F. Plowden (1996) *The State Under Stress* (Buckingham: Open University Press).
Foster, P. and P. Wilding (2000) 'Whither welfare professionalism?', *Social Policy and Administration*, 34 (2), pp. 143–59.
Friedson, E. (1994) *Professionalism Re-born: Theory, Prophesy and Policy* (Cambridge: Polity Press).

Gamble, A. (1988) *The Free Economy and the Strong State* (London: Macmillan).
Geddes, M. (1988) 'The capitalist state and the local economy: "restructuring for labour" and beyond', *Capital and Class*, 35, pp. 85–120.
Green, F. (2001) 'It's been a hard day's night: the concentration and intensification of work in late twentieth century Britain', *British Journal of Industrial Relations*, 39, pp. 53–81.
Harris, J. (1998) 'Scientific management, bureau professionalism, new managerialism: the labour process of state social work', *British Journal of Social Work*, 28, pp. 839–62.
Harris, J. and C. McDonald (2000) 'Post-Fordism, the Welfare State and the Personal Social Services: A Comparison of Australia and Britain', *British Journal of Social Work*, 30, pp. 51–70.
Harrison, S. (2002) 'New Labour, modernisation and the medical labour process', *Journal of Social Policy*, 31 (3), pp. 465–85.
Henkel, M. (1991) 'The new evaluative state', *Public Administration*, 69 (Spring), pp. 121–36.
Hoggett, P. (1991) 'A new management in the public sector?', *Policy and Politics*, 19 (4), pp. 243–56.
Hoggett, P. (1994) 'The politics of the modernisation of the UK welfare state', in R. Burrows and B. Loader (eds), *Towards a Post Fordist Welfare State* (London: Routledge).
Hoggett, P. (1996) 'New modes of control in the public services', *Public Administration*, 74 (1), pp. 9–32.
Hood, C. (1995) 'The "New Public Management" in the 1980s: variations on a theme', *Accounting Organisation and Society*, 20 (2/3), pp. 93–109.
Hood, C. (1998) *The Art of the State: Culture, Rhetoric and Public Management* (Oxford: Clarendon Press).
Hood, C., O. James, G. Jones, C. Scott and T. Travers (1999) *Regulation inside Government: Waste-Watchers, Quality Police and Sleaze-busters* (Oxford: Oxford University Press).
Hugman, R. (1994) *Power in the Caring Professions* (London: Macmillan).
Hutton, W. (2003) *The World We're In* (London: Abacus).
Jessop, B. (1992) 'Fordism and Post-Fordism: critique and reformulation', in A. J. Scott and G. Stoker (eds), *Pathways to Regionalism and Industrial Development* (London: Routledge).
Jessop, B. (1994) 'Post-Fordism and the state', in A. Amin, *Post Fordism: A Reader* (Oxford: Blackwell).
Kessler, I., J. Purcell and J. Coyle Shapiro (2000) 'New forms of employment relations in the public services: the limits of strategic choice', *Industrial Relations Journal*, 31 (1), pp. 17–34.
Kickert, W. (ed.) (1997) *Public Management and Administrative Reform in Western Europe* (Cheltenham: Edward Elgar).
Kirkpatrick, I., S. Ackroyd and R. Walker (2004) *The New Managerialism and Public Service Professions* (London: Palgrave).
Klein, R. (1989) *The Politics of the National Health Service* (London: Longman).
Laffin, M. (ed.) (1998) *Beyond Bureaucracy: The Professions in the Contemporary Public Sector* (Aldershot: Ashgate).
Lane, C. (1995) *Industry and Society in Europe* (Aldershot: Edward Elgar).
Lash, S. and J. Urry (1994) *Economies of Sigmond Space* (Oxford: Polity Press).
Lynn, L. (1998) 'The New Public Management as an international phenomenon: a sceptical viewpoint', in L. Jones and K. Schedler (eds), *International Perspectives on the New Public Management* (Greenwich, CT: JAI Press).

McLaughlin, K., S. P. Osborne and E. Ferlie (eds) (2002) *New Public Management: Current Trends and Future Prospects* (London: Routledge).

Newman, J. (2000) 'Beyond the new public management? Modernizing public services', in J. Clarke, S. Gerwitz and E. McLaughlin (eds), *New Managerialism New Welfare?* (London: Sage).

OECD (1995) *Governance in Transition: Public Management Reforms in OECD Countries* (Paris: OECD).

Offe, C. (1984) *Contradictions of the Welfare State* (London: Hutchinson).

Osborne, D. and T. Gaebler (1992) *Reinventing Government: How the Entrepreneurial Spirit is Transforming the Public Sector* (Reading, Mass.: Addison-Wesley).

Palan, R. and J. Abbott (1996) *State Strategies in the Global Political Economy* (London: Pinter).

Peck, J. and A. Tickell (1994) 'Searching for a new institutional fix: the after-Fordist crisis and the global–local disorder', in A. Amin, *Post Fordism: A Reader* (Oxford: Blackwell).

Pollert, A. (1991) 'The orthodoxy of flexibility', in A. Pollert (ed.), *Farewell to Flexibility?* (Oxford: Blackwell).

Pollitt, C. (1993) *Managerialism and the Public Services: The Anglo American Experience*, 2nd edn (London: Macmillan).

Pollitt, C. and G. Boukaert (2000) *Public Management Reform: A Comparative Analysis* (Oxford: Oxford University Press).

Power, M. (1997) *The Audit Society* (Oxford: Oxford University Press).

Rhodes, M. (2000) 'Desperately seeking a solution: social democracy, Thatcherism and the "Third Way" in British welfare', in M. Ferrera and M. Rhodes (eds), *Recasting European Welfare States* (London: Frank Cass).

Shaoul, J. (1999) 'The economic and financial context', in S. Corby and G. White (eds), *The Public Services: Themes and Issues* (London: Routledge).

Sinclair, J., M. Ironside and R. Seifert (1996) 'Classroom struggle? Market-oriented reforms and their impact on the teacher labour process', *Work Employment and Society*, 10 (4), pp. 641–61.

Stoker, G. (1989) 'Creating a local government for a post-Fordist society: the Thatcherite project?', in J. Stewart and G. Stoker (1989) *The Future of Local Government* (London: Macmillan).

Wallace, T. (1998) 'Fordism', in M. Poole and M. Warner (eds), *The IEBM Handbook of Human Resource Management* (London: Thompson Business Press).

Webb, J. (1999) 'Work and the new public service class', *Sociology*, 33 (4), pp. 747–66.

White, G. (1999) 'The remuneration of public servants: fair pay or new pay?', in S. Corby and G. White (eds), *The Public Services: Themes and Issues* (London: Routledge).

Whitfield, D. (2001) *Public Services or Corporate Welfare? Rethinking the Nation State in the Global Economy* (London: Pluto).

Winchester, D. and S. Bach (1999) 'Britain: the transformation of public service employment relations', in S. Bach, L. Bordogna, G. Della Rocca and D. Winchester (eds), *Public Service Employment Relations in Europe: Transformation, Modernisation or Inertia?* (London: Routledge).

Zeltin, J. (2003) 'Introduction: Governing work and welfare in a new economy: European and American experiments', in J. Zeltin and D. M. Trubek (eds), *Governing Work and Welfare in a New Economy* (Oxford: Oxford University Press).

# Part IV
# Labour and Society

# 9
# Feminization and Inequality in the New Regime of Work: From Exclusion by Design to Exclusion by Default

*Jean Gardiner and Miguel Martínez Lucio*

## Introduction

Most of the literature on Post-Fordism and the new economy has little to say about gender, except insofar as women are recognized as constituting a flexible labour force. One reason for this is that the literature considers changes in production independently of the social context in which these changes are taking place. While these changes might have secondary effects on women, they are often treated as being independent of social relations and social context. This is especially the case in the US and UK literature. The regulationist school does address the links between spheres such as production, consumption and social reproduction but pays little attention to the associated changes in gender relations (McDowell, 1991). The concern in the regulationist school appears to be to typologize relations between these spheres and to deduce the manner in which new accumulation regimes have emerged.

The development of a gender perspective on the new economy requires analyzing the linkages between work, family and welfare systems. This chapter will examine various perspectives on how gender relations are being reconfigured in the new economy and consider empirical evidence in support of these perspectives. Drawing from debates that are of particular reference to the UK, the chapter will deal with the following general developments. First, it will explore the notion of feminization of the labour force, a development that is sometimes seen as an outcome of changing workplace regimes. Second, it will focus on the question of individualization and risk, noting how individualization is gendered and uneven in its social impact. Third, it will consider the workplace itself and the manner in which new workplace regimes are underpinned by gendered notions of work. Finally, the work of Paul Thompson will be discussed in relation to disconnected capitalism. Thompson (2003) suggests that there is an absence of systematic cohesiveness in the new regimes of work and economy, with the result that social outcomes are uneven and impact on different groups in different ways.

Hence the chapter will suggest that regime change should not be seen as a comprehensive and systematic form of development, even if it is still exploitative and gendered. Many of the negative outcomes that are emerging are due to the fragmented nature of contemporary developments and the absence of overarching regulatory structures (see Chapter 2 of this volume). Any evaluation of gender and work must therefore consider four dimensions – labour market inclusion, individual change, collective processes, and socioeconomic context – if it is to address the complex way in which gender underpins workplace and social relations.

## Feminization

During the high male unemployment years of the 1980s and 1990s, when swathes of relatively well-paid men's jobs disappeared in the manufacturing and production industries, women were moving into mostly low-paid, part-time jobs in services (Balls, 1994). This growth of female employment occurred most rapidly in the deregulated labour markets of the UK and United States. These processes suggest some gender differentiation in terms of the impact of restructuring, with a decline in the proportion of jobs offering secure, life-time employment opportunities, notably for working-class men in industries such as mining and steel, whilst at the same time women's commitment to the labour market and continuity of employment increased (Cully *et al.*, 1999). However as noted above, most of the growth in female employment in the UK was in part-time jobs: in 2002, 43 per cent of female employees worked part-time, compared with only 9 per cent of male employees. Men retained their domination of higher-status, better-paid jobs in most European economies. The gap in earnings remained, with women in full-time employment earning approximately 80 per cent of men's hourly pay in the UK; the gap continues to exist to varying degrees in most European countries (EIRO, 2001). At the same time gender differences in human capital have diminished and there is declining support for human capital theory as an explanation of gender inequality in pay (Joshi and Paci, 1998). In the new economy, knowledge and skills are differentially rewarded on the basis of gender, thus countering the increase in highly qualified women (Purcell, 2002).

Economic analyses of the increase in the proportion of female employees associated with the new economy have identified three possible interpretations (Bruegel, 2001), all based on a primarily demand-led model of the labour market. The first interpretation is that because of the rigid gendering of jobs, feminization has resulted from a shift in demand from male to female jobs, for example the decline in male-dominated manufacturing industries has been accompanied by the expansion of female-dominated service industries. According to Lovering (1990), many new forms of high-profile employment, even in management areas such as marketing and public relations, have been driven by a highly gendered notion of this work, which has contributed to the establishment of gendered career paths that symbolically and materially reward men and women in different ways.

The second interpretation is the queuing model or reserve army of labour thesis, which holds that women move into men's work when demand exceeds supply or as men move out in search of better opportunities. Hence the inclusion of women is driven by economic necessity, not the gendering of work. Nor is it organized around any ethical turn or political shift in patriarchal structures.

The third interpretation is that women are the preferred workforce, either replacing men or moving into new industries, perhaps because they are viewed as more flexible or more willing to accept deskilling. The latter may be driven by a lack of political and industrial organization, or it may be a consequence of women continuing to play a strong role in the family, and therefore accepting downgrading in working conditions in order to balance work and private life.

All three interpretations are consistent with feminization of the labour force accompanied by continuing inequality in pay. As pointed out earlier, in the European Union women's pay is on average still lower than men's pay, and the factors outlined above have contributed to this. Whilst the presence of causal factors may vary, in the UK in the 1980s there was evidence of all three processes discussed above (Bruegel, 2001). Three-fifths of the increase in the proportion of female employees was accounted for by an increase in the proportion of women in particular occupations, and two-fifths was associated with structural change. This suggests that the gendering of jobs continues, but it is not fixed. Female occupations have grown faster than average, lending support to the queuing model, and they are most often graduate jobs. However in managerial and professional occupations men and women continue to be concentrated in different sectors and levels, reflecting traditional and new forms of gendering. Hence in quantitative terms, during the process of female inclusion in the new workplace and economic context, a number of new forms of exclusion and segregation have emerged. In order fully to comprehend the effect of the new regimes of work in gender terms we need to look beyond labour market factors and complement these with social and political factors.

## Individualization and flexibility

A number of sociologists, including Beck (1996) and Giddens (1998), have argued that individualization is a feature of late modernity in respect of both work and family. We need to understand how the nature of risk may be influenced by changes in the labour market and society more generally:

the exhaustion, dissolution and disenchantment of collective and ground-specific sources of meaning (such as belief in progress, class consciousness) of the culture of industrial society (whose lifestyles and ideas of security have also been fundamental to the Western democracies and economic societies until well into the twentieth century) leads to all the work of definition henceforth being expected or imposed on individuals themselves. (Beck, 1996, p. 29)

Individuals, it is argued, live in a society where they have to construct their own employment narratives and life plans in the face of growing instability and uncertainty. It is also argued that personal goals and aspirations are increasing in significance relative to gender in family and career decisions (Giddens, 1998). This assertion has taken hold in a range of academic and political circles, heralding for optimists an age of individualism and personal self-development, but an age of uncertainty and insecurity for the more pessimistic-minded (Sennett, 1998). According to some, individualization should not be equated with autonomy. Whilst institutional and normative constraints are weakened, enabling and requiring individuals to take responsibility for life-course decisions, the choices open to people remain highly gendered and class-related.

Wajcman and Martin (2002, p. 1000) found in their study of managers a high degree of conflict for women between gender-neutral career narratives and feminine identities outside the workplace:

> Our research reveals a persistent gender structuring of 'choices' about career and family in the new capitalism by focusing on identities as important sources of action. The new capitalism does not obliterate the effects of embedded organizational practices and cultures that favour men over women, even though they are increasingly illegitimate in the eyes of women and at least some men. However, it has indeed seen the emergence of apparently gender-neutral career identities, so that differences between men and women in career routes are less and less dictated by gendered differences in their self-images in work and the labour market. But, because private identities remain so integrally and fundamentally gendered, they are the increasingly dominant source of the quite different 'family–work' choices and dilemmas men and women face. In sum, the writings of Beck, Giddens and Sennett speak much more directly to the experience of men than women in the new capitalism.

Perrons (2003) has found a similar pattern of gender differentiation in the new media sector, where women are internalizing risk in a way that is much more complex and uneven. If gender differences in family identities are taken into account it is apparent that gender remains a significant dimension of labour market inequality. The new economy maintains practices and cultures that favour men because they have been shaped by a masculine life-course paradigm. Moreover with the spread of the internet and other forms of information technology, governments and employers may shrug off their responsibility for ensuring fair pay levels and working conditions – especially in respect of the work–life balance – by drawing attention to the emancipatory aspects of the new developments (Perrons, 2003, p. 73). In effect it is up to women to take advantage of these developments to adjust their lives around paid work. Hence the new individual confronts the risk society in a gendered manner.

Individualization and identity formation are taking place in different welfare regimes. Whilst there is a tendency in Europe for the universal breadwinner to replace the family breadwinner model, the welfare measures that provide people with support for labour market participation are very diverse and impact differently on the role of women in the new economic context. In countries where there is little public support for family care, women are more likely to postpone or reject motherhood. There is evidence of this in a steep decline in the birth rate in certain European countries, especially Spain, where social support from the state and employers has been uneven. Brannen et al.'s (2001) research on work and family identities amongst young Europeans reveals the extent of the variations in welfare entitlements in different countries.

The discussion of individualization throws new light on the issue of flexible labour, which is considered a central feature of the new economy. In one sense, flexibility is a prime example of the process of individualization, especially in the case of flexible working time. Deregulation and the diversity of working-time arrangements potentially enable employers and employees to match labour supply and demand. Yet some forms of flexibility continue to be highly gendered, for example men have less entitlement to family-friendly policies. Research on parental leave in Norway suggests that a rigid paternity leave entitlement is much more effective in encouraging men to take leave from work than a flexible entitlement (Brandth and Kvande, 2001). Research on European labour markets by Rubery et al. (1998) also suggests that regulating and limiting hours of work is more effective in achieving gender equality and a proper work–life balance than flexible working time arrangements. So the role of regulation appears to be very important to the forms of workplace flexibility chosen and how they impact differentially on women and men.

## New forms of work organization

This section looks at how gender relations in organizations are influenced by changes in work organization in the new economy. These changes are associated with the need for organizations to adapt to an environment of intensified competition, rapid product innovation and new forms of knowledge and information technology – an unpredictable environment in which there is less emphasis on standardization and continuity of production organized into vertical hierarchies and more emphasis on flexible, knowledge-based production in decentralized, 'disorganized' networks.

There has been a tendency in the literature on the new economy, post-Fordism and the new organization to exaggerate the scale of the shift in work organization and to underestimate the durability of bureaucratic and Fordist forms of organization. As Thompson and McHugh (2002) point out, since as long ago as the 1950s organizational theorists have been putting forward similar arguments about a rapidly changing environment compelling organizations to break up their bureaucracies (Drucker, 1959, 1968). The key is to identify through empirical investigation the ways in which continuity and change interact, and how horizontal network-type relations that supposedly foster creativity and innovation coexist with vertical hierarchies. The links between gender relations and new organizational forms are under-researched. Two aspects of this will be explored here: the implication of changes in employment practices associated with internal labour markets; and the development of non-market forms of organization, such as workplace communities.

Two changes in the structure of internal labour markets in the UK are of interest here: companies' increased use of temporary employment agencies as sources of recruitment, especially for jobs requiring lower levels of skill; and the reduction of opportunities for internal career progression as a result of delayering (Grimshaw *et al.*, 2001; see also Chapter 5 of this volume for a discussion of internal labour markets and externalization). There is increased emphasis on career progression through the external labour market, linked to a growing emphasis on individual responsibility for employability, the disruption of 'psychological' contract-based job tenure and vertical career ladders.

The impact of these changes has been uneven, for example the length of job tenure for women has increased slightly because shifts in employment practice have been more than offset by women's increased labour market attachment. Also, internal labour markets and career structures continue to predominate in the public sector (Thompson and McHugh, 2002). Moreover the influence of these changes on the relative position of men and women in the labour market is likely to be contradictory. On average men are more likely to have benefited in the past from the career opportunities offered by internal labour markets, both because greater continuity of employment over their working lives enabled them to climb the career ladder and because they were likely to be favoured for training and development as employers had higher expectations of their commitment to the organization. Also, Kingsmill (2001) has found that a disproportionate reward for length of service is one of the main explanatory factors in the pay gap between men and women doing similar work. This means that the historical configuration of the labour market continues to shape the contours of the new labour market in terms of social opportunities and political control. Finally, a case study of the British postal service has shown that the male-dominated seniority system has continued to shape people's choice about where to work and at what time (Jenkins *et al.*, 2002).

It is interesting to note in this respect that equal opportunities legislation and the concept of indirect discrimination have contributed to the shift in recruitment from the internal to the external labour market. In one sense, therefore, the decline in the internal labour market as a means of career progression has perhaps created a more level playing field between core male workers and peripheral female workers, from which some women and other underrepresented groups are likely to benefit. However this also means that core workers and men may experience greater insecurity and competition for jobs. Returning to the case of the British postal service (Jenkins *et al.*, 2002), the erosion of seniority as a criterion for internal job allocation has not led to meritocratic or open processes that enhance the voice and circumstances of either men or women.

Whether women will gain or lose from these trends is likely to depend on whether they can exploit their knowledge and skills to improve their employability and value to organizations that require their expertise. This is likely to be the case for only a minority of 'knowledge workers' who are able to construct 'portfolio careers' and create strategic networks and informal organizations to advance their careers.

Moreover a significant proportion of women in the labour force have benefited from career progression through the diminishing internal labour market, and women in some organizations may have been more adversely affected than men by restructuring because of the occupational areas in which they are concentrated. For example Woodall *et al.* (1997) report a case study in which decentralization and delayering had adversely affected women managers because they were concentrated in central services such as human resource management rather than in line management positions. Women who are in permanent employment are likely to have greater access to maternity and parental leave than those in temporary employment or constructing a portfolio career. The decentralization of organizations therefore undermines internal labour markets, the possibility of redeployment and supported career paths. Even in sectors that have traditionally had strong gender-defined professions, such as the airline industry, the stability of female professions has been eroded by a weakening of the core stable constituency of employees. This means that women have to mobilize their human capital assets and network more extensively in order to enter employment in key areas, whilst for others their already limited space within organizations will be further undermined and disorganized.

Post-bureaucracy is therefore likely to have conflicting implications for women's progress into and within organizations. If one accepts a rational-legal perspective on equality, which is the dominant perspective in equality legislation, women are more likely to prosper in an organization where roles, responsibilities and procedures are transparent and rule-based, rather than fluid, opaque and informal. However women's experience of bureaucracy is often of a highly gender-segregated environment in which higher-level jobs are defined as masculine and lower-level jobs as feminine, as with the boss–secretary relationship explored by Kanter (1977) and Pringle (1989). Alternatively women may be concentrated in jobs requiring expertise whilst positions of authority and high reward remain exclusively male (Savage and Witz, 1992). Organizations that exhibit a role culture whilst providing procedural equity are highly gendered.

Would organizations that are more oriented towards a task culture, where effectiveness and responsiveness take priority over adherence to correct procedures, therefore provide a more conducive climate for equality? There may be more scope in a task culture for jobs to become gender neutral because individual capability is the critical factor. However a task culture may be associated with long hours, with individuals being expected to commit themselves to successful completion of a job at the expense of work–life balance in order to placate and support the team. Women are likely to progress less well than men in such an organizational culture insofar as they tend to give greater priority, through choice or constraint, to family care commitments. The current vogue for teamworking has prompted an interest amongst labour sociologists to explore the tendency of teamworking to lead to collective self-exploitation. However as yet little attention has been paid to the gender dynamics of teamworking.

Regardless of whether teamworking disrupts the work–life balance, it has been suggested that women would benefit from a shift towards decentralized post-bureaucratic organization because the leadership styles associated with horizontal webs of relations are deemed to be more feminine, whilst those associated with hierarchies are interpreted as masculine. This argument is problematic if one takes a social constructionist view of gender identity. Wajcman (1998) demonstrates that the similarities between the styles of male and female managers are greater than the differences, and that it is organizational context and culture that principally influence management styles in practice, not the individual styles that managers bring with them into the organization.

Another aspect of the debate on the new economy and new organization is the emergence of non-market, non-cash-nexus forms of organization, such as workplace communities, which are considered by some to be vital to innovation and at the cutting edge of socioeconomic change, while at the same time representing a 'traditionalization' of the economic sphere. Adkins (1999) argues that this process is associated with a 'retraditionalization' of gender relations within and outside the workplace.

Lash (1994) argues that the new knowledge-intensive forms of production in late modernity, referred to as reflexive production, encourage the development of premodern, communal–traditional social relationships in the workplace because these relationships are conducive to information flow and acquisition. This is required by the fast pace of innovation, the emphasis on product design and the shift from a material labour process to a 'culturalized' labour process. Knowledge intensity involves self-reflexivity and self-monitoring on the part of workers, rather than monitoring according to rigid rules (Lash, 1994). Lash cites evidence from Japan and Germany that personalized relations of trust and an ethic of commitment to a community rather than to self, facilitate flows of information. Within this process symbolic exchanges, such as shared identity, are as important as cash-nexus exchanges such as promotion incentives. In the Japanese and German contexts, Lash notes but does not explore the exclusion of women from the communities of reflexive production. This provides a starting point for Adkins' suggestion that the new workplace communities reflect attempts to secure new gender identities, to 'narrate essentialized identity "truths" ' (Adkins, 1999, p. 136; see also Bauman, 1992; Giddens, 1994; Weeks, 1995) and to counter individualization. In the context of a breakdown of social structures, the notion of communities is gaining salience as a source of shared identity and belonging (Adkins, 1999, p. 127). Adkins' own research on the tourist industry in Britain

> revealed an intensification of the use of married 'teams' by companies for the management of tourist establishments. What is of significance here for my current argument is where such married teams are mobilized both the relations between 'managers' and the production of goods and services in such establishments are significantly based on family relations of appropriation; or on what might be regarded as non-market, non-cash nexus, traditional relations. (Ibid., p. 130)

Examples are also drawn from the tourist industry of women being expected to perform 'sexual labour', defined as work that includes a sexual element, such as visual sexual displays and responding to sexual innuendos. Adkins found that where sexual labour was part of the job, women tended to be viewed as an undifferentiated group of workers (ibid., p. 133). Male tourist workers, on the other hand, were not expected to perform sexual labour and hence were able to define their own individual attributes and competences, rather than being treated as a homogeneous group. Individuality is more achievable in male teams.

The concept of workplace communities offers important insights into the practices and processes through which work is reproduced as a gendered experience in new regimes of work. As Adkins notes: 'the current round of traditionalization in terms of the economic domain may be constitutive of and dependent on a retraditionalization of gender' (ibid., p. 135). In this respect the classic problem of 'gender-typing' is endemic and integral to new patterns of work.

## Gender and disconnected capitalism

The manner in which women have been quantitatively and qualitatively integrated into the new regimes of work must not be analyzed purely at the social level but should also take account of some of the developments that have taken place within capitalism and the economy. The more assertive proponents of Post-Fordism from the regulation approach and those with a more individualistic approach tend to reify developments of either a collective or an individual nature. We are presented with clear breaks and ruptures in the way in which modernist and organized – as well as Fordist – economies have emerged. Consequently exclusion and segregation are not solely the outcome of deliberate, interest-based actions by constituencies of men but are also due to the unevenness of change, the lack of a coherent model of development, and the absence of an articulatory focus for regulation (see MacKenzie and Martínez Lucio, 2003, for a discussion of articulation and regulation). A useful starting point for such an analysis is Thompson's (2003) work on disconnected capitalism.

According to Thompson, Fordism can be accepted as the least worst term to describe the set of connected and cohesive social relations that characterized the postwar boom years up to the early 1970s in the industrialized world. Thompson refers to a virtuous circle of mass production and consumption, which is overseen by the interventionist, welfare-Keynesian state (ibid.). One aspect of the interventionist role of states during that period, not discussed by Thompson, was their general support for a male breadwinner model of employment and welfare, in which women were engaged primarily in housework and family care and only marginally in the labour market. In the UK this was implemented through the Beveridge welfare system (Gardiner, 2000). There were of course variations between nations in this as in other aspects of Fordist projects, with greater and earlier integration of women into the labour market in some countries, such as Sweden and France, than elsewhere. However all Fordist projects had in common the capacity for the vast majority of the population to achieve self-sufficiency and security based on relatively stable gender divisions of labour.

As Thompson argues, what characterizes the new economy in the Post-Fordist era is the absence of system cohesiveness. That is, there has been a clear shift away from some aspects of the old economy without the establishment of a new paradigm or set of social relations with 'the capacity to generate mutual gains among key economic actors' (Thompson, 2003, p. 362). One aspect of this lack of cohesiveness that has received little attention in the debates on Post-Fordism is the way in which changing gender relations are influencing and are being influenced by the new economy.

What are the key features of the new economy identified and discussed by Thompson, and how are these features related to changing gender relations? One significant change is a 'qualitative intensification of labour', which may involve a drive on the part of companies to identify and use the tacit knowledge and skills of employees, rather than the traditional Taylorist drive to detach knowledge and skills from the workers. In some sectors, especially services, this may involve mobilizing workers as whole people who are capable of performing emotional labour, not just as labour embodying technical skills. Here there is a desire – absent under Fordism – to tap into the creativity and commitment of employees. The second key feature of the new economy is the need for quantitative flexibility and, associated with it, increased contingency of labour. This results as much if not more from pressure to meet the expectations of the capital market as from competitive pressures in product markets. The growth of networked firms, outsourcing and subcontracting illustrates this trend (see Chapter 5 of this volume).

The disconnection between these two features of the new economy is highlighted by Thompson, who argues that there is a tension between, on the one hand, the commitment that capital is seeking from employees to invest more of themselves and work collaboratively and, on the other hand, the lack of commitment on the part of employers to invest in the skills and career development of their employees (see also Blyton and Morris, 1992). In the context of job insecurity, it is increasingly the responsibility of employees themselves to invest in their own skills and maintain their employability. They also have to be aware that many of the skills that are valued by current employers may have limited recognition or value in the wider labour market, as well as limited scope for certification (Thompson, 2003).

How can this perspective on the new economy be applied to the feminization of the labour force in industrialized countries since the 1970s? First, it is significant that the Post-Fordist era has been associated with feminization. It could be argued that a number of linkages between the two have received little attention because each is addressed in a separate body of literature. Feminization is linked to quantitative and qualitative aspects of the intensification and increased contingency of labour, for example through the shift from male-breadwinner to dual-earner households and the mobilization of emotional labour. This draws in social relations beyond work and utilizes social hierarchies in order to develop a more contingent capitalism. Accumulation can be sustained even without cohesive regulatory process and organized economic relations, especially in the labour market, by gendering the employment relation in new ways that are still based on segregation. Hence the fundamental tensions in contemporary capitalism and its disconnections are sustainable and permit a reproduction of the workforce as it rests on gendered notions of labour – technical and social – and on social relations that are based on women experiencing insecurity and uncertainty due to the demands of their private sphere (see Chapter 11 of this volume for a parallel discussion of the family). Capitalism can afford to be disconnected and not concern itself with its consequences because of the nature of gender relations. Thus not only are these relations still sustained by the character of new regimes of work, they are also underpinned by it. The unevenness of current regimes is sustainable even if they are decentred, disconnected and unfair.

## Conclusion

The new economy coexists with a wide range of regulatory and welfare regimes that structure patterns of gender inequality and set the parameters for work and family choices. Across the various regimes, new discourses of equality, meritocracy and individualization coexist to varying degrees with the continuing reproduction of gendered family roles and identities within and outside work. Within the workplace, gender and sex remain powerful forces in respect of access to jobs and sectors of employment, as well as opportunities for individual development and progression. Gender-neutral career narratives are becoming more common in the case of highly educated cohorts entering professional and managerial occupations, but this is offset by highly gender-differentiated expectations and identities outside work, especially for those becoming parents. Within the workplace, retraditionalization and cultural exclusion coexist with the dismantling of traditional formal discriminatory practices. Women continue to be defined by their sex and not their individuality in workplaces where 'sexual labour' is considered an integral part of the labour process.

The key points emerging from this discussion are that organizational change is complex, problematic and contradictory in terms of its impact on gender relations, as in other areas. However what we are witnessing is a series of developments that suggest that the new capitalism and employment relations encourage an uneven feminization of the workforce whilst continuing to reproduce modes of gender exclusion and segregation. Understanding how gender relations are being reconfigured in the new economy requires further exploration of the gendered nature of individualization and of new forms of collective and communal identity at work. We have moved from a broad politics of exclusion and segregation to a new utilization of women at work that brings gender to the very heart of the labour process.

## References

Adkins, L. (1999) 'Community and Economy: A Retraditionalization of Gender?', *Theory, Culture and Society*, 16 (1), pp. 119–39.

Balls, E. (1994) 'No More Jobs for the Boys', in J. Michie and J. Grieve Smith (eds), *Unemployment in Europe* (London: Academic Press), pp. 116–29.
Bauman, Z. (1992) *Intimations of Postmodernity* (London: Routledge).
Beck, U. (1996) 'Risk Society and the Provident State', in S. Lash, B. Szerszyhski and B. Wynne (eds), *Risk, Environment and Modernity* (London: Sage).
Blyton, P. and J. Morris (1992) 'HRM and the Limits of Flexibility', in P. Blyton and P. Turnbull (eds), *Reassessing Human Resource Management* (London: Sage).
Brandth, B. and E. Kvande (2001) 'Flexible Work and Flexible Fathers', *Work, Employment and Society*, 15 (2), pp. 251–67.
Brannen, J., S. Lewis and A. Nilsen (eds) (2001) *Young Europeans of the Future* (London: Routledge).
Bruegel, I. (2001) 'The Full Monty: Men into Women's Work?', in M. Noon and E. Ogbonna (eds), *Equality, Diversity and Disadvantage in Employment* (Basingstoke: Macmillan), pp. 208–28.
Cully, M., S. Woodland, A. O'Reilly and G. Dix (1999) *Britain at Work: As Depicted by the 1998 Workplace Employee Relations Survey* (London: Routledge).
Drucker, P. (1959) *Landmarks of Tomorrow* (New York: Harper & Row).
Drucker, P. (1968) *The Age of Discontinuity* (New York: Harper & Row).
European Industrial Relations Observatory (EIRO) (2001) 'Gender Updates – an annual perspective' (www.eiro.eurofound.eu.int/2001/03/update/tn0103201u.html).
Gardiner, J. (2000) 'Rethinking self-sufficiency: employment, families and welfare', *Cambridge Journal of Economics*, 24 (6), pp. 671–89.
Giddens, A. (1994) 'Risk, Trust, Reflexivity', in U. Beck, A. Giddens and S. Lash, *Reflexive Modernization: Politics, Tradition and Aesthetics in the Modern Social Order* (Cambridge: Polity Press), pp. 184–97.
Giddens, A. (1998) 'Risk Society: the Context of British Politics', in J. Franklin, *The Politics of Risk Society* (London: Polity Press).
Grimshaw, D., K. G. Ward, J. Rubery and H. Beynon (2001) 'Organisations and the Transformation of the Internal Labour Market', *Work, Employment and Society*, 15 (1), pp. 25–54.
Jenkins, S., M. Martínez Lucio and M. Noon (2002) 'Return to Gender: An Analysis of Women's Disadvantage in Postal Work', *Gender, Work and Organisation*, 9 (1), pp. 83–104.
Joshi, H. and P. Paci (1998) *Unequal Pay for Women and Men* (Cambridge, Mass.: MIT Press).
Kanter, R. M. (1977) *Men and Women of the Corporation* (New York: Basic Books).
Kingsmill, D. (2001) *Report into Women's Employment and Pay* (London: Women and Equality Unit, Department of Trade and Industry).
Lash, S. (1994) 'Reflexivity and its Doubles: Structure, Aesthetics, Community', in U. Beck, A. Giddens and S. Lash, *Reflexive Modernization: Politics, Tradition and Aesthetics in the Modern Social Order* (Cambridge: Polity Press), pp. 110–73.
Lovering, J. (1990) 'A Perfunctory Sort of Post-Fordism: Economic Restructuring and Labour Market Segmentation in Britain', *Work, Employment and Society*, 4 (2), 9–28.
MacKenzie R. and M. Martínez Lucio (2003) 'Accomodation, Negotiation or Colonisation? The realities of regulatory change', paper presented at the sixth European Sociological Association Conference, Murcia, Spain, September.
McDowell, L. (1991) 'Life without father and Ford; the new gender order of post-Fordism', *Transactions of the Institute of British Geographers*, 16, pp. 400–19.
Perrons, D. (2003) 'The New Economy and the Work–Life Balance: Conceptual Explorations and a Case Study of New Media', *Gender, Work and Organization*, 10 (1), pp. 65–93.

Pringle, R. (1989) *Secretaries Talk: Sexuality Power and Work* (London: Verso).
Purcell, K. (2002) *Qualifications and Careers: equal opportunities and earnings among graduates* (Manchester: EOC).
Rubery, J., M. Smith and C. Fagan (1998) 'National working-time regimes and equal opportunities', *Feminist Economics*, 4 (1), pp. 71–102.
Savage, M. and A. Witz (1992) 'The gender of organizations', in M. Savage and A. Witz (eds), *Gender and Bureaucracy* (Oxford: Blackwell), pp. 3–62.
Sennett, R. (1998) *The Corrosion of Character* (London: W. W. Norton).
Thompson, P. (2003) 'Disconnected capitalism: or why employers can't keep their side of the bargain', *Work, Employment and Society*, 17 (2), pp. 359–78.
Thompson, P. and D. McHugh (2002) *Work Organisations: a Critical Introduction* (Basingstoke: Palgrave).
Wajcman, J. (1998) *Managing Like a Man* (Cambridge: Polity Press).
Wajcman, J. and B. Martin (2002) 'Narratives of Identity in Modern Management: The Corrosion of Gender Difference?', *Sociology*, 36 (4), pp. 985–1002.
Weeks, J. (1995) *Invented Moralities: Sexual Values in an Age of Uncertainty* (Cambridge: Polity Press).
Woodall, J., C. Edwards and R. Welchman (1997) 'Organizational Restructuring and the Achievement of an Equal Opportunity Culture', *Gender, Work and Organization*, 4 (1), pp. 2–11.

# 10
# A Post-Fordist Consumption Norm? Social Fragmentation, Individualization and New Inequalities

*Luis Enrique Alonso*

> Nothing can ensure the forming of cosmopolitan solidarity in the uncertainties of cultural modernity. (Tomlinson, 2003, p. 243)

**Introduction**

In contemporary Western societies, consumer practices stand at the centre of production and social reproduction. Paradoxically, however, consumption has held a relatively peripheral position in contemporary political debates. It is therefore necessary in any social analysis and intervention to remove consumption from its *a priori* reductionist role and aim for a theoretical version projected onto a specific field, that is tied to the social position of the various groups in the labour process and their struggle to define both material distribution and cultural recognition of their institutional contexts of reference.[1]

According to the French sociologist and anthropologist Marcel Mauss (1979), consumption is a 'total social fact'. It is both an objective material reality and symbolic, depending on the meaning and value that social groups confer on consumer objects and activities. Thus consumption is both quantitative and qualitative. Not only does a great deal of our time, money and emotions go into consumption, but also a significant portion of our identity and forms of expression are generated by and structured around it. Consumption is the battlefield for the social subjects' struggle for signification. It stems from the domain of production but instead of mechanically reproducing consumption with a certain degree of autonomy, it produces and reproduces power, domination and differentiation. Also, given the degree of maturity and complexity that consumer society has now attained, the traditional positions on consumption – typified by the critical theories of the Frankfurt school (alienation, manipulation, the closing or control of a social universe) and their symmetrical opposite (those who view consumption as sovereignty, total freedom and wealth, characteristic of the liberal individualistic *homo economicus* stance) – are insufficient. Both leave no room for considering the social subject's logic of confrontation, domination, resistance and change.

Availing ourselves of the concept of social usage, which is certainly no newcomer to modern social science, we shall observe two sides of consumption: the 'social reproduction' side and the 'strategy for action' side. Forms of consumption are group-specific, that is, they are social usages during a given period of time and in a given place. They are as much indicators of economic systems of accumulation as they are real practices of subjects using strategies to try to reproduce, increase or exploit the various types of capital associated with each social position (Bourdieu, 1972, 1979; de Certeau, 1990). Consumption is constituted as a 'habitus', one's social position translated into practice, and conversely one's practice translated into social position. It refers to the structuring process in which the players express their positions in the social system, given that the structural properties of the consumer system are both conditions and results of the conflictual practice of players seeking to increase their domain (or their resistance) in the field of social reproduction.

Therefore consumption has a specific political dimension. It is a social group's uneven struggle for the distribution of surplus and meaning. It is not merely an individual agent's free, abstract aggregation of preferences, as purported by rational choice theory, nor is it – as typically stated by those in the imperative world of Western, postwar, culturalist Marxism – merely a symptom of the material and symbolic alienation imposed by almighty capitalism on unidimensional persons with no attributes or powers. Instead consumption is a social usage – that is, an unequal, conflictive, specific form of material appropriation and the meaning of objects and signs generated in the social field from social positions determined by the labour process by social groups with different types of capital (be it economic, symbolic, social, cultural and so on). In this chapter, we shall consider the fundamentals of consumption associated with the transformation of the Fordist mode of regulation, its crisis, its rearticulation and its fragmentation following the theoretical premise that a society's way of life is not the mechanical result of a linear, continuous process following the dictates of abstract modernization and then globalization. Rather its evolution is presided over by an internal, conflictive relationship with the production and distribution of economic surplus. Strategies of conflict on the part of social players and historical cutoffs can therefore be found in consumption (Bourdieu, 2000; Edwards, 2000; Herpin, 2001).

## Fragmentation and lifestyles

The notion of a mass consumer norm, or any other norm from the golden age of Fordism, such as the 'standard package' as a unit of consumption, affected social integration – a mythical, demobilized middle-class lifestyle became an ideological (as opposed to aristocratic or bourgeois and now popular or working class) centrepiece of various discourses that also deradicalized social conflict. Thus an integrated, functional, constantly renewable ensemble of objects that were mass (and routinely) produced and distributed became the material support for the expansion of consumption as a synonym for the ideological triumph of mesocratization, i.e. of the tastes and practices of a supposedly universal and functional middle class based on income growth (Skeggs, 2004). In daily life, consumption sets the many boundaries encompassed by mature Fordism, that is, national industry, public enterprise, mass production, highly bureaucratic large companies, middle and working classes protected by social and labour rights, and so on. All of this occurred in the framework of international trade, with national industries vying for broader product markets and attempting to impose the competitive advantages of nations on supranational areas that were nevertheless still highly regulated by single states or agreements between states.

During the 1980s and 1990s this model was deconstructed and reconstructed again, but always with the underlying aim of boosting the rate of private earnings far above any social right or entitlement that had been consolidated during the Fordist period. The economic framework generated was a global trade area that was no longer dominated by industrial and material capitalism, but by financial, virtual and non-material capitalism, in which trade was not in goods at the international level but in a system of company networks operating transnationally. Trade was no longer between countries or national economies in the traditional sense, but an ensemble of integrated transactions with accelerated flows of information, patents and intellectual rights, components, technology and, above all, non-material financial resources.

Thus the Fordist model of the organization of production has gradually been replaced by new, diverse and highly fragmented divisions of labour (social, geographical and technical) that have configured a model, far removed from the fragile Keynsian social equilibrium, for restructuring production and the economy. A vigorous process of recommodification, privatization and deregulation has brought about an institutional and ideological framework for managing the labour force. The prevailing idea is to maximize mobility and adaptation (flexibility) to serve the strictly commodity-based interest (beginning with the labour market) of maximizing the short-term profitability of capital in a global scenario.[2]

Deregulation has paradoxically taken centre stage in the new Post-Fordist type of regulation. Rather than being a new, orderly criterion for the social articulation of production and consumption, over the last few years deregulation has resulted in a differentiated use of the workforce and its reproduction, unified only by the maximization of recommodification. On the production side, Post-Fordism has consisted of more than a simple 'technologification' of the labour process. It has also recomposed the codes for relations between companies and the market, meaning that a new social and technological framework (Boltanski and Chiapello 1999) has – either through robotization and computerization or through the dispersion into networks of smaller-sized companies coordinated through contractual agreements – introduced highly customized production models. These models have enough flexibility to satisfy constantly changing, complex and segmented market demands. Flexibility, speed, adaptation and change have become the new production paradigms as opposed to the continuity, linearity, long-term profitability and stability of the Fordist model. Thus all resources have had to be adapted to a change in market dynamics and scale. This began with the workforce losing most of its historically and institutionally secured guarantees. The workforce has become yet another resource, fluctuating according to market cycles and needs. Interestingly and paradoxically, Post-Fordism has reinstated the workforce management that the Fordist cycle had abolished in many of its areas and sectors, making it widespread.

With regard to consumption, a series of dynamics completing the Post-Fordist regulation model can be found, though on a relatively haphazard basis in the context of institutional upheaval. These dynamics are fragmentation, individualization, virtualization and globalization. Therefore consumer society as a model for social integration and welfare (an opulent working class, mass market, full employment, a host of goods and services for anonymous consumers, a decommodifying Keynesian state, and so on) has gradually given way to a post-Fordist pattern of flexible manufacturing and specialization. This pattern includes a segmented purchasing model in which the unifying, integrating social universe that had served as a point of reference for conceiving consumer society has been undermined. Thus while middle-class taste, virtually non-differentiated products, the mass manufacture of large series of products and little attention to the aesthetic and symbolic design of products characterized the typical Fordist model, Post-Fordism is characterized by segmented markets, structural unemployment, a trend towards dualization and social vulnerability, differentiated or customized goods and services, the adaptation and constant renewal of business niches and a recommodified state.

In this context, social identities have become much more fragmented and there has been a large increases in the number of perceptions attached by the various social groups to the act of consumption and the social and cultural effects of consumption. Centralized marketing mechanisms have been replaced by networks and other new means of distribution. In this sense, mass consumption and mass culture must be considered from a much less integrated standpoint. At the same time, new lifestyles and (neo-elitist and individualist) differentiated consumption have become embedded in the set of differentiated purchasing standards that have taken shape in these new times of Post-Fordist consumption.[3]

Meanwhile the financial sector has expanded and new types of relatively specialized, highly remunerated jobs have been created in this sector. Simultaneously the high-technology sector has spawned a new breed of promotion-driven cosmopolitans. These developments have served to break the unifying symbol of Fordist national mass consumption (based on the ideological value of a growing, integrating middle class) and legitimized ostentatious consumption, which is much more integrated into daily life than the traditional bourgeoisie's conspicuous consumption. Analogously, in the face of this 'revolt of the elites' (Lasch, 1996), and given the cutback or containment of traditional workers' wages, the expansion of 'atypical' groups of workers, the systematic consolidation of fragile or weak segments of the labour market and the increase of social exclusion and new poverty phenomena, popular consumption has tended to disorganize and lose its social cohesiveness. We have moved on to a sort of 'lawless consumption' – that is, consumption degraded by voracity and overbuying. This dearticulation of the Fordist worker and social citizenship has led to a single identity among salaried workers, that of the hedonistic, amnesia-ridden subconsumer.

During the Post-Ford era most consumption has continued to be dominated by Fordist-like mass-produced and universal standardized products, but at the same time this product base has eroded in terms of its quality, social recognition and status-generating capacity. Since deregulation, mass-produced products such as traditional household appliances, utilitarian cars and the like have lost some of their appeal while differentiated product and service ranges have mushroomed in the quest for more profitable market niches and social segments. Here recommodification strategies have become ubiquitous in Post-Fordism. This has given rise, along with the multi-dimensional degradation of universal (both public and private) supply, to exclusive consumption patterns in the case of products whose exclusive nature is part and parcel of their commercial lure. While integration was the hallmark of Fordist consumer society, fragmentation and daily representation of inequality are the main features of Post-Fordist consumer rhetoric, and this fragmentation has blurred traditional class identities, beginning with the industrial working-class itself.

The Post-Fordist social adjustment that has gradually replaced large-scale agreements and macrocorporate regulations with endless commodifying strategies, multiregulations and microcorporate practices has resulted in an individualization of social identities and lifestyles, as manifest in new consumer patterns and products.[4] The once stationary objects have become portable (cellular phones, laptop computers, light weight video and music players, and so on), allowing consumers to become increasingly mobile. As consumption has become more linked to rapidly changing milestones in people's lives than to the familiar and orderly, personal biographies have lost their linearity and predictability (Attali, 1999). Access to digital supports and extremely light and easy to handle technology increases the breadth of a given buyer's personal choice. Similarly the stable, fixed, long-term functions of objects have been lost or become more complex. The separation of working and leisure time has also blurred. The home is no longer a haven of comfort and leisure, but rather a potential arena for the prolongation of work. Computers are used for both work and leisure, thus blending the private and public spheres. Thanks to microtechnology, any place can be a place of work. The innocent Fordist discourse of comfort, peace, tranquillity and the enjoyment of family life has given way to a production-driven discourse on the duty to consume in order not to be left out of the competition of the labour market, the symbolic market and the social relations market.

Congruous with these developments, the design of objects and the discourses justifying their use has evolved from a functionalist and opulent styling to a new pragmatic, effect-seeking, hyperconsumerist, cynical *raison d'être* that represent the major signifier of the era: postmodernism.[5] In the postmodern context there is no need to provide reasons to consume since consumerism has become the *raison d'être* for everthing else leading to a playful, and self-complacent aesthetic. Reasonless consumerism seems to be the major sign of identity (or rather lack of identity) of the postmodern realm of reference.[6] This hedonistic, narcissistic and individualistic postmodernism, aiming to turn consumerism and fashion into the cultural and artistic logic of Post-Fordism (deployed against progress, collective values, representative values, linearity, reason and so on), is nothing other than the imposition of the logic and aesthetics of commodification and commercialization. And this logic materializes in the area of project design and the aesthetics of goods (and services).

## Consumption and virtual society: from standard consumption to lawless consumption

Directly related to the above mentioned phenomena are the 'virtualization' and 'semiotization' of consumer processes (Baurriaud, 2001; Kerckhove, 1999) and the generation of a new spirit of capitalism. If in the welfare age there was a transition from production-driven capitalism to consumption-driven capitalism, then in the Post-Fordist, postindustrial, postmodern era there has been a transition to a sort of 'fiction capitalism'. Investment in image and symbolic eroticization have blurred the boundaries between consumption as an economic activity and consumption as a cultural phenomenon. Brands have broadened and become independent from their production and even their marketing. These 'metabrands' are above objects, functions and especially subjects. They create a mythology of their own. As Klein (2001, 2002) rightly states this mythology systematically distorts and conceals national inequalities, the social cost of hegemony, and their undermining of the weakest groups in society. All of this has come in the name of maintaining both affordable prices in the West and astronomical profits for firms.

This virtualization is yet another process in the entrepreneurialization and 'artificialization' of all areas of daily life. It has replaced direct social relations with relations that are totally mediated by digital merchandise and its icons. 'Life on the screen' and 'virtual communities' indicate that the factual dimension (contact and relation) of the social sphere has been colonized by Post-Fordism, deployed as a network capitalism that first individualized consumer culture and then went on to reconstruct it technologically.[7] We have gone from the typical passive, receptive consumer of the mechanical and electrical age (and even the age of early electronics), to the appearance of a self-produced, active and interconnected consumer. The seemingly endless increase in choice has come hand in hand with an increase in the power of the market and the companies that monopolize codes and technologies. This virtual, Post-Fordist culture has unleashed commodity-driven capacity for generating images, information and exchanges at a spectacular pace, virtually free of any control. It has also generated social references and supposedly democratic institutions that are not concerned with resistance or alternative uses of this digital technology. The Italian sociologist Paolo Virno (1996) speaks of Post-Fordism as a sort of communicative or cognitive twist in capitalism in the sense that there has not only been an increase in the channels, information and intellectual capital involved in production, but also a unification of working time and consumption, and a re-establishment of spheres of public and private life. This marks a break with the idea of clear delineation of the traditional factors of Fordism (factory, working hours, tools, status, consumer objects, and so on). These factors are currently intertwined leading to a capitalism leaping into the immaterial: its ultimate frontier.

Certain classes, nations and economically, culturally and linguistically dominant regions have bolstered their power in this virtual deployment of cosmopolitan capitalism, while certain social groups and territories that have historically been disadvantaged are at increased risk of being harmed and excluded. The social property upon which Fordism based its accumulation has been partially diluted. This engenders the symmetrical effects of exclusion and social disaffiliation. During Post-Fordism, market views of time and space have gradually become the true regulators of many spheres of life. Time considered as 'real' time experiences an acceleration of flows and an increase in the reflexivity of commercial channels in daily life. Insofar as space is concerned, distances shrink, production becomes mobile/relocated and consumption expands through the non-material (computer networks) or highly material (shopping malls, as the new cathedrals of consumption).[8]

## Globalization and differential consumption

The trends described thus far are inscribed in the globalization of the world economy, and this globalization is dominating the furthering of commodification strategies in all social and geographical areas. Thus the nation state has gradually lost its potential for intervention, with the paradoxical exception of the use of public power to recommodify and privatize. Nation states are therefore caught in an international financial crossfire. The public sector is unable effectively to intervene in the social sphere because it would cease to be financially efficient in an environment of increased competitiveness.[9] Inequality at the international level has worsened and a new map of the world has appeared. Rather than nations in the strict sense of the term, what we find are territories where a few integrated zones (large areas with high levels of competitive innovation) prevail while more vulnerable zones are absorbed by policing and more direct forms of surveillance. Most of the map is made up of excluded zones that lie outside the phenomenon of globalization. Information highways do not run through these areas because they were not designed to. Global and local have merged into 'glocal', a blurry area with barely any institutionalization or democratic definition. Yet these areas are increasingly salient to people's daily lives, as opposed to the state, which persists in terms of politics and law and order but is increasingly vague in terms of its social obligations vis-à-vis its citizens.

The Keynesian commitment to social welfare and job security has gradually given way to a risk society and an increasingly 'individualised self-construction of biographies' (Beck, 1992, 1999). In this society the individual is responsible for matters such as training, health care, pensions and personal security, which have become goods to be purchased in the growing service sector. Thus there has been an increase in 'defensive consumption', – that is, consumption designed to provide security against the excluding policies introduced during the crisis of the welfare state.[10] There has also been an increase in 'amnesiac' and 'dissipated' consumption, desperate consumption that is neither calculated nor fits into individuals' life design or future perspectives. Life is lived in the 'fast lane'. In addition waste has increased just as neoliberal, antidistributive policies have led to austerity and cutbacks in services for the most unprotected segments of Western society. Meanwhile ostentatious consumption, tied to the volatile profits of the new financial and technological economy, has become the hallmark of the new managers and brokers of the 'symbolic economy' and its ascendant classes.

This globalization has effects that go far beyond the homogeneity purported by self-congratulatory exponents of the internet society. It has also generated new social inequalities and a hierarchy of lifestyles and consumer patterns at the national and international level (Lash and Urry,

1994; Lash 2002). New segments of transnational consumption, new capital-intensive classes in human, social and symbolic terms, are gradually breaking away from the increasingly fragmented and vulnerable middle classes, and the working class. Many of their segments become new sub- and under-classes pushing to be included in the commodity-driven, purchase-based globalization but existing within depreciated, marginalized lifestyles (Bauman, 2004). Therefore the globalization process has had a twofold effect on consumer norms. First, a segment of the population, varying in size depending on a country's place in the ranking of the international division of labour, has been positively tied to the global economy and global patterns of consumption (the acquisition of new products and technology, international mobility, high purchasing power, and so on). Second, a much larger segment of the population (and entire geographical areas) has borne the social costs of globalization and defensively adapted its lifestyle to widespread commodification.

In short, what once defined the Fordist welfare state – functional middle classes, integrated working classes, full industrial employment, the opportunity for social ascent, and general access to goods and services designed for non-differentiated consumers in a decommodified state – have faded away. Meanwhile Post-Fordism has generated a symmetrical although somewhat diffuse model: globalization, interconnection, segmented labour markets, social dualization, structural unemployment, a differentiated, stratified supply of goods and services (including customized ones), a commodifying, entrepreneurializing state, and so on. Simultaneously many of the social identities traditionally anchored in standardized industrial consumption have been blurred,[11] and centralization has been replaced by networks of production, distribution, information and so on. National consumer norms have been diversified and fragmented, structured around elite, international, cosmopolitan consumer norms, selective information and symbolic ostentation. And lifestyles and consumption have become increasingly defensive and removed from traditional local patterns.

Time and space have been configured in different ways. New consumer products (software, intangible goods, computer goods, audio and video products, entertainment goods and so on) are now launched globally and their distribution is stepped up to obtain profits before the next innovations come on the market. In the case of industrial products that were central to Fordism, such as cars and household appliances, the production of components has been increasingly transferred to Brazil, Mexico and countries in Southeast Asia and Eastern Europe. Meanwhile global advertising campaigns have instilled up-market preferences among the elite in a large number of countries, accompanied by falling sales of medium- and low-quality consumer goods. This reflects a growth model that is geared primarily to high-income global consumers and a relative weakening of the middle- and lower-income segment in commodity terms.

In contrast to the national middle classes that emerged after the Second World War, which were characterized by a centripetal discourse and lifestyle and uniform social and purchasing practices, from the 1980s an increasingly international society began to configure itself in a centrifugal and segmented fashion. Lifestyles, consumer patterns and purchasing models expressing social identity were first fragmented and then differentiated. While Fordist-mass consumption patterns continued – as illustrated by standardization strategies and 'McDonaldization' – they have now been degraded and limited by divergent strategies that have gained ground to bring about a new structuring of classes, ranging from culturally hegemonic lifestyles to defensive and vulnerable consumer patterns among those who have been put on the fringe of the labour market by deregulation and growing job insecurity, including immigrants, the long-term unemployed, underemployed young people and so on.[12]

## Conclusion

If the Post-Fordist regulation model is notable for anything, it is for its vacuity and social weakness. In the case of consumption, this translates into discontinuity, where innovations are powerful but their impact is uneven. Therefore to present Post-Fordism as a type of general ultratechnological organization (together with its nihilistic cultural correlate – postmodernism), is to overlook its fragmented social nature. Although it is degraded, intensified and made flexible, the strictly Fordist material underpinning is still the main social stabilizer of the regulation of forms of lifestyle. However, it also encompasses a tremendous variety of segmented, juxtaposed consumer strategies leading to a highly disintegrated, even anomic character. This social order has based itself on a broadening out and deepening of the market but we have seen few innovations in terms of social rights, forms of security or consumer styles that are not directly tied to markets (or even social resistance of attempts at total commodification). During Fordism mass consumption coincided with the building of a sort of social citizenship, but during Post-Fordism the diverse consumption standards, habitus and lifestyles have been constituted without the parallel development of a new social citizenship capable of democratically institutionalizing forms of social action, consumer practice, or regulation that do not stem directly from a pure individualism or purchasing culture (Touraine, 1997; Foucauld and Piveteau, 2000; Schnapper 2002).

To highlight this issue is not to engage in Fordist nostalgia, as Fordism was based on ecological and social premises that are no longer acceptable, including the massive use of energy. There were also citizens who acknowledged no social rights other than those stemming from participation in waged work. Sexual discrimination was extensive, and economic and production-driven industrialism had major health effects. However Fordism does serve as a reference to compare the social nature of capitalist reproduction with the extreme disarticulation of social consumption and cultural patterns that the Post-Fordist model has generated. 'Cyberhouseholds', technology networks and privatization of the means of living have individualized practices and fragmented group purchasing culture to the point of collapse. They have widened symbolic and social barriers. It is true that the Post-Fordist model's ability to generate profits rapidly has increased the volume, availability and choice of goods for better placed social groups. However it has also increased the power of those who dominate the technological, cultural and linguistic codes, while enlarging the collection of social groups, countries and regions that are excluded from the benefits of intensive growth.[13]

In the light of the above, there is a need for a new consumption policy. Consumption can no longer be relegated to the back seat or viewed as a mere side effect of other social, economic and political dynamics that are deemed more important. Consumption is a source of both public and private welfare, however it is also a major generator of individual and group risks. The deepening of social inequalities, unsafe agricultural practices, environmental damage and commercial fraud and malpractice highlight the need for political and social control, and for better monitoring and control of production (Peretti-Watel, 2001; Ewald, 2002).

Consumption is a fundamental part of social identities and lifestyles. A society without consumption is impossible, but a society centred solely on consumption runs the risk of becoming a sham, of losing its solidarity and becoming nothing other than an agglomeration of selfish practices. Thus for societies that have made consumption their holy grail the time has come for political reflection (with the participation of all social partners) and formal and informal consumer education. They must rid themselves of the moral, social, economic and environmental risks brought about by being a servant of consumption, as in the total market paradigm, and instead make consumption a servant of society, as should be the case in any democratic community. Instead of instrumentally subverting human abilities to private profitability, consumption can be used as a rational means of developing them (Sen, 1985, 2000; Nussbaum, 2000).

Despite the above, consumer society is changing and maturing. New consumers – that is, responsible consumers who are interested in simplicity, health, a good price–quality relationship, and critically learning what are now highly complex codes of product markets (Nodé-Langlois and Rizet, 1995; Rochefort, 1996, 1997) – seem to be displacing stereotyped consumers. But these new consumers cannot be developed in an individual or isolated basis. Only by engaging with the political sphere to think through and build new alternatives can this materialize. Therefore, only participation, education, social mobilization, and knowledge of our true scope for choice in the market can democratically 'open' the sphere of consumption.

Everyday life is the modern realm of consumption, but it is also the realm for creating new social movements, new types of coexistence, and new methods for gaining knowledge and self-knowledge. Consumption is embedded in all aspects of life, not merely the market. Welfare, education, health and consumption are not isolated concerns that merely coincide in the minds of theoreticians. They are integrated facets of everyday life and must be at the heart of public policies to meet social needs and demands.

## Notes

1. Particularly relevant to this chapter are the sociological conceptualizations of consumption by Campbell (1987), Bocock (1995), Corrigan (1997), Lury (1997) and McCraken (1998). All these works contain multidimensional reflections on consumption as a complex social phenomenon.
2. Discussions of the crisis and transformation of Fordisim using the metaphor of a network (of society, economy, technology and communications) and the change this marks vis-à-vis the notions based on the power of large, isolated market dominators can be found in Castells (1995, 1998), Langlois and Robertson (1995) and Veltz (1996).
3. The issue of lifestyles as a basic concept in postmodern consumption is addressed from various approaches in Cathelat (1986, 2001), Featherstone (1991), Chaney (1996, 2002) and Lash (1997).
4. The issue of individualization has come to the fore in sociology – see Beck (1999) Beck and Beck-Gernsheim (2000) and Bauman (2001) Particularly relevant to consumer issues are Lipovetsky (1990) and Quessada (1999).
5. Postmodernism has become one of the principal topics of contemporary social science. The works by (McGuigan (1992, 1999), Jameson (1992, 1996, 1999), Smart (1992), Lyon 1996), Harvey (1998, 2002, 2003), Bauman (2001) are of particular interest.
6. The metaphors of speed, fragmentation and chaos prevail in the postmodern cultural environment. See Cleick (1987, 1999), Hayes (1993) and Cohen and Stewart (1995) for these metaphors and their impact on social practices. A good analysis of the political implications of this change in paradigm can be found in Balandier (1988, 2001).
7. For the digital revolution and its effects on the identity of social groups and types of expression and purchasing, see Turkle (1997) Sustein (2001), Castells (2001), and Shapiro (2003).
8. The question of large shopping malls becoming the predominant factor structuring urban time and space in the postmodern environment is dealt with in depth by Crawford (1992), Ferreira (1996), Longstreth (1997) and Ritzer (2000, (2001). The loss of specific social references is studied by Augé (1998, 2001).
9. Discussions of the strictly spatial dimension of globalization dealt with in this chapter – the creation of a new structuring of geographical inequality – can be found in Sassen (1991), Harvey (1996, 2003) and Soja (2000).
10. For the crisis of the welfare state and its implications for lifestyles; see Leonard (1997), Mann (2000), Lund (2002), Shipman (2002), Deacon (2002).
11. On the transformation of lifestyles due to symbolic saturation and an excess of signs see Morace (1993), Calabresse (1993), Maffesoli (1997), Baudrillard (2000, 2001) and Dubar (2002).

12. On the fragmentation of labour and the inability to ensure stable identities for growing segments of the population, see Lash and Urry (1987), Gorz (1995, 1998), Aznar (1998), Barbier and Nadal (2000), Sennett (2000, 2002) and Alonso (2001).
13. This issue is dealt with from different standpoints in García Canclini (1995), Fitoussi and Rosanvallon (1996), Sabel and Zeitlin (1997), Storper and Salais (1997), Luttwak (2000), Castel and Haroche (2001).

## References

Alonso, L. E. (2001) *Trabajo y posmodernidad. El empleo débil* (Madrid: Fundamentos).
Attali, J. (1999) *Fraternités*. (Paris: Fayard).
Augé, M. (1998) *Los 'no lugares'. Espacios del anonimato* (Barcelona: Gedisa).
Augé, M. (2001) *Ficciones de fin de siglo* (Barcelona: Gedisa).
Aznar, G. (1998) *Emploi: la grande mutation* (Paris: Hachette/Pluriel).
Balandier, G. (1988) *Le Désordre. Éloge du mouvement* (Paris: Fayard).
Balandier, G. (2001) *Le Grand Système* (Paris: Fayard).
Barbier, J.-C. and H. Nadel (2000) *La flexibilité du travail et de l'emploi*, (Paris: Flammarion).
Baudrillard, J. (2000) *Pantalla total* (Barcelona: Anagrama).
Baudrillard, J. (2001) *D'un fragmente láutre* (Paris: Albin Michel).
Bauman, Z. (2000) *Trabajo consumismo y nuevos pobres* (Barcelona: Gedisa).
Bauman, Z. (2001) *La sociedad individualizada* (Madrid: Cátedra).
Bauman, Z. (2004) *Wasted Lives, Modernity and its Outcasts* (Cambridge: Polity Press).
Baurriaud, N. (2001) *Esthétique relationnelle* (Paris: Les Presses du Réel).
Beck, U. (1992) *Risk Society. Towards a New Modernity* (London: Sage).
Beck, U. (1999) *Word Risk Society* (Cambridge: Polity Press).
Beck, U. and E. Beck-Gernsheim (2000) *Individualisation* (London: Sage).
Bocock, R. (1995) *El consumo* (Madrid: Talasa).
Boltanski, L. and E. Chiapello (1999) *Le nouvel esprit du capitalisme* (Paris: Gallimard).
Bourdieu, P. (1972) *Esquisse d'une théorié de la pratique* (Geneva: Droz).
Bourdieu, P. (1979) *La Distintion. Critique sociale du jugement* (Paris: Minuit).
Bourdieu, P. (2000) *Les structures sociales de l'économie* (Paris: Seuil).
Calabresse, O. (1993) *La era neobarroca* (Madrid, Cátedra).
Campbell, C. (1987) *The Romantic Ethic and the Spirit of Modern Consumerism* (Oxford: Blackwell).
Castel, R. and C. Haroche (2001) *Propiété privée, propiété sociale, propiété de soi* (Paris: Fayard).
Castells, M. (1995) *La ciudad informacional* (Madrid: Alianza).
Castells, M. (1998) *La era de la información (vol. 2). El poder de la identidad* (Madrid: Alianza).
Castells, M. (2001) *La galaxia internet* (Barcelona: Areté).
Cathelat, B. (1986) *Socio-styles sistem* (Paris: Edtions de L'Organisation).
Cathelat, B. (2001) *Publicité et societé* revd edn (Paris: Payot).
Certeau, M. de (1990) *L'invention du quotidien* (Paris: Gallimard/Folio).
Chaney, D. (1996) *Lifestyles* (London: Routledge).
Chaney, D. (2002) *Cultural Change and Everyday Life* (London: Palgrave).
Cohen, J. and I. Stewart (1995), *The Collapse of Chaos: Discovering Simplicity in a Complex World* (Harmondsword, Penguin).
Corrigan, P. (1997) *The Sociology of Consumption* (London: Sage).

Crawford, M. (1992) 'The world in a shopping mall', in M. Sorkin (ed.), *Variations on a Theme Park: The American City and the End of Public Space* (New York: Farran), pp. 5–34.
Deacon, A. (2002) *Perspectives in Welfare* (Buckingham: Open University Press).
Dubar, C. (2002) *La crisis de las identidades* (Barcelona: Bellaterra).
Edwards, T. (2000) *Contradictions of Consumption* (Buckingham: Open University Press).
Ewald, F. (2002) 'Le risque dans la société contemporaine', in Y. Michad (ed.), *L'Individu dans la société d'aujourd'hui* (Paris: Odile Jacob), pp. 9–25.
Featherstone, M. (1991) *Consumer Culture and Postmodernism* (London: Sage).
Ferreira, R. (1996) *Centres comerciaux: #afiles urabines de la postmodernite* (Paris: L'Harmattan).
Fitoussi, J.-P. and P. Rosanvallon (1996) *Le nouvel âge des inégalités* (Paris: Seuil).
Foucauld, J.-B de, and D. Piveteau (2000) *Une société en quête de sens*, 2nd edn (Paris: Odile Jacob).
García Canclini, N. (1995) *Consumidores y ciudadanos. Conflictos multiculturales de la globalización* (Mexico: Grijalbo).
Gorz, A. (1995) *Metamorfosis del trabajo. Búsqueda del sentido* (Madrid: Sistema).
Gorz, A. (1998) *Miserias del presente riqueza de lo posible* (Buenos Aires: Paidós).
Harvey, D. (1989) *The Condition of Postmodernity* (Oxford: Blackwell).
Harvey, D. (1996) *Justice, Nature and the Geography of Difference* (Oxford: Blackwell).
Harvey, D. (2002) 'The Art of Rent: Globalization, Monopoly and the Commodification of Culture', in L. Panich and C. Leys (eds), *A World of Contrations. Socialist Register* (New York: Monthly Review Press).
Harvey, D. (2003) *Espacios de esperanza* (Madrid: Akal).
Hayes, N. K. (1993) *La evolución del caos. El orden dentro del desorden en las ciencias contemporáneas* (Barcelona: Gedisa).
Herpin, N. (2001) *Sociologie de la consommation* (Paris: La Découverte).
Jameson, F. (1991) *El posmodernismo o la lógica cultural del capitalismo avanzado* (Barcelona: Paidós).
Jameson, F. (1992) 'Postmodernism and Consumer Society', in P. Brooker (ed.), *Modernism/Postmodernism* (London: Longman), pp. 163–79.
Jameson, F. (1996) *Teorías de la postmodernidad* (Trotta: Madrid).
Jameson, F. (1999) *El giro cultural. Escritos seleccionados sobre posmodernismo* (Buenos Aires: Manantial).
Kerckhove, D. (1999) *La piel de la cultura* (Barcelona: Gedisa).
Klein, N. (2001) *No Logo. El poder de las marcas* (Barcelona: Paidós).
Klein, N. (2002) *Vallas y ventanas* (Barcelona: Paidós).
Langlois, R. N. and P. L. Robertson (1995) *Firms, Markets and Economic Change* (London: Routledge).
Lasch, C. (1984) *The Minimal Self* (New York: Norton).
Lasch, C. (1996) *La rebelión de las élites y la traición a la democracia* (Barcelona: Paidós).
Lash, S. (1997) *Sociología del posmodernismo* (Buenos Aires: Amorrortu).
Lash, S. (2002) *Critique of Information* (London: Sage).
Lash, S. and J. Urry (1987) *The End of Organized Capitalism* (Cambridge: Polity Press).
Lash, S. and J. Urry (1994) *Economies of Signs and Space* (London: Sage).
Lipovetsky, G. (1990) *El imperio de lo efímero. La moda y su destino en las sociedades humanas* (Madrid: Anagrama).

Longstreth, R. (1997) *City Center to Regional Mall: Architecture, the Automobile and Retailing in Los Angeles* (Cambridge, Mass.: MIT Press).
Lund, B. (2002) *Understanding State Welfare. Social Justice and Social Exclusion?* (London: Sage).
Lury, C. (1997) *Consumer Culture* (Cambridge: Polity Press).
Luttwak, E. (2000) *Turbocapitalismo. Quiénes ganan y quiénes pierden en la globalización* (Barcelona: Crítica).
Lyon, D. (1996) *Postmodernidad* (Madrid: Alianza).
Maffesoli, M. (1997) *Du nomadisme*, Paris: Librairie Générale Francaise/Le Livre de Poche).
Mann, K. (2000) 'The Welfare State and Postmodernity', in C. Pierson and F. C. Castles (eds), *The Welfare State Reader* (Cambridge: Polity Press).
Mauss, M. (1979) *Sociología y Antropología* 2nd edn (Madrid: Tecnos).
McCracken, G. (1988) *Culture and Consumption* (Bloomington, Ind.: Indiana University Press).
McGuigan, J. (1992) *Cultural Populism* (London: Routledge).
McGuigan, J. (1999) *Modernity and Postmodern Culture* (Buckingham: Open University Press).
Morace, F. (1993) *Contratendencias. Una nueva cultura de consumo* (Madrid: Celeste).
Nodé-Langlois, N. and L. Rizet (1995) *La consommation* (Brussels: Le Monde-Marabout).
Nussbaum, M. C. (2000) *Women and Human Development. The Capabilities Approach* (Cambridge: Cambridge University Press).
Peretti-Watel, P. (2001) *La société du risque* (Paris: La Découverte).
Quessada, D. (1999) *La Societé de consommation de soi* (Geneva and Paris: Verticales).
Ritzer, G. (1996) *La McDonalización de la sociedad* (Barcelona: Ariel).
Ritzer, G. (1998) *The McDonaldization Thesis* (London: Sage).
Ritzer, G. (2000) *El encanto de un mundo desencantado. Revolución de los medios de consumo* (Barcelona: Ariel).
Ritzer, G. (2001) *Explorations in the Sociology of Consumption* (London: Sage).
Rochefort, R. (1996) *La société des consommateurs* (Paris: Odile Jacob).
Rochefort, R. (1997) *Le consommateur entrepeneur* (Paris: Odile Jacob).
Sabel, C. and J. Zeitlin (1997) *World of Possibilities: Flexibility and Mass Production in Western Industrialization* (Cambridge: Cambridge University Press).
Sassen, S. (1991) *The Global City* (Princeton, NJ: Princeton University Press).
Schnapper, D. (2002) *La démocratie providentielle. Essai sur l'égalite contemporaine* (Paris: Gallimard).
Sen, A. (1985) *Commodities and Capabilities* (Amsterdam: North-Holland).
Sen, A. (2000) *Desarrollo y libertad* (Barcelona: Planeta).
Sennett, R. (2000) *La corrosión del carácter. Las consecuencias personales del trabajo en el nuevo capitalismo* (Barcelona: Anagrama).
Sennett, R. (2002) 'Trabajo y tiempo de trabajo en el siglo XXI', in AA.VV, *Claves para el siglo XXI* (Barcelona: UNESCO/Crítica), pp. 387–91.
Shapiro, A. (2003) *El Mundo en un Clic* (Barcelona: Random House/Mondadori).
Shipman, A. (2002) *The Globalization Myth* (Cambridge: Icon).
Skeggs, B. (2004) *Class, Self, Culture* (London: Routledge).
Smart, B. (1992) *Postmodernity* (London: Routledge).
Soja, E. (2000) *Postmetropolis. Critical Studies of Cities and Regions* (Oxford: Blackwell).
Storper, M. and R. Salais (1997) *Worlds of Production The Action Frameworks of the Economy* (Cambridge, Mass: Harvard University Press).

Sunstein, C. R. (2001) *Republic. Com* (Princeton, NJ: Princeton University Press).
Tomlinson, J. (2003) *Globalización y cultura* (Mexico: Oxford University Press of Mexico).
Touraine, A. (1997) *Pourrons-nos vivre ensemble? Égaux et differents* (Paris: Fayard).
Turkle, S. (1997) *La vida en la pantalla* (Barcelona: Paidós).
Veltz, P. (1996) *Mondialisation villes et territoires. L'Economie d'archipel* (Paris: Presses Universitaires de France).
Virno, P. (1996) *Parole con parole* (Milan: Bollati-Boringhieri).

# 11
# The Feminization of Work, Changes in Family Structure and the Transformation of the Welfare State in the Post-Fordist Environment

*Gerardo Meil Landwerlin*

## Introduction

The relationship between the Fordist production model and the Keynesian welfare state as a model for the later development of capitalism was forged on a concrete historical model of social reproduction that hinged on what is colloquially known as the 'traditional family'. This model, based on a gendered division of work, was seen by functionalist sociologists such as Parsons and Bales and new political economists such as Becker as the most appropriate one for the development of capitalism and the maximization of social and individual welfare. Even though the Post-Fordist debate has overlooked changes in this area, deep social changes have taken place in the wake of the crisis of the Fordist model. Family life has been deeply affected by what has been described as individualization (Beck, 1986). Marriage is no longer a privileged framework for the personal and social self-fulfilment of women and it no longer holds out the prospect of financial security in exchange for loss of independence. Traditional social mores can no longer ensure that men and women will marry, have children and take care of other family members as the social pressure to do so has reduced and they have become increasingly aware of the direct and opportunity costs that these responsibilities entail. Thus the family structure around which the Keynesian welfare state was developed has undergone substantial change. This chapter will address the main aspects of this and the challenges it poses to the 'conservative' welfare state model (Esping-Andersen, 1990, 1999).

## The transformation of family life

Family life in developed countries, just as other spheres of society, is undergoing deep changes. All dimensions of family life are affected, including social representations and ideals and everyday interactions among family members. The traditional model for organizing family life, understood as a lifetime, joint cohabitation project with complete separation of gender roles, has shifted to a much less clearly defined model that is mainly characterized by the reduction of social control over individuals' lives and increasing freedom to construct one's own life project. In this sense there has not been so much of an emergence of a new, egalitarian model as the privatization of choice in terms of building one's own family biography (Lüscher *et al.* 1988; Meil, 1999).

The emergence of the modern nuclear family during industrialization involved the privatization of family life, though it was still subject to tight social control and based on the bourgeois or traditional family model. Social and cultural change during the 1960s brought about a second, deeper privatization of life projects in general and family life in particular. It also called into question the validity of the social norms that had hitherto kept private life under tight social control. 'What will the neighbours say?' – the manifestation of individuals' internalization of social control – was gradually replaced by 'It's none of their business', signalling a social space in which individuals were free to define and organize their own life projects and their life as couples and families. In other words life projects and lifestyles were privatized and the previous model of family life was no longer binding. Entering, remaining in or ending a marriage became more flexible, governed mainly by negotiation and agreement by consenting individuals. Social condemnation of deviation from the model established by norms of the past was no longer legitimate.

All this has led to a reduction in the significance of the family as an institution, in the socially established ways of understanding and organizing family life. However the same cannot be said for the subjective significance and importance that family life has for individuals. Despite privatization, coupledom has not ceased to be the model for organizing adult life. Being single, living alone, living in communes or 'flexible couple biographies' (Beck, 1986; Beck-Gernsheim, 1998) have not emerged as widely accepted alternative models to stable coupledom, which – be it expressed through marriage, civil union or cohabitation – is still the framework in which most individuals seek to satisfy their need for affection and sexual gratification.

Nonetheless, with the 'new conjugal pact' (Roussel, 1989) there is greater emphasis on the fulfilment of both partners, of the individual egos as opposed to 'we' the couple or family. Thus a new model of parenthood has emerged in which women are no longer expected to dedicate all their time to their family and are free to pursue their own careers, while fathers take greater responsibility for the physical care of their children. This greater emphasis on the individual is also associated with an understanding of the couple in consensual and hedonistic terms. The new conjugal pact focuses more on the partners' emotional leisure and consumption needs than on the household production of goods and services. Behind this new model lurks not only the commodification of women's work and household production but also fundamental changes to social values, which are also shifting towards greater individual freedom and the right to make one's own choices as an individual (Beck, 1986).

A corollary to the above is social acceptance of consensual divorce when the emotional ties that formed the basis of the relationship have disappeared. Although for some couples children pose a significant obstacle to divorce, the change in values underpinning the new conjugal pact marks a change in the part played by children in binding a relationship. Culturally speaking, marriage and having a family is no longer required as a social security measure for women.

In parallel with this there has been a separation of sexuality, marriage and procreation, all three of which once belonged to the single notion of the family. Premarital sexual relations are no longer penalized and have become the norm in romantic relationships. Moreover they begin at an increasingly early age while the age of marriage is postponed. This liberalization of sexual relations came hand in hand with the ready availability of effective means of birth control and acceptance of family planning as a social norm. The social norm that now governs procreation is that one should only have as many children as one can properly care for and educate, judged by increasingly demanding standards.

Sexual relations have therefore been separated not only from marriage but also from procreation. While single motherhood is now accepted by most people, this does not mean that it has attained the status of a behavioural model, merely that it has been destigmatized. Meanwhile marriage no longer necessarily implies procreation, and motherhood for career, financial or any other reason is no longer socially stigmatized.

However these widespread changes have not automatically translated into a general crisis of the family structure, of how families actually live. Moreover the situation varies from country to country and one cannot speak of a trend towards convergence (Roussel, 1992; Hantrais, 1997). Below we shall briefly consider the main traits of the structural changes: the growth of cohabitation, the reduction in the size of families, the increase of divorce and single parent families, and the increasing participation of women in the job market. All these factors are absent from the assumptions that underpin the welfare state.

First, marriage has lost its monopoly as the legitimate way of organizing life as a couple and cohabitation has become an accepted alternative in many countries. As shown in Table 11.1, the prevalence of cohabitation varies greatly from one country to another, with clear differences between Northern and Southern Europe. Cohabitation first became prevalent, in Scandinavian countries and then in Northern Europe, both for the first union and for subsequent ones. In Southern Europe cohabitation has

Table 11.1 Type of first union entered into by women, selected European countries, 1995 (per cent)

| | Women aged 25–29 | | | Women aged 35–39 | | |
| --- | --- | --- | --- | --- | --- | --- |
| | Marriage | Civil marriage | Cohabitation | Marriage | Civil marriage | Cohabitation |
| Sweden | 7 | 41 | 52 | 8 | 62 | 30 |
| Norway | 24 | 40 | 35 | 62 | 30 | 7 |
| Finland | 17 | 43 | 40 | 31 | 46 | 23 |
| France | 12 | 30 | 58 | 48 | 34 | 19 |
| Austria | 19 | 41 | 40 | 30 | 42 | 28 |
| Switzerland | 19 | 44 | 37 | 30 | 52 | 18 |
| Western Germany | 16 | 38 | 46 | 38 | 33 | 29 |
| Eastern Germany | 15 | 35 | 50 | 21 | 26 | 53 |
| Italy | 86 | 8 | 6 | 91 | 5 | 4 |
| Spain | 80 | 8 | 12 | 91 | 4 | 5 |
| Latvia | 50 | 34 | 17 | 67 | 26 | 8 |
| Lithuania | 75 | 9 | 16 | 78 | 10 | 12 |
| Hungry | 76 | 14 | 10 | 84 | 9 | 7 |
| Poland | 95 | 3 | 2 | 96 | 3 | 1 |

become a little more common for second unions, but it is still a minority choice for first-time couples. The conversion of cohabitation into marriage with the birth of children, particularly in the case of first unions, is not universal, although it is common in Central and Southern Europe, where welfare state provisions are based on the principle of derived rights – that is, family members are entitled to welfare provision through the socially insured person upon whom they are dependent (Lauterbach, 1999; Kiernan, 2000).

Also, the size of families is shrinking, with a decrease in the average number of children being born and an increase in the number of women who end their child-bearing years without becoming mothers. In 2003 the average number of births per women born in 1940 ranged from 2.0 to 2.6 children in the 15 EU countries (with the exception of Ireland, where the average was 3.3), compared with 1.5–2.1 for those born in 1965 (Table 11.2). In the same year the proportion of women born in 1940 who had had no children ranged from 5–6 per cent in Ireland and Portugal to 14 per cent in Finland, while among those born in 1965 the figures ranged from 7 per cent to 18 per cent, having substantially increased in all EU countries except Sweden and France. In line with this, households consisting of two adults with dependent children have lost their relative weight in the EU household structure, falling from 36 per cent in 1988 to 28.7 per cent in 1999.

Table 11.2  Fertility among women born in 1941–45 and 1961–65, 2003

|  | Average numbered births per woman | | Percentage of women without children | | Percentage of women with 1 child | |
|---|---|---|---|---|---|---|
|  | 1941–45 | 1961–65 | 1940–44 | 1955–59 | 1940–44 | 1955–59 |
| EU-15 | 2.14 | 1.73 | n.a. | n.a. | n.a. | n.a. |
| Belgium | 2.02 | 1.78 | 8.5 | 11.2 | 28.3 | 31.7 |
| Denmark | 2.14 | 1.90 | 9.8 | 12.8 | 17.0 | 19.5 |
| Germany | 1.84 | 1.56 | n.a. | n.a. | n.a. | n.a. |
| Greece | 2.00 | 1.80 | n.a. | n.a. | n.a. | n.a. |
| Spain | 2.40 | 1.60 | 7.4 | 11.0 | 8.4 | 23.2 |
| France | 2.30 | 2.04 | 8.0 | 7.9 | 18.5 | 20.4 |
| Ireland | 3.30 | 2.24 | 5.3 | 14.7 | 13.9 | 9.5 |
| Italy | 2.10 | 1.54 | 11.5 | 12.6 | 17.7 | 24.6 |
| Luxembourg | 1.80 | 1.68 | n.a. | n.a. | n.a. | n.a. |
| Netherlands | 2.10 | 1.78 | 11.1 | 17.7 | 12.5 | 15.0 |
| Austria | 2.00 | 1.64 | n.a. | n.a. | n.a. | n.a. |
| Portugal | 2.30 | 1.84 | 6.2 | 7.0 | 25.7 | 28.4 |
| Finland | 1.94 | 1.92 | 14.3 | 17.9 | 19.4 | 16.0 |
| Sweden | 2.00 | 1.98 | 12.6 | 13.1 | 16.3 | 15.5 |
| United Kingdom | 2.20 | 1.90 | 10.7 | 18.5 | 13.0 | 12.4 |

Source: Eurostat, Newcronos Database, Luxembourg (2003).

Table 11.3  Divorce rate and length of broken marriages in the EU, 1959–61 and 1996–98

|  | Divorce rate per 1000 marriages (%) | | Average length of broken marriages (years) | |
|---|---|---|---|---|
|  | 1959–61 | 1996–98 | 1970–74 | 1995–99 |
| EU-15 | n.a. | 36.2 | – | 12.3 |
| Belgium | 7.2 | 57.3 | 13.1 | 13.8 |
| Denmark | 18.5 | 36.9 | 10.7 | 12.0 |
| Germany* | 10.7 | 43.9 | 9.1 | 12.2 |
| Greece | 4.1 | 19.1 | 14.2 | 11.8 |
| Spain | – | 17.1 | – | 14.8 |
| France | 9.6 | 41.9 | 11.8 | 13.8 |
| Italy | – | 11.9 | 23.7 | 17.0 |
| Luxembourg | 5.9 | 46.2 | 11.6 | 12.6 |
| Netherlands | 6.3 | 39.3 | 14.0 | 12.4 |
| Austria | 14.1 | 44.0 | 8.3 | 11.1 |
| Portugal | 1.0 | 21.8 | 14.5 | 14.2 |
| Finland | 11.4 | 57.2 | 11.2 | 13.2 |
| Sweden | 17.3 | 64.8 | 12.0 | 12.2 |
| United Kingdom | 6.8 | 53.0 | 13.4 | 10.0 |

* Including Eastern Germany from 1991.
Source: Eurostat, Newcronos Database, Luxembourg (2003).

At the same time the proportion of marital breakdowns has grown steadily (Table 11.3). While at the beginning of the 1960s the divorce rate was generally below 10 per cent (with the exception of the Scandinavian countries), with several countries not recognizing the right to divorce and most countries only allowing divorce when one of the parties had committed a fault, by the mid 1990s the number of divorces had increased sixfold in the EU as a whole, although the rates varied greatly from country to country. While in Southern Europe the divorce rate is still quite low – 'fewer than 24 divorces per 1000 marriages – in most of the remaining EU countries it is substantially higher, reaching a rate of 50 per cent, or more. It is important to note, however, that many marital separations in Southern Europe never culminate in divorce, making the divorce statistics an unreliable indicator of marital breakdown. In Spain, where there must be legal separation before divorce, the annual legal separation rate between 1982 and 1997 increased by 7.9 per cent, while the increase in the annual divorce rate over the same period was 3.1 per cent.

*Table 11.4* Employment rate of women aged 20–49, by number of children, second quarter of 2001 (per cent)

|  | 0 children | | 1 child | | 2 children | | 3 or more children | |
| --- | --- | --- | --- | --- | --- | --- | --- | --- |
|  | 1985 | 2001 | 1985 | 2001 | 1985 | 2001 | 1985 | 2001 |
| EU-15 | n.a. | 66.9 | n.a. | 68.2 | n.a. | 62.2 | n.a. | 45.1 |
| Belgium[1] | 52.6 | 65.8 | 55.3 | 70.4 | 51.3 | 87.2 | 33.1 | n.a. |
| Denmark | 77.3 | 79.0 | 77.8 | n.a. | 79.7 | n.a. | 66.0 | n.a. |
| Germany[2] | 69.2 | 72.6 | 46.6 | 74.6 | 35.4 | 63.4 | 27.7 | 45.8 |
| Greece[3] | 48.2 | 52.3 | 41.1 | 53.0 | 37.5 | 50.8 | 36.0 | 40.4 |
| Spain[3] | 38.1 | 55.7 | 28.2 | 49.5 | 23.1 | 46.0 | 18.3 | 39.6 |
| France[4] | 68.4 | 69.4 | 67.3 | 73.1 | 57.9 | 65.7 | 28.6 | 40.7 |
| Ireland | 64.2 | 65.9 | 29.2 | n.a. | 18.4 | n.a. | 13.8 | n.a. |
| Italy | 48.2 | 53.6 | 43.9 | 53.1 | 35.4 | 46.6 | 27.4 | 34.2 |
| Luxemburg | 62.6 | 69.8 | 38.9 | 65.8 | 29.4 | 56.3 | 26.7 | 36.1 |
| Netherlands | 62.3 | 81.9 | 32.0 | 71.9 | 26.9 | 68.9 | 19.3 | 59.1 |
| Austria | n.a. | 76.9 | n.a. | 78.3 | n.a. | 67.9 | n.a. | 58.8 |
| Portugal | 55.9 | 69.4 | 59.7 | 79.6 | 57.4 | 71.7 | 47.5 | 63.5 |
| Finland | n.a. | 75.5 | n.a. | n.a. | n.a. | n.a. | n.a. | n.a. |
| Sweden | n.a. | 79.4 | n.a. | n.a. | n.a. | n.a. | n.a. | n.a. |
| United Kingdom | 76.9 | 81.3 | 53.1 | 69.4 | 47.3 | 66.5 | 32.2 | 46.7 |

*Notes*:
1. Last quarter of 2000.
2. From 1991 includes the former East Germany.
3. First quarter of 2001 and second quarter of 1986.
4. First quarter of 1985.
*Source*: Eurostat, Newcronos Database, Luxembourg (2003).

As a result of improved medical treatment, single-parent families stem increasingly from divorce and separation rather than the death of one of the parents. However, given the lower birth rate the proportion of households with one parent and dependent children is decreasing. Meanwhile there has been an increase in the number of households with two or more adults (childless couples, mothers with one or more adult offspring, fathers with adult offspring, and so on).

Finally, the family model with separate gender roles is less common among recent generations, although this is often less to do with the division of domestic labour than with the ending of the traditional male role of sole breadwinner. While there are large differences among countries, there is a clear trend in all of them towards the full involvement of women in paid work (Table 11.4; see also OECD, 2002). However women's careers are still highly contingent on family circumstances, meaning that women with dependent children tend to be overrepresented in the most unstable and irregular jobs, as well as in part-time work, and are also hit harder by unemployment (Drew and Emerek, 1998; OECD, 2001).

In summary, family change is taking place in all countries to varying degrees. A number of models for beginning, remaining in and ending family life as well as greater freedom to define one's life course can be observed in all countries. Social norms no longer guarantee that family responsibilities will be taken on. Instead this sphere of life has been privatized and is up to personal choice. The traditional family model is less and less prevalent among the younger generations, and this has strong implications for the welfare state, particularly in its conservative form.

## The family model that underpins the conservative welfare state

Two basic principles are used in developed welfare states to organize the redistribution of income and the provision of social services: universal access to services based on the principle of citizenship, by virtue of which all citizens have the same right to services according to their age, state of health and so on; and the social security insurance principle, whereby social services (mainly income guarantee schemes) are granted on the basis of national insurance contributions. In the case of the latter, benefits are available to all contributors and their dependants, but payments must be made over a given period of before claims can be made. It is argued that there has been convergence of the two systems over time. In countries where the system is organized according to the citizenship principle there has been a tendency to introduce complementary contribution systems, while in countries whose systems are based on the social security principle certain universal coverage has been introduced (typically for health and family services), but the distance between the two systems remains large and therefore it cannot be said that there is convergence (Schmidt, 1988; Esping-Andersen, 1990; Ministerio de Trabajo y Seguridad Social, 1993).

Because all citizens are entitled to social protection, universal welfare systems tend not to be underpinned by any explicit conception of the family, although this does not mean that they do not discriminate against women (Sainsbury, 1995; O'Connor, 1996). Meanwhile contributory systems typically rest on the traditional family model: individuals marry and have children, the marriage lasts a lifetime and the wife – whose work is restricted to the household, bringing up children and caring for any other family member who needs help – is financially dependent on her husband. As noted above, social protection is assured for all those who pay into the system, as are all financially dependent family members in the household. Individuals who are not insured in this way have no protection. However the trend to universalize protection has broadened the groups of persons paying into the system and raised the age for entitlement. There has also been some development of means tested social assistance.

Basing social protection on the traditional family model is done in different ways according to the regulations in the countries in question. It has also changed over time as financial resources have become scarcer, the principle of sexual non-discrimination has emerged as a basic social value and legislation has been adapted to reflect family change. The way in which the regulations on widow(er) pension entitlements have evolved is illustrative of this. During the first phase of the establishment of the social security system, widows' pensions were paid only to the legally married wives of deceased contributors, provided the former did not remarry or take on paid work. The aim of these payments and orphans' entitlements was to replace the salary of the deceased breadwinner. After the issuing of EU Directive 79/7/EEC on non-discrimination and equal treatment for men and women (and after court rulings in different countries along the same lines), men obtained the right to a widower's pension, although unlike women they were also allowed to engage in paid work.

Although current pension regulations are no longer modelled on the traditional family, the very existence of widows' and widowers' pensions, the fact that they are not paid to a person who was not legally married to the contributor, and the loss of these and other entitlements with subsequent marriage make it evident that social protection is still organized around family links. One example of this is public care for the elderly. For many years elderly people had to rely exclusively on family members or market services for care.

Welfare state adaptations to family change have been limited and have taken different forms in different countries. The most noteworthy measures have been the application of EU Directive 79/7/EEC and, more generally, the development of social protection for mothers and consideration of the difficulty of combining family life with a career. However the family changes discussed above have posed to the conservative welfare state challenges of a much broader nature. These challenges will be discussed in the next section.

## Challenges posed to the welfare state by changes in the family

As space limititations prevent an exhaustive investigation we shall restrict the discussion to what we consider to be the three major challenges: the fall in the birth rate to below replacement level, the massive inclusion of women in the job market, and the increase in separations and divorce.

With regard to the first of these, our aim here is to discuss the demographic challenge to the pension system posed by the falling birth rate and the consequest rise in the proportion of elderly persons in the population, and also to draw attention to one of the facets of the public pension system that is rarely alluded to: the so-called 'demographic contribution' made by families to the social security system (Nell-Breuning, 1980; Meil, 1989). Families typically not only pay contributions in cash but also in kind, insofar as they bring up their children as future workers, who through their national insurance payments will contribute to the system's functioning.

During the early years, social security systems were similar to private insurance schemes in that they were based on the capitalization principle, meaning that payments made into the system were capitalized on the financial market in order to pay pensions once the insured risks had matured. But over time this model has become unviable. Due to wars, inflation, the universalization of social security and other factors, all social security systems have ended up being financed on a pay-as-you-go basis – that is, income from current contributors is used solely to finance current beneficiaries. Therefore the distribution system has also been termed 'a contract between generations' or 'generational solidarity' (Venturi, 1954): a generation of working adults provide their older generation with economic resources through their work on the assumption that when they themselves are elderly, their children's generation will do the same. But basing the contract between generations on only two generations assumes that the economy will expand and that there were be sufficient growth in the population to ensure an equilibrium between the second and third generations. In fact after the Second World War, thanks to exceptional demographic and economic trends (Kaufmann, 1988), it was possible to universalize and increase welfare provisions irrespective of demography. However the ageing of the population, which is a consequence of increased longevity as well as the drop in the birth rate, is threatening to create an imbalance in the foundation upon which public pension systems are based. As the drop in the birth rate begins to have an impact on the size of the working population it will affect the terms in which the generational contract, which considers only one generation of adults and the elderly, was drafted, making the contract increasingly unsustainable. This is not a 'war between generations'; it is an inversion of the population pyramid that threatens to dash the social security system, not only because its 'head' is unduly weighty but also because of its 'feet' of clay.

Although the number of contributors may increase due to women and legal immigrants joining the labour force, thus providing some scope for improving the imbalance between contributions and pensions (under the hypothesis of an expanding job market), this will not be viable in the long term unless the birth rate at least approaches if not surpasses the replacement level. However, because of the family and cultural changes described earlier there is no longer any guarantee that couples will have the number of children necessary to ensure generational replacement. The destigmatization of renouncing motherhood, the indifference of many in society to the social benefits of having and bringing up children (Kaufmann, 1990), the privatization of the costs of having children (Iglesias de Ussel and Meil, 2001) and the aspiration of women to have full-time careers, among other factors, have substantially raised both the direct and the opportunity costs of having children. But those who help maintain the viability of the pay-as-you-go system are couples who choose to have children. Therefore social security is not merely a contract between two generations but between three, which means that payments into the social security system are not all-inclusive and that other contributions are made. In addition to contributions in money there are contributions in kind, that is, there is a 'deomographic contribution' that must be taken into account (Nell-Breuning, 1980; Müller and Burkhardt, 1983; Meil, 1989).

Closely linked to the issues discussed so far is the increasingly widespread tendency of both partners to work outside the home. The fact that more women are joining the workforce provides some solution to the growing imbalance between contributors and beneficiaries. Work outside the household also provides women with their own resources and reduces their financial vulnerability, and therefore their possible dependence on the social security system. The challenges posed by women's paid employment to the social security system stem from the problem of combining family commitments with their careers, and the consequences this has for their current and future income (e.g. pension).

In terms of guaranteeing income, social protection depends on paying into the system and meeting increasingly stringent criteria in respect of the number of years of contributing and the amount paid into the system before becoming eligible for benefits, as recommended by the European Commission (2000). The problem of combining family life with work, which given the traditional gender roles mainly affects women, has repercussions for individuals' contributions. The significance of this varies from case to case and depends not only on the extent of family responsibilities but also, among other factors, on the time of life at which these responsibilities occur, the job market situation, the financial situation of the family, the division of labour between partners and the resources available to combine work and family life. Any reduction of working time, whether through working fewer hours, temporarily leaving the labour force and so on, will translate into an incomplete contribution record and a diminution of individual protection. In this regard, those who take on the fewest family responsibilities incur the lowest costs in labour terms and will enjoy greater social protection in the form of pensions and unemployment benefit. To illustrate this, consider two couples: a childless, full-time working couple with no older family members to care for, and a couple with several children and dependent elderly relatives. Upon retirement the first couple will have accumulated not only personal savings but also sufficient social security contributions to draw two pensions, plus a widow's or widower's pension upon the death of one of the partners. In contrast the second couple's family responsibilities make it impossible for them both to work. Therefore their personal savings will be far less (or even non-existent), and upon retirement they will only be entitled to one pension, and eventually a widow's or widower's pension.

What ramifications do cases such as the latter have on the future of the social security system and society as a whole? First, from a feminist point of view (Sainsbury, 1995; Lewis and Ostner, 1995; O'Connor, 1996), while social rights are formally guaranteed because there are no official barriers to women entering the job market and enjoying the benefits deriving from social security contributions, in practice the fact that women are expected to attend to family responsibilities means that less money is flowing into the system. Although this is compensated for when their children join the labour force, the women themselves suffer financial consequences.

Second, there is likely to be a further increase in the inclination not to procreate, which in the longer term will severely threaten the social security system. Moreover there may be a decrease in the motivation to care for elderly family members, which will impose a heavy burden on the state, especially in light of the ageing population and the resulting increase in the number of elderly persons requiring care. The state already pays for services for the elderly (residential care, day care centres, palliative services and home care) when family care and private insurance are absent, and substantial increases in this over time will eventually put an overwhelming strain on the social security system unless counter measures are introduced soon. This could involve compulsory private insurance for care in old age, or increased social security contributions.

Third, the increase in the number of women in permanent employment will call into question the legitimacy of the widow's pension. Introduced for the first time in Germany in 1911 (Venturi, 1954), it was designed to compensate the loss of income suffered by women following the death of their husband, who was usually the principal or sole breadwinner. It was therefore based on the traditional family model, a model that, while still prevalent among the older generation, is rare among younger generations.

Fourth, as discussed earlier divorce has become more commonplace and socially accepted. Although couples do not embark on marriage believing that it will end in separation, the possibility of divorce has raised the potential costs of taking on family responsibilities and unpaid (and non-socially protected) domestic work. Therefore, paid employment and contribution to the social security system may come to be seen by women as essential to having a guaranteed income, especially as orphans' and widows' pensions are not paid when there has been separation or divorce. Indeed divorce has become a major source of poverty – in nearly all the EU countries (with the significant exception of the Nordic countries) single parent households are overrepresented among the poorest households (Eurostat, 2000). Several commentators have referred to divorce as a 'new social risk', among them the Council of Europe (1989; see also Esping-Andersen, 1999). However, welfare state systems, and particularly liberal and conservative ones, have barely been adapted to take this into account.

## Conclusion

Family life is undergoing deep changes that are affecting the very foundations of society. The inadequacies of the welfare state and the disappearance of the traditional family are having severe social consequences in the form of reduced motivation to take on extended family responsibilities and a reluctance by some women to have children. As a consequence of the latter the birth rate has fallen far below the generational replacement level. This is threatening the viability of the social security system as it will be unable to meet the needs of the ageing population. In addition the rise in the divorce rate has brought with it an increased risk of childhood poverty. At the core of adapting to the new family realities is the combining of family life with paid employment and income redistribution mechanisms; and the welfare state should be adjusted to facilitate this.

### References

Beck, U. (1986) *Risikogesellschaft* (Frankfurt am Main: Suhrkamp).
Beck-Gernsheim, E. (1998) *Was kommt nach der Familie? Einblicke in neue Lebensformen* (Munich: Beck Verlag).
Council of Europe (1989) *La Sécurité Sociale dans une société en mutation* (Strasbourg: Council of Europe).
Drew, E. and R. Emerek (1998) 'Employment, Flexibility and Gender', in E. Drew, R. Emerek and E. Mahon (eds), *Women, Work and the Family in Europe* (London: Routledge).
Esping-Andersen, G. (1990) *The Three Worlds of Welfare Capitalism* (Cambridge: Polity Press).
Esping-Andersen, G. (1999) *The Social Foundations of Postindustrial Economies* (Oxford: Oxford University Press).
European Commission (2000) *The future evolution of social protection from a long-term point of view: safe and sustainable pensions*, COM (2000) 622 final (93) 551 (Brussels: European Commission).

Eurostat (2000) *Income poverty and social exclusion in the European Union* (Luxemburg: Eurostat).
Hantrais, L. (1997) 'Exploring Relationships between Social Policy and Changing Family Forms within the European Union', *European Journal of Population*, 13, pp. 339–79.
Iglesias de Ussel, J. and G. Meil (2001) *La política familiar en España* (Barcelona: Ariel).
Johnson, N. (1987) *El Estado de Brenestar en Transicíon* (Madrid: Ministerio de Trabajo y Seguridad Social).
Kaufmann, F. X. (1988) 'Sozialpolitik und Bevölkerungsprozess', in B. Heck, (ed.), *Sterben wir aus? Die Bevölkerungsentwicklung in der BRD* (Freiburg: Herder)
Kaufmann, F. X. (1990) *Zukunft der Familie* (Munich: Beck Verlag).
Kiernan, K. (2000) 'European Perspective on Union Formation', in L. J. Waite, (eds), *The Ties that Bind, Perspectives on Marriage and Cohabitation* (New York: Aldine de Gruyter), pp. 40–58.
Lauterbach, W. (1999) 'Die Dauer nichtehelichen Lebensgemeinschaften. Alternative oder Vorphase zur Ehe?', in T. Klein and W. Lauterbach (eds), *Nichehelichen Lebensgemeinschaften. Analysen zum Wandel partnerschaftlicher Lebensformen* (Opladen: Leske and Budrich).
Lewis, J. and I. Ostner (1995) 'Gender and the Evolution of European Social Policies', in S. Leibfried and P. Pierson (eds), *European Social Policy: Between Fragmentation and Integration* (Washington, DC: Brookings Institution).
Lüscher, K., F. Schultheis and M. Wehrspaun (eds), *Die postmoderne Familie* (Konstanz: Universidad Konstanz).
Meil, G. (1989) 'Seguridad Social y familia', *Revista de la Seguridad Social*, 42, pp. 43–56.
Meil, G. (1999) *La postmodernización de la familia española* (Madrid: Editorial Acento).
Ministerio de Trabajo Y Seguridad Social (MTSS) (1993) *La mujer y la protección social* (Madrid: Ministerio de Trabajo y Seguridad Social).
Müller, H. and W. Burkhard (1983) 'Die 3-Generationen-Solidarität in der Retenversicherung als Systemnotwendigkeit und ihre Konsequenzen', *Sozialer Forstchritt*, pp. 73–7.
Nell-Breuning, O. (1980) 'Soziale Rentenversicherung in familien und bevölkerungspolitische Sicht', in K. Schenke and W. Schmähl (eds), *Alterssicherung als Aufgabe für Wissenchaft und Politik* (Stuttgart: Kohlhammer).
O'Connor, J. (1996) 'From Women in the Welfare State to Gendering Welfare State Regimes', *Current Sociology*, 44 (2), pp. 1–124.
OECD (1995) 'Long-term leave for parents in OECD countries', in *Employment Outlook* (Paris: OECD), pp. 171–200.
OECD (2001) *Employment Outlook* (Paris: OECD).
OECD (2002) *Employment Outlook* (Paris: OECD).
Roussel, L. (1989) *La famille incertaine* (Paris: Odile Jacob).
Roussel, L. (1992) 'La famille en Europe Occidentale: Convergence et divergences', *Population*, 47 (1), pp. 133–52.
Sainsbury, D. (1995) *Gender Equality and Welfare States* (Cambridge: Cambridge University Press).
Schmidt, M. (1988) *Sozialpolitik, Leske und Budrich* (Oplanden: Leske & Budrich).
Venturi, A. (1954) *Los fundamentos cientificos de la Seguridad Social* (Madrid: Ministerio de Trabajo y Seguridad Social).

# 12
# Individualism and Collectivism in the Sociology of the Collective Worker

*Paul Stewart**

## Introduction

Since the myriad oppressions in our lives are determined by much of what occurs in the realm of material production, even when we are not in it, or even apparently part of it, one of the promises of labour process analysis is to offer an account of the relation between economic power and these various oppressions. Yet one of the difficulties with many of the current labour process analyses is that they have subordinated concerns with the broad interrelationship of social and material power to discussions of individual subordination, power and identity. Individual fear and insecurity, illness and quality of life at work are inextricably tied, just as much today as formerly, to the particular form and pattern assumed by material exploitation. It is principally by accounting for the texture of the current phase of work intensification, control and subordination that these crucial problems at the heart of the labour process can be understood. Thus whereas the 'missing subject' cannot be the subject of analysis, the problems of the subject him- or herself can be sought in the pursuit of the missing collective worker, the proper subject of labour process analysis.

It is difficult to imagine a less propitious period for social movements with an organic relationship to labour. Despite the commitment of considerable organizational and financial resources to addressing the problem of trade union decline in the UK (see the TUC's Organising Academy and agenda for union renewal), union membership is in decline, although there has been limited and marginal growth in some 'in-fill' and new sectors (for a discussion see, *inter alia*, Heery, 1998a and b; Danford *et al.*, 2002; Fairbrother and Stewart, 2002). While this limited membership growth is welcome, grounds for optimism are tempered by the fact that it has to be set against a background of structural weakness, reflected on one dimension by falling union density.

When unions have recognized the compelling needs of workers in new industries, changing labour market characteristics – including the social composition of the labour force – have severely tested their scope for representation (Heery, 1998; Conley *et al.*, 2001). That we need to register a problematical traditional collectivism is axiomatic in any discussion of the nature of collectivism today, and notably in the context of workplace associations, identities and conflicts. Of course the current debate on union form, structure and strategy also offers possibilities for more sanguine assumptions, notably when union renewal is premised on local and workplace realignment around worker-centred agendas (see, *inter alia*, Fairbrother and Yates, 2001; Danford *et al.*, 2002). Moreover, and inevitably, broader sociological concerns about the changing nature of the social structure and class relations have significantly impacted on the way in which not only material conditions but also identities of, among others class, gender and ethnicity (including confessional and secular affiliations) can be debated. As we shall see later when discussing the configurations of a new politics of production (Stewart and Martínez Lucio, 1998), the existence of significant possibilities for a collectivist agenda challenge the post-structuralist assumption that there is little scope for a new collectivist workplace politics. The word 'little' is important here as most post-structuralists would never go so far as to rule out the possibility of collectivist representation. Rather its occurrence is seen as accidental, since what distinguishes a number of post-structuralist readings of collectivism from modernist metanarratives is that collectivist practices are seen as non-essential and indeterminate.

Of course not all post-structuralists would view collectivist accidents of fate as bestowing the good fortune assumed by errant collectivists. This is because collectivism is seen to cause as many existential problems for actors as management agendas (Knights and Willmott, 1989). The significance of this for a discussion of the prospects for trade unionism is that – irrespective of whether they survive and renew, or atrophy and decline – the problem is that their fate and that of the collective worker has been conflated (Martínez Lucio and Stewart, 1997).

One difficulty with a number of objections to the idea of the centrality of the collective worker is that they derive from a mechanistic view of the collective worker. In contrast to Marx, these objections see the concept of the collective worker as revealing in some sense the expression of workers acting collectively, or indeed as emanations of the sum total of worker subjectivity.[1] This functionalist and reductionist view, misses the point that it is by linking new patterns of exploitation to workplace struggles that the character, form and trajectory of the collective worker can be understood. John Holloway (1995) elegantly encapsulates the tension of this dialectic in his essay 'Capital Moves', in which he argues that the scope of capitalist strategies is always limited by the nature of the social and political spaces in which it confronts labour struggles. Yet the horizons of the latter are themselves determined by the limitations imposed by the coherence of capital's hegemony in the context of any particular conjuncture (see also, in a similar register, Harvey, 2000). Capital may always want to 'move', but this is because it needs to do so as a result of the struggles against its ability to valorize. The current attempt by capital in the era of neo liberalism to tie down labour can be summed up by the sobriquet 'lean production'.

The *longue duree* of neo liberalism has framed the economic and institutional context in which lean production has thrived, albeit in distinctive ways depending on the political economy of time and space. Moreover it should be noted that lean production is less an end than a strategy. It is the culmination of an ensemble of management strategies that are often, though not alone, concerned with stripping labour out of the labour process, and this explains why so much of what is described as lean production can be interpreted as an assault on labour standards. One might therefore begin to understand how management strategies (amongst others, human resource management, team working, total quality management) are seen as engaged in social and economic struggles. Simply, while the nature of the functional division of labour can tell us something about the space and temporal features of the collective worker, it can also allow us to map the form taken by workplace collectivism. Moreover it is the material conditions of the collective worker that gives the clue as to how a strategic collectivism might develop. The recent discovery of 'the subject' has developed out of a one-sided and misplaced view of the nature of the current period of economic and workplace restructuring. This is ironic given the collective nature of assaults on the individual by contemporary management agendas.

In arguing the case for the conceptual centrality of the collective worker, we are going beyond the aspiration to identify and make sense of individual insecurities, dissent and struggles insofar as these are located in the nature and pattern of contemporary labour processes. More than this, rather than individual securities and insecurities having either inchoate or discursively non-structural origins, individuals' meanings are to be derived from the way in which contemporary labour processes constitute, divide and give material affirmation to individual workers. Attempting to understand the structured nature of employee conflicts and hence the nature of the labour process cannot begin and end with the individual employee.

So why is it that the problem of the collective worker remains unresolved in the labour process debate? Two common assumptions are used to underscore the problemmatical use of the concept of the collective worker: that the possibilities for traditional action are limited; and that even if one could collectivize individual antagonisms, in the longer term nothing would be resolved for individuals. There is currently a dominant individualistic interpretation of how management subordinates and controls (or as Ackroyd and Thompson, 1999, might say, in the attempt to do so they fail abysmally). This interpretation can be said to revolve around four dimensions of management–worker relations: *individualizing labour processes* (fragmentation of work), which broker *individualizing ideologies*; *anticollectivism* via performance-related pay, temporal flexibility (such as working time accounts) and other interpersonnel competitive 'carrots'; and *company-centred collectivism* (neocorporatism dependant on identification of the individual with the company). However the case being made here is against the notion that these issues of changing structure are explicable in terms of the pursuit of the subject, the revelation of identity or the interpretation of discursive practices. In some accounts, revelations of individuality are taken as ciphers of opposition (Knights and McCabe, 2000) and in others resistance is the marker of struggle and opposition (Ackroyd and Thompson, 1999), but together they depend on a turn away from the fate of the collective worker, the central drama in the labour process.

If Marxist orthodoxy frequently denied agency, the new consensus has, perhaps ironically, dealt a similar blow to collectivism – it is ultimately intelligible only in terms of individual employee expression. It might be that even if the collective worker does have import for the post-structuralists, this is no more or no less significant than the actions of individual workers. Or at best the collective worker *qua* collectivist trade union practice is but one form of collectivism, merely one pattern of group or collective activity amongst others.

This chapter is concerned with three approaches to labour process analysis that can be distinguished by the way they treat the question of the relationship between individualism and collectivism. In one significant account – Ackroyd and Thompson (1999) – the centrality of the collective worker is downplayed in terms of its analytical and empirical strength. In another account – O'Doherty and Willmott (2001) – individualism is given more prominence since it is considered to be axiomatic in any account of the development of contemporary labour processes. Whilst the first takes collectivism to be problematic, reintroducing it in however limited a form, the second sees collectivism, however unlikely its appearance, as inherently problematical from the standpoint of the individual. Both accounts see the notion of worker collectivism as a limited form of representation, dependent as it is on an outdated view of the conceptual efficacy of the collective worker. The third perspective however – the critical social relations (CSR) approach (Stewart, 1998; Danford *et al.*, 2002, 2004) – holds out greater prospect for understanding the relationship between workplace subordination and social struggle. In this account the collective worker is primarily understood in the context of social struggles over recent processes of employment and community restructuring. The CSR approach sees recent management strategies as sites of indeterminate conflict that are no more evidence of individualism than they are signs of the end of oppositional collectivism. We shall consider each of these three approaches in turn, beginning first with O'Doherty and Willmott.

## The decline of collectivism and the rise of the subject

Since individualists obviously feel that labour process analysis should be about people as individuals, they argue that labour-process Marxists in the UK can never understand this because of their obsession with reducing people to emanations of the economic structure. This obsession supposedly ignores the very problem (individual subordination) that the labour process is supposed to help resolve. Yet the irony is that by focusing on the individual the very basis of individual subordination is missed since the causes of this are analytically closed down. This is nowhere more obvious than in the arguments made by O'Doherty and Willmott (2001) and – with rather different intent – Knights and McCabe (2000). But at least for the latter the shibboleth of collectivism acts to ward off the charge that one is not taking the structural basis of exploitation seriously.

Before we approach the question of struggle and social justice we need to address O'Doherty and Willmott's account of the way in which the individualism–collectivism debate has been refracted through the prism of sociology's agency–structure conundrum, emerging in labour process debates as the subjectivism–objectivism divide. O'Doherty and Willmott (2001, p. 457) interpret this dilemma as inhibiting any proper account of 'agency, subjectivity and resistance' that they hope to resolve in their quest for what they see as the problem of the 'missing subject' (ibid.). Post-structuralism offers some relief for those concerned to re-emphasize what should be the central problem for labour process analysis since it can lead us away from various inflections of the dualism(s) noted above (ibid., p. 461). Not only will recognition of the verities of post-structuralism allow a shift away from the sterility of both the irresolvable sociological and Marxist dilemma encapsulated in the binarism structure–agency, but also (in a telling phrase), 'by opening up the question of subjectivity, the conceptual inheritance of "system", "structure" and "objectivity", can be de-reified in a way that enables us to better understand the enigmatic "space" where capitalism both finds its source *and* gets reproduced and maintained' (ibid.)

So the claim is that post-structuralism offers the chance to escape the old couplet of agency–structure in order better to comprehend the 'enigmatic "space" where capitalism . . . both finds its source . . . *and* gets reproduced' (ibid.) This allows them (and us) to think, unlike Ezzy (2001 pp. 471–2), in a 'processual', 'complex' and 'paradoxical' way (O'Doherty and Willmott, 2001). This can be characterized as advancing a 'radical critique with a capacity to appreciate and address inequitable and exploitative relations that are always-already immanent in our practices – immanent in that they have provided for by the sense of who we are and what we value' (ibid., p. 470).

The presumption is that post-structuralism at one and the same time breaks the enigma of the complexity of exploitation and the fate of the exploitee(s), and allows us a way out of the 'traditional sociological dualistic division whose originary dislocation is the product of a more profound theoretical intolerance towards thinking the processual' (ibid.) It is not entirely clear in what respects this claim to bypass the Scylla and Charybdis of individualism–collectivism by invoking the ideal of the subject will enable greater insight into the contemporary conditions of the collective worker. On the contrary, a passing reference to collective workers, far from presaging a safe passage, merely confirms their shipwrecked journey from an optimistic landscape of social struggle to the wasteland of the helpless individual. While O'Doherty and Willmott claim not to have abandoned the metanarrative of collectivism (ibid., p. 462), since at no point are we offered any understanding of how this fits into the pattern of domination, the only realistic conclusion is that they do indeed jettison any attempt to understand the relationship between the collective worker and the missing subject. Moreover, contrary to the view that an emphasis on the collective worker conflates a discourse of collectivism with an account that supposedly recognizes 'how, within the contradictions of the labour process, "privatised efforts" may emerge that are self-defeating in so far as they impede, undermine or displace collective self-transformation as a strategy of emancipatory change' (ibid., p. 462), the CSR perspective does not see subjectivity as either secondary or inconsequential. As Martínez Lucio and Stewart (1997) argue, the crucial point is that new management strategies are recombining around distinct notions of the individual as an employee of 'our company' *sui generis*. One consequence of individualizing strategies is not that collectivism does not matter, but rather that the sense of these strategies cannot be externally understood; that is, understood outside the relationship between capital and labour in the labour process, and notably in the spaces and temporalities embracing and defining the social reproduction of labour and capital in the community and elsewhere.

It is interesting that the empirical demise of collectivism, especially in terms of labour's institutional fragmentation, is identified by 'individually negotiated contracts, flexitime, and performance-related pay' (ibid., p. 462), and that these are motifs of an individualizing dynamic (see below). But the telling thematic is betrayed by the knowing gesture. O'Doherty and Willmott tell us that capitalism's fragmenting and individualizing tendencies 'can accentuate existential insecurity to the point where privatised efforts to gain a secure identity take precedence over collective efforts to transform the historical conditions that promote such self-defeating tendencies' (ibid.) Certainly they can, if they try, but how can one know? There is a gesture here to a radical agenda rooted in a critique of capitalist social relations, but this is betrayed by an unwillingness to follow the promised logic through, for how else are we to understand the asymmetric attachment to 'the individualising tendencies of capitalist relations of production' (ibid.)? If there is a relationship between what they take to be these individualizing tendencies and the collective worker, if the latter is not intended rhetorically how might it explain the double-sidedness of these individualizing tendencies? In contrast to this individualizing reductionism, the objective of contemporary labour process analysis must be to try to elucidate three aspects of the relationship between capitalism's intimately entwined individualizing and collectivizing tendencies. This is best understood as an interwoven as opposed to a binary relationship.

Firstly, it is true that the ecology of the collective worker, including social relations, patterns and forms of life, confront powerful strategies aimed at fragmenting the ensemble of working-class power not only in work but also outside it (Glucksmann, 2000; Stephenson and Stewart, 2001). For the sake of brevity, individualizing strategies – we can list them all, including those pointed to by O'Doherty and Willmott (2001) – can be summed up in terms of human resource management and other abominations (let us not leave out our old intimate that is a consequence of these – lean production). But we also know from case studies that even where union organization is absent or weak these strategies are often broken, stymied or otherwise confounded by a range of worker practices that can be accounted for in terms of a collectivist ideology (see Ackroyd and Thompson, 1999; Stephenson and Stewart, 2001). Moreover where so-called individualizing practices are present, union activity not only engages with them but is also more robust (for one interpretation of this see *Gallie et al.*, 1998). Certainly, collectivist ideologies may not always be present in terms of traditional collectivist ideology, but this is to make the point that collectivist ideologies and strategies cannot be represented apart from the contrary tensions that pull labour away from economic and sometimes social antipathy with capital. And these tensions are derived from the nature of a labour process that seeks both to fragment and to unify labour. The fragmentation can be seen in the changing pattern of the division of labour, in a range of sectors, including postal services, nursing and public health, and the automotive industry. The unifying dynamic can be witnessed in the coordination and drive dynamic of the organization, and especially in the relationship between planning strategies (for example human resource management) and punishment agendas (see Danford, 2002, for a discussion of the relationship between new management strategies and recollectivization agendas).

Secondly, and relatedly, what is it about these attempts at recombining worker confessional identities around so-called individualizing human resource practices that makes them incompatible with collectivist strategies aimed at their removal, whether traditional or what could be called 'new collectivism'? After all, collectivist strategies, as much today as formerly, always and necessarily engage with capital on its own hegemonic terrain. Moreover it should be remembered that workers, just as much as sociologists, can orientate themselves towards radical collectivist and individualistic or non-work identities and practices at one and the same time.

Thirdly, it is only by linking the current conditions of people at work – 'exploited' (Stephenson, 1996), 'stressed out' (Nichols, 1997; Green, 2001), 'overworked' and 'injured' (Lewchuk *et al.*, 2001; Lewchuk and Robinson 1996) – that we can really begin to grapple with the nature of individual experiences of the fragmentation of work and employment. Why is individual isolation so often referred to in terms that can also be interpreted as rewards: flexitime and individual contracts? Is it really true that these create insecurity in a personalized and individualized way? After all, they are 'inducements'. Are they really so different in kind from the factors of fragmentation and unification that characterize such practices as piecework and measured day work? The threats that are inextricably tied to these inducements, it can be argued, unify labour at the same time as they fragment it. It is also significant that most union struggles today are provoked by management strategies that focus on temporalizing and fragmenting labour. If, as Doogan (2001) argues, employment insecurity (interpreted in terms of tenure) did not in fact vary during the 1990s, where might the source of workers' insecurity and disaffection actually reside?

One possibility is that it is precisely the necessary conditions for introducing management strategies aimed at employee fragmentation that are the cause of this insecurity. More specifically, these are targeted at control of effort and are associated most prominently with hybrid forms of lean production. While the ideology, rhetoric and practices associated with lean production are most developed in the automotive industry (Rienhart *et al.*, 1997; Lewchuk and Robertson, 1996; Lewchuk *et al.*, 2001; Yates *et al.*, 2001) their reach has now extended into a range of private and public sectors (Danford *et al.*, 2002; see Nichols, 2001, on a related observation). It is by engaging with these and other management agendas for restructuring that the new politics of production might be developed.

Yet against a background of personal and interpersonal subordination rooted in the configurations of this new politics of production, it would be odd to attempt to determine the form and character of subjectivity by beginning with a search for the 'missing subject' *qua* individual identity. That this might provide the proper focus of labour process theory seems to miss the obvious point that bridging the agency – structure binarism cannot be done by such a project. Of course tracking down the missing subject is not the same as denying the wider structural pattern of exploitation and subordination that would follow privileging it above structure. O'Doherty and Willmott (2001) counterpose their emphasis on the subject to the reified subject identified in the 'anti-realist' critique of labour process orthodoxy. It is not their attempt to delineate patterns of social and political struggle in terms of subjective action that is at fault – who, after all, makes social struggles, let alone the revolution? Understanding what O'Doherty and Willmott define as exploitative relations is not hampered by seeking out the missing subject, but it is undermined by assuming this to be *the* critical absence in contemporary labour process debate. What is problematical is not subjectivity *per se*, but how we assess the nature of subjectivity (Martínez Lucio and Stewart, 1997). O'Doherty and Willmott

(2001) get near the problem when they note that the connection between action and structure are not reducible.

Rather than seeing the problem as one of accounting for capitalist social relations from the standpoint of the subject, we need to approach from a different direction. We can best conceptualize the nature and dynamism of capitalist social relations according to those who, in O'Doherty and Willmott's terms, have a 'sense of who we are and what we value' (ibid., p. 470), by defining domination in work in this society as a central part of the constitutive relations of capitalism. This is a clearer way of avoiding reification of the 'conceptual inheritance of "system", "structure" and "objectivity"' (ibid., p. 461). To view the site for the production and reproduction of capitalist social relations as an 'enigmatic space' (ibid.) misses the point that restoring the subject from its former role as the absent presence leads to a collapsing of history and process to that of the subject.

## What do they know of labour processes who only labour processes know?

Put somewhat differently, what can any individual tell us about capitalist exploitation from their private suffering of the production process? They can tell us much that may be similar to our own experiences, but what stands out in the different personal accounts of exploitation is that they are only resolved in the context of collective agendas, usually by resistance. Then again, when do individual grievances and existential crises not have a collective character? Who we are and what we value cannot, *pace* O'Doherty and Willmott (2001) and Knights and McCabe (2000), be accounted for – in the context of a labour process analysis rooted in a critique of capitalist exploitation – in terms of subjectivity. I myself can tell little of the capitalist labour process, but I can, as a consequence of my individual experiences, tell a more or less interesting story about the nature, form and consequences of exploitation on me. The point has been made so many times in regard to labour-centred accounts of exploitation that it hardly seems necessary to repeat it here, but perhaps it is because we need to re-emphasise that an analysis of the social relations of domination cannot begin with the subject. While the subject of (class?) struggle may be the subject of analysis, the individual subject as the object of analysis cannot deliver this. This is because those who suffer in silence are only so many silences, and it is as a consequence of the compulsion and domination that produce the myriad silences that the many subjectivities make sense of their circumstances. But only, that is, when we begin from the understanding that what this describes is capitalist social relations that exemplify both the separation and unity of individuals both in and beyond work.

So far from tying the pursuit of the missing subject to a materialist account, O'Doherty and Willmott (2001) fail on two counts. First, instead of resolving their central objective (the sociological paradox of dualism), by pursuing the missing subject their account merely reinforces the divide they wish to abolish. Second, and in consequence, in attempting to sublimate one form of dualism (agency – structure) and one form of reductionism (economic) these appear again as a form of methodological individualism. To claim that the idea of the collective worker has some analytical virtue in relation to the search for the missing subject, commensurability must be demonstrated more convincingly. The second account we shall examine – Ackroyd and Thompson (1999) – has the distinction of linking the missing subject to collectivism in one form or another.

## The problem with conflict at work: individualism and collectivism in the labour process

> [T]he distinctive subculture of employees is becoming a more pointedly critical and overtly satirical counter-culture. (Ackroyd and Thompson, 1999, p. 103)

Is this really the case, and is it all that remains for workers to throw at capital in their struggles with management today? It seems unlikely that workers really are more obsessed with 'identity' today than in former times.

Miguel Martínez Lucio and I argued that when Thompson and Ackroyd (1995) portrayed conflict as a cipher for individual autonomy, conflict functioned both as a means by which the employee could be redeemed as a subject of analysis and as an indication of the persistence of resistance to management (Martínez Lucio and Stewart, 1997). Commendable though Thompson and Ackroyd's turn away from discourse as the focus of analysis was, it did not go far enough, since like those they criticized (whom they termed neo-Foucauldians) they fell prey to an undue emphasis on the subject, grounded in a notion of the employee. But this abstract subject of the employment relationship, the employee, was not the same as the concrete subject, labour. Our argument derived from an attempt to distinguish between an approach that began from the sociality of individuals acting within an exploitative domain of capitalist social relations, and an approach that rooted the sociality of the individual within the organisation *sui generis*. (Ackroyd and Thompson subsequently developed their thesis, adding caveats that sought to place the organization within the wider context of the capitalist political economy, but this was not the same as beginning with *this* capitalist economy.) Moreover we were concerned to counter the methodological individualism in which individual identity (and its attendant crises), group-based though it may be, is seen as the key to understanding the ontological nature of individual motivation and action. For us it was important to emphasize how individual identity cannot be understood as autonomous of the particular conditions of the labour process, both internally and more broadly within the wider political economy, or at least that part of it described by Glucksmann (2000) as the total social organization of labour.

Thompson and Ackroyd's 1995 publication was a response to what they saw as the inadequacy of neo-Foucauldian attempts to account for the perceived demise of workplace collectivism. According to Thompson and Ackroyd, the neo-Foucauldians misunderstood the character of subjectivity in the workplace, not only in declaring its analytical primacy but also in assuming that the ubiquity of managerial domination pre-empted the death of traditional collectivism. For Thompson and Ackroyd, this conclusion derived from both a poorly developed conceptual apparatus and a misreading of historical and contemporary evidence. To be sure, they argued, traditional patterns and forms of collectivism were considerably diminished, but that did not imply either that they would always be so or that other forms of collectivism were absent. This was a crucial idea, despite evidence that might well lead us to the contrary view. While the thematic proposition – resistance is there if you care to look for it – was clear enough, the stages of the argument, including the possibility that workplace identity might continually create patterns of collectivism, were undertheorized. In *Organisational Misbehaviour* (Ackroyd and Thompson, 1999) the concept of misbehaviour is developed to perform a number of useful analytical functions when addressing the problem of the relationship between individualism, collectivism and the workplace. Whilst a superficial reading might allow for the trivialization of the notion of misbehaviour, contrary to Knights and McCabe (2000, p. 434) no moral attribution is intended. It is best understood as framing the debate on workplace conflict in terms that encompass (and define) the nature of behaviour and the failure of the broader sociological debate to make sense of conflict.

'Misbehaviour' is a triple entendre, as in the sense of behaviour having been 'missed' by orthodox approaches to the study of organizational behaviour and the sociology of work. Since these disciplines are obsessed with the normative problem of order they fail to see other significant dimensions of employee behaviour. Secondly, misbehaviour can be viewed as referring to the proposition that even when orthodoxy does see employee activities as diverging from company expectations it simply misunderstands the true nature of this behaviour, laying down guidelines for organizational rectitude so as to expel misbehaviour. Finally, and relatedly, the notion of misbehaviour can be seen as an example of missed opportunity by traditionalists (orthodoxy). When the latter witness divergent behaviour they interpret this not only in ethical terms but also, and more conceptually damaging as a consequence, as deriving from employee ineptitude.

Ackroyd and Thompson (1999, pp. 27–9) intriguingly develop a theme of the multiplicity of forms of conflict (leading to various forms of collectivism) rooted in patterns they term 'self-organised' group behaviour.

Collectivism is nevertheless approached methodologically in terms of identifying conflictual patterns of behaviour that could be defined as trade-union-centred but which Ackroyd and Thompson call 'responsible autonomy' deriving from the activity of formal and externally directed self-organized groups (ibid., pp. 56–61). 'Irresponsible autonomy' (ibid., pp. 67–70), by contrast, is identifiable in, *inter alia*, banter and ritualistic behaviour, and while a good degree of 'irresponsible autonomy is inwardly directed and ceremonial in nature', some is marked by being both 'recalcitrant and aimed at management and its systems.' (ibid., p. 67). But crucially, especially as this form of autonomy has become more prevalent with the demise of traditional collectivism (and hence formal self-organized autonomy, notably in the form of trade unions), it allows for the continued pursuit of autonomy in forms that were previously essential to 'sustain[ing] a similar outlook amongst employees' and are now vital 'to a satirical and distanced evaluation of the activities of management and the policies of companies' (ibid., p. 63). The result is the maintenance of autonomy – albeit autonomy recast in specific antimanagement forms – and its representation in informally self-organized groups that continue in their various ways to be exemplified by particular forms of conflict. From a traditional standpoint this is pessimistic since it signals a retreat from what are viewed as the impossible limitations of class analysis. An optimistic scenario is offered instead:

> [T]he inability to resist general encroachment of [their] institutional powers should not be confused with the removal of the informal organisation of groups in workplaces. It would be an error to assume that taking away the institutional aspects of worker power is the same thing as weakening or effectively removing workers' capacity for self organisation. Because the conditions for the production of responsible autonomy have now gone, it does not mean that the pursuit of autonomy will disappear. (Ibid., p. 61)

While it is true that a 'general encroachment' by management should not be confused with the eradication of workers' identity and autonomy, it is not obvious that the conditions for institutional autonomy have therefore gone. It is plainly absurd that management wants to control workers' consciousness. As Scott (2001) succinctly puts it, management is more interested in workers' product than their souls. Yet even if it is not after workers' souls, management nevertheless continues to spend considerable sums on eliciting their other assets and usually some of this is spent on ideological assaults on alternative worker-centred ideologies. Nor is it immediately obvious that the scope for self-organization (in the form of 'irresponsible autonomy') is very different from the scope for autonomy (not to mention its concrete expression) in traditional terms – because we know that a joke, is a joke, . . . isn't a joke. Or to put it another way, while irresponsible autonomy may well be different in terms of the focus of struggle at one level, it is difficult to see how broader (class-traditional) struggles might be separated from these. Certainly Ackroyd and Thompson cover themselves by emphasizing inherent links where the latter grow out of the former, but they remain theoretically sure that they are distinct analytically and historically. Realistically, humour, 'passions of romance' and various other rituals are all that workers have left in the struggle, not for class power but for group power that provides the possibility of securing individual identity:

> There is some evidence for a change in the new pattern of workplace resistance of the kind [they now investigate]. The increased saliency of joking behaviour, and the innovation of new forms of such behaviour, are evidence of a shift in emphasis away from the traditional contestation between employees and managers. (Ibid., p. 100)

This seems to be mistaken – how could one possibly argue that humour is now more important than previously in any workplace? We can misconstrue many things about the past, but it is hard to see how workers in any workplace have become more jocular just because unions are weak or non-existent. Then again, if the 'workplace is an arena in which the struggle over the appropriation of identity is becoming more prevalent' than struggles that until 'recently [were] centrally concerned with material issues' (ibid.), it is fairly easy to separate identity, material relations and workplace struggle. Yet while Ackroyd and Thompson trounce the Foucauldians, management seems to have had some success in marginalizing a new worker-centred counteragenda that focuses on the new politics of production (ibid., p. 101). The exclusion of traditionalism is a commonplace assumption deriving from an ideational – material symbiosis exemplified *par excellence* by total quality management. From this standpoint, since employees must be taken seriously, or at least rhetorically, and since conflict of a broader type is excluded because of employees' need for affirmation, an asymmetrical focus on identity by the two social actors links employers' desire for quality production (part of the new competitive edge) to employees' desire for identity affirmation. For Ackroyd and Thompson, this symbiosis emphasizes the extent to which traditional conflict is excluded from the picture.

To what extent can it be argued that this view, in common with the previous account of subjectivity and its relationship to work, eschews or at best downplays the importance of the socioeconomic and cultural determinants of work and non-work patterns of identification? These include patterns of affiliation such as occupational association and friendship networks that do not necessarily lead to conflict (misbehaviour) of any kind, although they can be understood as fundamental to an individual's class identity. Although they do provide the basis for conflict, it can be argued that the absence of conflict is not due to the success of strategies of domination, as suggested by some neo-Foucauldians. Neither does the absence of conflict have particular significance *per se* for the dynamics of class or social group views. People may not primarily seek autonomy at work but rather an absence of conflict, since it is just as reasonable to argue that people may achieve autonomy outside work.

Yet organized collectivism, inspired or not by misbehaviour or trade union practices, is not obviously a response to an inherent or ontological desire for autonomy by employees. Sometimes conflict and resistance (which are not the same thing, as we know) are simply not there, no matter hard one looks.[2] However their absence is not indicative of the absence of other world-views, notably those espousing collectivism (Stephenson and Stewart, 2001). Does this mean that Ackroyd and Thompson (1999) are right to argue that the crucial point is how different groups come together in work, or are created in work in ways that are inherently oppositional yet not fundamentally concerned with the collective worker? Perhaps this has nothing as such to say about conflict, so what needs to be emphasized is that all forms of group activity are equally valid and significant in their own terms. We can challenge this assumption by considering collectivism from another vantage point.

## Discussion and conclusion

The wider political economy is of course regime-bound so that we can understand it from the standpoint of patterns of domination and struggle. Thus neoliberalism today, which in some ways is distinct from and in others continuous with Thatcherism, can be said to offer an extension to the tableau in which the notion of citizenship and its corollary, social exclusion, are in unique ways played out in work and the labour process. Not only are they played out in work and the labour process, but they also serve to characterize the form, content and to some extent the pattern of different capitalist regimes. How can we characterize the dominant work and employment regime that prevails at the moment, and what constitutes the nature of citizenship and the place of the collective worker within it? We know that a significant factor, notably in highly routinized work activities (though there are variations according to sector and function), is lean production. Lean production, however, should not be simply viewed as a strategy for control but principally as the culmination of an ensemble of social relations of contestation concerned with stripping out labour (rationalization more broadly) through an assault on postwar labour standards across all sectors. Lean production combines many elements of human resource management, but in the current period, and in the context of labour process debates, the question of labour standards is fundamental since they and labour controls are always and everywhere contested. It is in terms of the struggles and contests, formal and informal, that the problem of the sociology and ecology of the collective worker comes into play.

Originating in the automotive industry, lean production can be said, paradoxically, to have reached its apotheosis under the aegis of the neoliberal productionist agenda – paradoxical because it depends on highly centralized authority structures while typically neoliberal responsibility relations govern the actions of individual workers (that is, considerable responsibility but no real authority). Blairism and its attendant discourses of social partnership are increasingly framing the agenda in which workplace insecurities, subordination and struggles are framed. These struggles necessarily mediate the intimacies of the production process in which labour is bound by what we term new-wave lean production. This regime combines Taylorist routinization with intensified human resource management, resulting in a decline in the quality of working life. While this description can tell us something of the form and circumstances of the collective worker the outlook may be bleak. Whether it will or will not be is necessarily sector-, market- and workplace-specific. The latter is crucial since in many ways it will determine the potential for advancing social and workplace struggle. While we can better depict the pattern of opposition to the conjuncture of lean production against a wider discussion of the nature of union organization, we are now beginning to develop some knowledge of what this new politics of production will be. If it is to link into the drivers of new-wave lean production it will address at least three central contradictions: work intensification versus quality of life at work; company-sponsored collectivism (corporatism) versus employee disaffection; and employee/individual responsibility versus collectivism in everyday life (Stephenson and Stewart, 2001)

In order to understand these dualisms we need to explore the following. First, we now know something about the limited scope of key management practices notably human resource management, business process re-engineering and lean production, but what role has labour played in delimiting these? An analysis of this needs to be anchored on an understanding of various neoliberal regimes, including the problematizing of nation, culture, conjuncture (Smith and Thompson, 1998) and firm strategy (Durand et al., 1998; Boyer and Fressenet, 2002; Lewchuk et al., 2001). That is, in what ways has labour been recollectivized and what shape has this taken? (For a discussion of collectivism – individualism see Therborn, 2001, pp. 87–9.) To the extent that we can identify the relationship between new production regimes and a more robust workplace union agenda, what is happening in key sectors in relation to the collective worker?

Second, the current phase of neoliberalism has had a distinct impact on the reproduction and production of the collective worker, both in and out of employment, and in terms of its effects on the nature and shape of communities. An understanding of the interrelationship of the two is essential to making sense of the new patterns of exploitation and subordination, as well as telling us something about the character of new sites and strategies of struggle. As Holloway (1995) already alluded to, capital can run and run, but it cannot easily hide from labour. Yet in its running it also regroups and takes aim. This is sometimes mediated by state/legal strategies and institutional and organizational assaults, but ideological stands are also significantly involved – even if they are not successful in a straightforward way. Whilst we should query the possibility that management can actually get to our souls, some new institutional agendas are contrived specifically for this purpose. Undoubtedly, human resource practices and lean production create workplace stress and diminise the quality of working life, and struggles over these are bringing together old and new ideological confrontations in what are invariably termed 'hearts and minds' campaigns.

Finally, if capital cannot easily hide, how might it be confronted? If labour process theory is to be something other than, as Nichols (2001) witheringly but appropriately puts it, an intellectually interesting way of talking about work, it must uncover the forms and patterns of the social production of surplus value and address the types of exploitation to which this production gives rise. It should also concern itself with struggles against and challenges to this exploitation, and with the sociological and political relationship between work and non-work beliefs and practices.

To make use of this knowledge we shall have to address the question of social justice on the basis of a collective agenda. In other words we must examine individuals' personal experience of alienation in a call centre, an insurance bureau or a hospital, and connect their emotional and physical pain to the sociology and politics of the collective worker. To move beyond ethics (we know why capital has power) and beyond the issue of where power resides, we need to examine the question of justice because this will enable us to investigate how power, both in and outside work, is maintained and how it can be and is being challenged, most notably by struggles to promote economic and institutional democracy, ranging from involvement in product planning to bargaining over employment conditions for workers in outsource firms.

All of this is to say that the labour process problem of subject – object/subjectivity – class structure is neither equivalent to sociology's eternal dualist conundrum, agency – structure, nor soluble by shifting to the problematic of the subject. To understand the labour process the associated problems of individual action, structure and strategy need to be unravelled in the context of the inherent contradictions and infrequently realized struggles of the collective worker. For labour process debates, this must be the major show in town. While a number of accounts identify the Holy Grail of labour process analysis as the missing subject, this simply replaces what they perceive to be a misplaced focus on the collective worker with what could be described as a misconstrued notion of the subject.

## Notes

\* An earlier version of this chapter was published in 2002 as 'The Problem of the Collective Worker in the Sociology of Work in the UK', *Sociologia del Lavoro*, 34(2), March.
1. 'With the progressive accentuation of the co-operative character of the labour process, there necessarily occurs a progressive extension of the concept of the bearer of that labour, the productive worker. In order to work productively, it is no longer necessary for the individual himself to put his hand on the object, it is sufficient for him to to be an organ of the collective labourer, and to perform any one of its subordinate functions' (Marx, *Capital*, vol. 1).
2. Ackroyd and Thompson (1999, p. 162) are somewhat ambivalent here, sometimes accepting of this truism but mostly sure that resistance is there if one looks hard enough.

## References

Ackroyd, S. and P. Thompson (1999) *Organisational Misbehaviour* (London: Sage).
Boyer, R. and M. Fressenent (2002) *The Productive Models: The Conditions of Profitability* (Basingstoke: Palgrave Macmillan).
Conley, H., E. Heery, R. Delbridge and P. Stewart (2001) 'The AUT and Part-Times', mimeo, Cardiff Business School.
Danford, A., M. Richardson and M. Upchurch (2002) *Trade Unionism and the New Work Place* (London: Routledge).
Danford, A., M., Richardson, P., Stewart, S. Tailby and M. Upchurch (2004) 'High performance work systems and workplace partnership: a case study of aerospace workers', *New Technology, Work and Employment*, 19:1, March.
Doogan, K. (2001) 'Insecurity and Long term Employment', *Work, Employment and Society*, 15(3), pp. 419–41.
Durand, J.-P, P. Stewart and J. J. Castillo (1998) *Teamwork in the Automobile Industry* (Basingstoke: Palgrave).
Ezzy, D. (2001) 'A Simulacrum of Workplace Community: Individualism and Engineered Culture', *Sociology*, 35(3), pp. 631–50.
Fairbrother, P. and P. Stewart (2002) 'The Dilemmas of Social Partnership and Union Organization: Questions for British Trade Unions', in P. Fairbrother and C. Yates (eds), *Unions Facing the Future* (London: Continuum).
Fairbrother, P. and C. Yates (eds) *Unions Facing the Future* (London: Continuum).
Gallie, D., M. White, Y. Cheng, and M. Tomlinson (1998) *Restructuring the Employment Relationship* (Oxford: Oxford University Press).
Glucksmann, M. (2000) *Cotton and Casuals: The Gendered Organisation of Labour in Time and Space* (Durham: Sociology Press).
Green, F. (2001) 'It's Been a Hard Day's Night: The Concentration and Intensification of Work in Late Twentieth-Century Britain', *British Journal of Industrial Relations*, 39(1), pp. 53–80.
Harvey, D. (2000) 'Reinventing Geography', *New Left Review*, 4 (July/August), pp. 75–97.
Heery, E. (1998a) 'Campaigning for Part-Time Workers', *Work, Employment and Society*, 12(2), pp. 351–66.

Heery, E. (1998b) 'The Relaunch of the Trades Union Congress', *British Journal of Industrial Relations*, 36(3), pp. 339–60.
Holloway, J. (1995) 'Capital Moves', *Capital and Class*, 57 (Autumn), pp. 136–44.
Knights, D. and H. Willmott (1989) 'Power and Subjectivity at Work: From Degradation at Work to Subjectivity in Social Relations', *Sociology*, 23 (4), pp. 535–58.
Knights, D. and D. McCabe (2000) ' "Ain't Misbehavin"? Opportunities for Resistance under New Forms of "Quality" Management', *Sociology*, 34(3), pp. 421–36.
Lewchuk, W. and D. Robertson (1996) 'Working conditions under lean production: A worker-based bench marking study', *Asia Pacific Business Review*, 2(4), pp. 60–81.
Lewchuk, W., P. Stewart and C. Yates (2001) 'Quality of working life in the automobile industry: a Canada–UK comparative study', *New Technology, Work and Employment*, 16(2), pp. 72–87.
Martínez Lucio, M. and P. Stewart (1997) 'The Paradox of Contemporary Labour Process Theory: The Rediscovery of Labour and the Disappearance of Collectivism', *Capital and Class*, 62 (Summer), pp. 49–77.
Nichols, T. (1997) *The Sociology of Industrial Injury* (London: Mansell).
Nichols, T. (2001) 'The Condition of Labour – A Retrospect', *Capital and Class*, 75 (Autumn), pp. 185–98.
O'Doherty, D. and Willmott, H. (2001) 'Debating Labour Process Theory: The Issue of Subjectivity and the Relevance of Poststructuralism', *Sociology*, 35(2), pp. 457–76.
Reinhart, J., C. Huxley and D. Robertson (1997) *Just Another Car Factory? Lean Production and its Discontents* (Cornell University Press).
Scott, A. (2001) 'Organisation: Between Charismatic, and Bureaucratic Nerchution', mimeo, IOL Workshop Institut für Soziologie, Innsbruck.
Smith, C. and P. Thompson (1998) 'Re-evaluating the Labour Process Debate', *Economic and Industrial Democracy*, 19, pp. 551–77.
Stephenson, C. (1996) 'The Different Experience of Trade Unionism in Two Japanese Transplants', in P. Akers, P. Smith and C. Smith (eds), *The New Workplace and Trade Unionism* (London: Routledge).
Stephenson, C. and P. Stewart (2001) 'The whispering shadow: collectivism and individualism at Ikeda-Hoover and Nissan UK', *Sociological Research Online*, 6:3 (16 pages) www.socresonline.org.uk
Stewart, P. (1998) 'Out of Chaos comes Order – From Japanisation to Lean Production', *Employee Relations*, 20(3), pp. 213–23.
Stewart, P. and M. Martínez Lucio (1998) 'Renewal and Tradition in the New Politics of Production', in C. Warhurst and P. Thompson (eds), *Workplaces of the Future* (London: Macmillan), pp. 65–83.
Therborn, G. (2001) 'Into the 21st Century', *New Left Review*, 10 (July/August), pp. 87–110.
Thompson, P. and S. Ackroyd (1995) 'All Quiet on the Workplace Front? A Recent Critique of Trends in British Industrial Sociology', *Sociology*, 29(4), pp. 610–33.
Williams, R. (1979) *Politics and Letters* (London: Verso).
Yates, C., W. Lewchuk and P. Stewart (2001) 'Empowerment as a Trojan Horse: new systems of work organisation in the North American automobile industry', *Economic and Industrial Democracy*, 22(4), pp. 517–41.

# 13
# Trade Unionism and the Realities of Change: Reframing the Language of Change
*Miguel Martínez Lucio*

## Introduction

Discussions on trade unionism during the last two decades have been based on either agony or disdain. Unions have been refashioned and restructured by a variety of developments that have weakened their class identity and role in the regulation of labour – or such is the assertion of many narratives that portray the demise of unions as inevitable. This demise has been studied across various dimensions, three of which will be reviewed in this chapter.

First, studies of the micro level of change have focused on the transformation of production processes and workplace roles. Discussions at this level have dealt mainly with management's creation of a new labour process and system of workplace representation that has questioned the legitimacy of trade union representation and roles. The literature in this area is extensive, drawing from industrial/labour relations and industrial sociology. However this literature has often paid scant regard to the macro and social role of trade unions and the pressures on this role.

Second, within political science there is an ongoing concern with the declining political role and social influence of unions. This is explained with reference to the changing economic context and the move towards a less socially oriented state system. Whilst questioned as a coherent development, many see this declining role as either complementing the micro-level decline in terms of political influence, or establishing the basis for a mainly symbolic and management-led role within the enterprise. Hence the study of decline must be located with reference to these two sets of dynamics and levels.

Third, in social and cultural terms extensive social restructuring and the decline of working-class identity, masculine cultures and geographical/spatial changes are seen to underpin these changes. This approach views organizational and political changes as corresponding to a broader process of social disaggregation.

This chapter will outline and synthesize these developments. It will also evaluate the academic changes and political transformations that have underpinned the developments, arguing that they are based on a narrow view of trade union roles. We are currently hearing a very different set of embryonic arguments that do not see the problem as one of decline and social disorganization, but rather of changing boundaries in terms of roles and identities. These changes test the past role played by traditional trade unionism. The problem is that in economic and social terms there are less clear boundaries and more complex social structures that require a new and more complex response from the labour movement. The chapter will therefore outline the pessimistic views of change and then make a more optimistic point about the role of organized labour. The main task, it is argued, is to frame new developments and solidarities. For this reason the chapter will consider the nature of the discussions themselves – and the way the language of decline has been framed – and the manner in which academic discourse has been influenced by a desire to ignore the complexities of change, the political continuities, and the realities and diversity of organized labour.

## Post-Fordism and the crisis of trade unionism

The crisis of labour is at the heart of Post-Fordism, but the issue of trade unionism is not. Indeed the classic texts on Post-Fordism and regulation say very little about trade unionism and its crisis. For example in the Anglo-Saxon context, texts such as Jessop's *The Future of the Capitalist State* (2002) discuss unions only in a tangential manner. The main lines of argument about economic change concern the fragmentation of consumption, economic globalization, the decline of Fordist regulation and the shift towards a new market-oriented regulatory system. The social, economic and political roles of organized labour are either ignored or are only addressed in terms of their functionalist role in sustaining the regulatory process in the wage relation (Aglietta, 1979).

While joint regulation and the economic activity of trade unions were functional to Fordist modes of regulation and regimes of accumulation, according to some observers they are dysfunctional to the development of Post-Fordist variants, and will remain so if they fail to develop an entrepreneurial dimension and focus on labour reproduction and skill formation (Sabel, 1982). The absence of agency in regulation theory and its reliance on a functionalist perspective have been the subject of much discussion (see for example Bonefeld, 1987; Jessop, 1988). That unions could respond to political change and economic transformation was rarely a topic of discussion in the 1970s and 1980s. Instead the main line of argument was the declining role of trade unions as social and political actors, and not their reinvention as political or regulatory actors.[1]

During the 1970s and early 1980s a series of texts argued that the fate of trade unions was synonymous with the fate of the working class. The changing economic and social circumstances of the industrial working class in terms of the emergence of a leisure society, increasing automation and declining industrial values were seen to be leading to a fundamental transformation of industrial identity and social politics (Gorz, 1982). Central to traditional working-class identity had been the role of unions as representatives of industrial communities and as a crystallization of working-class customs and interests. The culture of bargaining, with its masculine posturing, the centrality of wages to the process of struggle and the role of collectivism, as manifested in the mass assembly, were all perceived to be threatened by the scaling down of industrial communities and their social relations. Some questioned this viewpoint and suggested that if anything the industrial and Taylorist spirit was emerging in new sectors such as the service sector, thus enlarging the working class (Beynon, 1992). However the tendency was to alert us to the decline of collectivism. According to Valkenburg (1995, p. 131):

> Individualization undermines traditional views of solidarity and trade union democracy. According to the traditional viewpoint, solidarity is based on interests that are supposed to be objective and common. Solidarity means that trade unionists perceive these common interests as such, that the unions embody them in a collective policy, and that this policy directs the actions of all involved.

This decline in social terms was driven – or paralleled, depending on one's point of view – by political changes at the macro and micro levels. At the macro level there was a decline in corporatism. The role of unions had been enshrined, to varying degrees, in the macroeconomic policy making processes in Western Europe (Lehmbruch, 1984). A form of societal or neocorporatism based on independent social partners (Schmitter, 1974) and macro-level political bargaining (Hyman, 1983) underpinned the Fordist state of postwar liberal-democratic Europe. In some cases the unions played a large part in the coordination and articulation of economic and social policy and regulation, as in Sweden (Lash and Urry, 1987). However the crisis of Fordism gave rise to a relative withdrawal of the state from direct economic regulation and to the questioning of neocorporatism as a basis for decision making. In countries such as the United Kingdom this withdrawal was extensive, and in other countries there was a questioning of union roles within the state. The trade union movement was therefore exposed to a more market-oriented state, interested in privatization and developing more commercially driven social services. And even if there was a state role, as Jessop (2002) argues, in terms of providing the basis for capital accumulation, as in the Schumpeterian workfare state (with its reformulation of regulation to facilitate increasing competition through indirect state roles in spatial and supply terms), in organized terms labour was not considered to be integral to it.

More specifically, the crisis of social democracy and the failure of communism in the 1980s were seen to accelerate these developments. The decline of neocorporatism as a concrete development in European politics was questioned by some, as will be discussed below, and many preferred to see the decline as a major shift in the political role of unions and their presence in the regulatory process:

> Of course the real culprit – everyone's favorite *deus ex machina* – was (and still is) *globalisation*. Sharpened international competition . . . [and] the overt threat to move to another site put great pressures on workers to make concessions. . . . The upshot of these trends seemed quite clear to many analysts in the 1980s. At best 'national corporatism' had to shift from the macro to the meso level of aggregation. And even then, the question remained whether the process would stop there or disintegrate even further until the only 'systematic dialogues' left would be taking place at the level of firms and the 'voluntary and active assent', so obviously necessary for improving competitiveness in a more globalised marketplace, would emerge from the interactions of individual workers and employers – stalked by the shadow of future dismissals and plant closures. (Schmitter and Grote, 1997, pp. 28–9)

Changing relations between employers and unions in the workplace therefore paralleled macropolitical developments. Whilst unions were being removed from a broader political role, they were being confronted by a similar dynamic at the micro level. Increasingly, difficult economic and market circumstances were forcing employers to adopt less pluralistic approaches to industrial relations in their companies. The American industrial relations literature was replete with references to deunionization, union marginalization and political shifts to a more conservative view of work (see for example Weinstein and Kochan, 1995). Meanwhile the Thatcher government in the United Kingdom brought an authoritarian approach to industrial relations with legislation that undermined collective rights and representative processes. Even in socialist Spain and France, the 1980s saw governments follow a broad policy of market adaptation that limited the role of unions and their integration into the decision-making processes of the state (Smith, 1999). Hence unions had to confront the challenge of how to reconstruct their historical role within the firm and 'socialize' capital from below.

Ongoing economic restructuring therefore pushed unions in the 1980s and 1990s into a defensive role and collective mobilization became tied to more instrumental and short-term interests. Within the firm, it was argued that the development of new technologies, and information technology in particular, required a new type of employment relation that challenged the logic of traditional collective representation. In the case of the United Kingdom, Purcell (1993, p. 72) argued that trade unions were being confronted by a new individualistic employment relation that countered the logic of collective mobilization and organization:

> The evidence is that support for the institutions of collective bargaining have been removed by the Government as legislator and employer, and by employers themselves to a great extent, while employers associations have largely collapsed. It is this shift in ideology toward market individualism that underpins explanations of market deregulation, privatisation and the opening of international markets. . . . [I]t was the ideas of market individualism which offered the direction of change and led to the end of institutional industrial relations.

Bacon and Storey (1996) agreed that unions were, as boxers often say, 'on the ropes', but not because of any new individualistic logic amongst workers or regulators. Rather the new management practices took a collectivist logic and form that robbed the unions of their collective robes. Direct communication, company-based meetings and team working emerged as alternative forms of collective representation and involvement that appealed to workers in terms of their corporate identity and not just their individual interests. These new management practices – known variously as human resource management or toyotism – to one degree or another attempted to tie workers' rights to the identity and needs of the firm, denying any autonomous trade union approach to such matters (Martínez Lucio and Simpson, 1993). Regulation theorists remained relatively calm on such matters due to the inherent pessimism that underpinned much of the tradition. Unions were faced with a new regime of work and they had either to conform or to negotiate in a context where the economic was paramount over the social. Given that not much had been said about organized labour when discussing Fordism, there was perceived to be no need to say anything substantive about them in the new context.

Hence at the micro level there was a new type of accommodation between capital and labour. The extent of this accommodation ranged from a consensual understanding of the constraints of the market and the need for a more business-oriented view of industrial relations (Kochan and Osterman, 1994; see Martínez Lucio and Stuart, 2004, for a discussion), to the marginalization of labour and fatalistic acceptance by unions of the need to sustain jobs through work intensification and restructuring (Bassett, 1986; Garrahan and Stewart, 1992). The consequence was dual in nature: the decentralization of the economy in terms of production and service delivery narrowed and limited the capacity of unions, whilst the increasing globalization of capital and ownership structures locked labour into a local and parochial position as it competed for investment and resources against other workers (for an example of the latter see Mueller and Purcell, 1992).

As a result of all this, unions faced a major challenge in terms of their identity, purpose and role. In addition their independence and autonomy were questioned (Martínez Lucio and Weston, 1992).[2] This led to a variety of discussions on the declining relevance of organized labour in social, economic and political terms. The gap between contemporary culture and politics, on the one hand, and the role and identity of unions, on the other, was quite broad. Unions may have adapted in order to negotiate concessions from capital, but the 1980s and 1990s were replete with examples of the failure of organized labour to reinvent itself (Hyman, 1989).

Much of this concern was derived from analytical and empirical interpretations of developments in work places and labour markets, but much was also derived from two other phenomena. The first was the crisis of the Marxist left in the broader sense of the term, and the transformation of social democracy through such discourses as the 'third way' (Martínez Lucio and Stuart, 2004). The intellectual allies of trade union action became less in number, and even those in the antiglobalization lobby were wary of the institutionalist politics of trade unions and their obsession with regulation in a narrow sense. Second, in the academic world there was a marginalization, perhaps not always effective, of labour studies. Within sociology, cultural studies, broadly speaking, became paramount and more attractive to students and academics. Trade unions were seen as marginal to the gender, sexual, symbolic and informational dimensions of society. Meanwhile business schools, via organizational studies and human resource management studies, began to address labour issues from a different dimension, with industrial and labour relations being redefined as an area of study. This may be somewhat of a generalization, especially as in the Anglo-Saxon context industrial relations specialists continued to exert a strong influence in such areas as human resource management, but it was noticeable that changes in postmodern organizational studies and psychological approaches to the study of work left labour studies relatively isolated. Thus the social and political changes discussed earlier and in tandem with these intellectual developments resulted in a reduced interest in unions within policy and academic circles, with traditional forms of union action being seen as anachronistic.

In summary, the decline of organized labour cannot be understood from the prism of one dimension of social and political analysis. For example, as is customary in the institutionalist Anglo-Saxon tradition, the declining role of collective bargaining in quantitative terms is not a sufficient basis for analysis. Union decline or change is multidimensional. It has a social dimension in terms of the changing nature of the working and professional classes; it has a political dimension in terms of the shifting role of the state and allied political parties; it has a regulatory dimension in terms of the institutional reach and effectiveness of employment regulation; it has a corporate dimension in terms of the internalization of industrial relations; it has a cultural dimension in terms of the way in which union action is seen as disconnected from social and political change; and it has a global dimension by virtue of the fact that global corporate structures and new forms of informational processes have outflanked unions and their local character and presence.

## Rereading the crisis of labour

Unfortunately for those who seek a simple narrative of transformation, social and political change is often complex. The reality of trade unionism needs to be approached with a more open mind. The application of the notion of fate to social studies should be questioned. Fine (2003) argues that it is too easy to criticize unions for their lack of strategic impetus and their focus on wages: for example trade unions play a subtle role in conditioning capital and ensuring the development of rights through implicit critiques of control at the level of production and campaigns on welfare rights and the decommodification of welfare services. Fine asserts that the boundary between wage and non-wage issues, even in the most institutionalized industrial relations system, is never that clear.

Moreover why should the changing nature of social boundaries, such as the emerging centrality of consumption, the changing nature of the workplace and the decline in traditional skill-based hierarchies at work be solely a challenge to labour? Do not the demands generated by rapid technological change, consumer identity, decentralized and global production and ongoing skill formation challenge the structures and identity of capital and management as well?

For example if we focus on one specific dimension of these changes, the feminization of work, then the new demand for rights and representation in the workplace is creating a whole new set of challenges to both labour and capital, yet regulation theory and the critiques of trade unionism appear oblivious to the complexity of this. Hence the developments outlined in the previous section are really a broad set of challenges and, dare one say, opportunities. If we move away from the discussion of labour as trade unions, for example, and focus on 'concrete and living labour' we cannot attribute its decline to any technological turn. What we can see is the emergence of new understandings of labour, such as the debate around emotional labour (Hothschild, 1983; Noon and Blyton, 1998). At the heart of the new relation between the firm and the customer is a new type of interaction that stresses the role and behaviour of employees. The position of labour may be changing but it is by no means less central to production and service delivery.

Leaving aside the qualitative dimension of work, since the mid 1990s the European Union has experienced an alarming shortage of labour in key sectors and immigrant workers have been essential to avoiding a major breakdown in key services. Hence in structural terms the role of labour and the potential strength of labour are significant, although the realization of this potential may be another matter.

These developments have forced firms to elicit a new individual commitment from their workers and a political commitment to resolving the tensions brought about by the expansion of the service economy and the need for skill formation and labour reproduction. The details of this are outlined below, but of relevance here is the fact that the social changes, new production regimes and labour market developments do not in themselves automatically undermine the role of worker representation. They must be viewed in a very different way – as changes in the pattern of voices, rights and processes that constitute work and employment. This does not mean that unions are always at the centre of these changes, or that the changes are not being used by employers to marginalize unions and individualize employment relations, but it does mean that we need to map social and economic changes in such a way that we can identify the responses of institutions to them. Rights at work are not in decline, rather they are increasing and in that respect they present a whole new terrain of engagement for social actors. Moreover they present academics and observers with a challenge to any binary notion of political change they may hold.

## The new agendas of labour

Much has been written and spoken about the new agendas of labour. Normally this is depicted in managerialist terms as the growing trade union role of organized labour within the firm in respect of new functional areas such as training. However the term is used here more loosely to outline the potential offered to trade unionists by the fundamental contours and fault lines of workplace and economic developments. There are six levels at which one can detect new types of union activity and possibilities in the changed economic and social context and which are explained below (Table 13.1). That is not to imply that union renewal is consistently occurring and developing across a range of organizational and social levels. What does appear to be the case is that there are instances of innovation and response that suggest that the new regime of work is as rife with contradictions as any previous regime.

The decentralization of production and a greater focus on labour involvement are notable features of the new regime. Although these may not be consistent features, or empowering ones, as far as workers are concerned (Parker and Slaughter, 1988; Stewart and Garrahan, 1995; Cully *et al.*, 1999), there has been greater emphasis on line management and local decision making in industry. Fairbrother (1994) argues that decentralization can contribute to a greater degree of activism in the workplace and a renewal of branch activity due to the number of issues and problems that emerge as a consequence. The reassertion of management prerogative through new workplace practices has forced unions to reconsider their agendas and develop suitable and even innovative responses. In a study of the automotive industry, Stewart and Martínez Lucio (1998) note that the development of teamworking and quality requirements have led to a new politics of production where health and safety issues, questions of working time and general problems with workplace dignity have become much more significant and contested (Stewart, 2004). This points to a whole new agenda on questions of health and safety that potentially challenge managements' prerogative. In this respect the demand for deeper and more extensive collective bargaining on issues such as health and safety, training and development, worker involvement and much more is underpinning many of the discourses on union renewal and change (Martínez Lucio and Weston, 1992; Martínez Lucio and Stuart, 2004). Hence decentralization in the broad sense of the term, coupled with firms having greater exposure to economic and market pressures, has given rise to a new set of initiatives and issues in the trade union movement.

This is partly due to the nature of the decentralization being discussed. Decentralization is not a fragmentary process that isolates workers. It is a development, no matter how inconsistent, that exposes workers to the nature of the market and the new pressures on the organization. It may distance the workplace from the centre of the organization, but ironically it exposes it to the issue of consumption. In this respect whilst management attempts to influence that link by emphasising individual and competitive relations, it opens a whole new set of possibilities concerning consumption politics, showing how difficult it can be for management to focus the involvement of workers around production issues. Service delivery, its purpose and its quality have been exposed to broader interventions. Hence attempting to base the aim, purpose and means of work and labour on the needs of the customer can lead to workers calling for more socially oriented objectives and purposes, although such developments as total quality management and greater emphasis on management control may also have the ironic effect of giving workers a more instrumental and Taylorist view of work. The flood of information on service, quality and organizational purpose may prompt a greater alertness to change that will not necessarily be dictated by employers and managers. In the European public sector, management-led change has given rise to counter discourses in areas such as health and education. New forms of conflict are emerging that are media-focused, strategic and linked to consumer as well as producer interests, as in strikes in the airline industry, which have been known to link health and safety concerns with customer interests (see Kirkpatrick and Martínez Lucio, 1995; Linstead, 1995).

The changes and fractures in the boundaries between production and consumption, and the manner in which organizations have decentralized, are therefore much more political than at first suggested by the Post-Fordist debate and its corollaries. Also relevant is the boundary between the state and society in respect of regulation. Throughout Europe, to varying degrees the role of the state has shifted. We know much about privatization and the managerialization of the state (see Chapter 8 of this volume), and about the emergence of the Post-Fordist state, with its targeted intervention and decentred approach to service delivery and regulation. Yet paralleling this process has been the development of regulatory transfer (Martínez Lucio and MacKenzie, 2004), a feature of which is increased union involvement in matters such as pension rights, employment benefits and employment flexibility measures; coupled with a move, albeit uneven, to involving trade unions and employers in state intervention as an attempt to modernize and enhance its effectiveness in such areas as health and safety, training and employment contracting. The strategy is normally to operationalize new forms of intervention within employment relations whilst simultaneously trying to extend the remit of what has been a very narrow system of joint regulation in the firm and the workplace. The approach is driven in terms of involving unions in the role of the state as administrators, and, in the stronger cases, even policy makers.[3] This strategy has evolved from the long held interest by unions in widening the remit of collective bargaining, which had hitherto not always achieved broad representation amongst workers.[4]

Then there is the pessimism brought about by globalization. According to Schmitter and Grote (1997), globalization will fundamentally undermine national regulatory systems and actors. The concern is that unions are locked into national institutions and national remits in terms of their organizational habits. The discourse on internationalism is primarily rhetorical in respect of the role of unions in the regulation of the employment relation, and it ignores the impact of international capital and transnational coordination on labour politics. It fails to see that new forms of networking are emerging in transnational corporations and that management behaviour, sometimes unintentionally, has alerted trade unionists to the need for international coordination and information exchanges (Martínez Lucio and Weston, 1994, 1995). It also fails to understand that common changes among organizations and by the state (for example the adoption of new forms of quality management and privatization) lead to greater international labour collaboration. Some, such as Waterman (2001), have spoken of the emergence of a new international unionism as a consequence of these and other political developments; a new trade union identity and approach based on synergies with social movements nationally and locally is the subject of a variety of interventions (Wills, 1998; Lambert and Webster, 2001). It is too early to suggest a Copernican revolution in

Table 13.1  Two interpretations of change

|  | Post-Fordist positions | Alternative developments |
|---|---|---|
| Workplace | Decentralization in the firm and the workplace | The enhancing of collective bargaining and a new politics of production |
| Social context of work | Fragmented social boundaries and the decline of conflict | New forms of social unionism and links between production and consumption issues; new forms of strategic labour conflict |
| Management and labour utilization | New forms of labour utilization through the quality and consumer paradigm | The development of a new consumer politics and alternative views of quality management |
| State and regulation | Changing state roles and decentralization | Operationalizing the state and service provision through social actors such as unions |
| The global dimension | Globalization – the new international dynamic and gaps in labour organization | Networked unionism and flexible/innovative soliderity |
| The communication sphere | New forms of communication and a decline in public space and collectivism | Virtual representation and new internet-based collaboration |

the labour movement on such matters, but there are signs that the new international order of production is giving rise to novel developments. This has been facilitated by the spread of information technology and its use by the labour movement as part of its new communication strategy (Lee, 1996; Greene et al., 2001).

In summary, we should pay greater attention to the tensions and possibilities facing the trade union movement, or the threats and opportunities as the management gurus put it.

## Conclusion: the possibilities and limits of unions

The objective of the chapter has been simple: to show that the changes facing unions are much more complex, multifarious and unstable than was first imagined. There is a need to take stock of these changes and show how they offer both threats and opportunities.

We have noted that the crisis stems from ideology and history, and that it predates Fordism. Hyman (1989), whilst sympathetic to labour, once alluded to some historical factors coming home to roost. That is, strategic direction and innovation remain a challenge to unions given their reactive nature and, on occasion, their sectionalist tendency. The real issue is how unions should respond to the new possibilities and find a democratic discourse of emancipation that embraces the diversity of work and society on the one hand and the need for justice and change on the other (Hyman, 1999).

The challenges facing unions are varied. Unions continue to play a role and have a purpose in the representation of workers but pressures can be seen to emerge not just from the disorganization, decentralization and disintegration of social and economic relations but of their 'multiplication' leading to a broader set of worker issues and identity. The workplace is still a political environment and matters of representation and rights continue to emerge, but in an increasingly complex way. Moreover the boundaries of the workplace with regard to consumption and social issues have become increasingly porous, requiring a new organizational logic by unions. However, it clearly does not mean that work has become a marginal concern being de-politicized and fragmented. At the macro level unions are positioning themselves in curious ways within the supply side regulation of the economy. These new roles may vary and be in great part merely administrative and supportive of state roles, but they do present possibilities for the rethinking of educational processes and learning dynamics within the new economy. In an area such as training, the role of political engagement has been central (Stuart, 1996; see also chapter 7 of this volume).

In the 1980s Panitch (1981) argued that the new political role of organized labour in the neocorporatist state had given rise to a tension between the social democratic conformism of union leaders and the militant responses of their members and workplace representatives. In many respects the corporatist state constituted a politicization of organized labour as internal contradictions subsequently emerged in terms of union governance as unions were drawn into new decision-making arenas, although this did not always result in positive gains *vis-à-vis* employers, the state or even their own members, as evidenced by incomes policies in the 1970s and 1980s.

The current developments are indeed opportunities for labour, but they raise internal debates. Just as unions have not withered or become marginal, neither have their internal politics. The development of a union movement with a need to (re)develop workplace institutions and their relations with social actors within the sphere of consumption, calls for a new organizational logic and a new language of democracy. In addition, the informal processes that emerge around trade union networking add a further layer of demands for reorganization and new forms of democratic engagement.

Trade unions do not face political decline due to any tensions that may exist with allied left parties, they in fact face a new political exploration based on the new demands made on them. Hence if we trace our steps back to the question of Post-Fordism in the broader sense, its discussion has been unacceptable when referencing trade unions. It has failed to apply its own broader views of capitalist change, which show how tensions can emerge that can in turn provide new possibilities for organized labour. The question will be whether a new service or market form of trade unionism, which is commercially driven, can adapt better to the demands from new constituents (inside and outside the remit of work) and to new state roles than an alternative, network-based and mobilization based union approach. Or it could be that other actors capture this space of representation (Martínez Lucio and MacKenzie, 2004). This is the dilemma facing organized labour as it grapples with Post-Fordist developments. In order to understand this we need to evaluate the way we frame and signpost the question of change, moving away from the binaries characterizing the debate, and re-engage with the political debate about organized labour.

### Notes

1. One could attribute this to the Marxist tradition of viewing trade unions as inward looking, sectarian, capable of wage-consciousness only, and generally tied to the subjective interests of the working class (for a discussion see Hyman, 1971).
2. Some argued that any such discussion should be located in an understanding of the historical limitations of unions (Hyman, 1971). There had always been question marks over the political and strategic qualities of organized labour, let alone their sectionalism and instrumentalism. If anything the problem was a cultural one in that during the previous 20 years capital had reinvented itself and engaged with postmodern developments in a way that labour had not (Boltanksi and Chiapello, 1999). It therefore became a vogue for commentators to show the limitations of organized labour in broader terms. This corresponds to a broader vogue for postmodernist tales of organizational decline in general: 'declensionist narratives' (Putnam, 2000, p. 24).
3. The fragmented role at the level of the state is accompanied supposedly by a fragmented role within the corporation (Alonso, 1994). Within the employment relationship a move away from the political in traditional terms is apparent – although this does not by any means signify the end of the political but rather the construction of a new set of contradictions and tensions (Martínez Lucio and Stewart, 1997).
4. In terms of union choice and strategy, this has had the effect of creating a more realistic position in which unions try to find specific trade-offs to achieve new institutional roles at the company, sectoral and state levels. Thus trade unions are assimilating the political in terms of state activity and the function of regulation. Whether this will radicalize unions is however another question.

### References

Aglietta, M. (1979) *A Theory of Capitalist Regulation* (London: NLB).
Alonso, L. E. (1994) 'Macro y Micro Corporatismo', *Revista Internacional de Sociologia*, 8–9.
Bacon, N. and J. Storey (1996) 'Individualism and Collectivism and the Changing Role of Trade Unionism', in P. Ackers, C. Smith and P. Smith (eds), *The New Workplace and Trade Unionism* (London: Routledge), pp. 1–40.
Bassett, P. (1986) *Strike Free* (London: Macmillan).
Beynon, H. (1992) 'The End of the Industrial Worker?', in N. Abercombie and A. Warde, *Social Change in Contemporary Britain Cambridge* (Cambridge: Polity Press).
Boltanksi, L. and E. Chiapello (1999) *El Nuevo Espíritu del Capitalismo* (Madrid: AKAL).
Bonefeld, W. (1987) 'Reformulation of State Theory', *Capital and Class*, 33, pp. 96–127.

Castells, M. (1998) *The Rise of Network Society* (Oxford: Blackwell).
Cully, M., S. Woodland, A. O'Reilly and G. Dix (1999) *Britain at Work: As Depicted by the 1998 Workplace Employee Relations Survey* (London: Routledge).
Fairbrother, P. (1994) *Politics and the State as Employer* (London: Mansell).
Fine, B. (2003) 'Contesting Labour Markets', in A. Saad-Filho, *Anti-Capitalism: A Marxist Introduction* (London: Pluto Press).
Garrahan, P. and P. Stewart (1992) *The Nissan Enigma* (London: Mansell).
Gorz, A. (1982) *Farewell to the Working Class* (London: Pluto Press).
Greene, A. M., J. Hogan and M. Greco (2001) 'E-collectivism and Distributed Discourse: New Opportunities for Trade Union Democracy', paper presented at the TUC/LSE Conference on Unions and the Internet, London, 12 May.
Hothschild, A. R. (1983) *The Managed Heart: Commercialisation of Human Feeling* (Berkeley, CA: University of California Press).
Hyman, R. (1971) *Marxism and the Sociology of Trade Unionism* (London: Pluto Press).
Hyman, R. (1983) 'State and Unions in Britain: The Collapse of Corporatism?, in T. Akkermans, P. W. M. Nobelen and S. Kroese (eds), *Corporatisme en Verzorgingsstaat* (Antwerp: SK).
Hyman, R. (1989) *The Political Economy of Industrial Relations* (London: Macmillan).
Hyman, R. (1999) 'Imagined Solidarities: Can Trade Union Resist Globalisation?', in P. Leisink (ed.), *Globalisation and Labour Relations* (Cheltenham: Edward Elgar).
Jessop, B. (1998) 'Regulation Theory, Post-Fordism, and the State: More than a Reply to Werner Bonefeld', *Capital and Class*, 34, pp. 147–69.
Jessop, B. (2002) *The Future of the Capitalist State* (Cambridge: Polity Press).
Kirkpatrick, I. and M. Martínez Lucio (1995) 'The Politics of Quality in the British Public Sector', in Ian Kirkpatrick and Miguel Martinez Lucio (eds), *The Politics of Quality and the Management of Change in the Public Sector* (London: Routledge).
Kochan, T. A. and P. Osterman (1994) *The Mutual Gains Enterprise: Forging a Winning Partnership among Labour, Management and Government* (Boston, Mass.: Harvard University Press).
Lambert, R. and Webster, E. (2001) 'Southern Unionism and the New Labour Internationalism' in P. Waterman and J. Wills (eds), *Place, Space and the New Labour Internationalism* (Oxford: Blackwell), pp. 33–58.
Lash, S. and Urry J. (1987) *The End of Organised Capitalism* (Cambridge: Polity Press).
Lee, E. (1996) *The Labour Movement and the Internet: The New Internationalism?* (London: Pluto Press).
Lehmbruch, G. (1984) 'Concertation and the Structure of Corporatist Networks', in J. E. Goldthorpe (ed.), *Order and Conflict in Contemporary Capitalism* (Oxford: Oxford University Press).
Linstead, S. (1995) 'After the Autumn Harvest: Rhetoric and representation in an Asian Industrial Dispute', *Studies in Cultures, Organisations and Societies*, 1, pp. 231–51.
Martínez Lucio, M. and R. MacKenzie (2004) 'Unstable Boundaries? Evaluating the "New Regulation" within Employment Relations', *Economy and Society*, February, pp. 77–97.
Martínez Lucio, M. and D. Simpson (1993) 'La dimension social de las nuevas practicas de gestion y su relevancia para la crisis de las relaciones laborales', *Sociologia de Trabajo*, spring, pp. 49–78.
Martínez Lucio, M. and P. Stewart (1997) 'The Paradox of Contemporary Labour Process Theory: The Rediscovery of the "Employee" and the Disappearance of Collectivism', *Capital and Class*, May, pp. 49–77.
Martínez Lucio, M. and M. Stuart (2004) 'Swimming against the tide: social partnership, mutual gains and the revival of "tired" HRM', *International Journal of Human Resource Management*, 15 (2), pp. 404–18.

Martínez Lucio, M. and S. Weston (1992) 'Human Resource Management and Trade Union Responses: Bringing the Politics of the Workplace Back into the Debate', in p. Blyton and P. Turnbull (eds), *Reassessing Human Resource Management* (London: Sage), pp. 215–32.

Martínez Lucio, M. and S. Weston (1994) 'New management practices in a multinational corporation: the restructuring of worker representation and rights?', *Industrial Relations Journal*, June, pp. 110–21.

Martínez Lucio, M. and S. Weston (1995) 'Trade Unions and Networking in the Context of Change: Evaluating the Outcomes of Decentralisation in Industrial Relations', *Economic and Industrial Democracy*, May, pp. 233–52.

Mueller, F. and J. Purcell (1992) 'The Europeanisation of manufacturing and the decentralisation of bargaining: multinational management strategies in the European automobile industry', *International Journal of Human Resource Management*, 3 (1), pp. 15–43.

Noon, M. and P. Blyton (1998) *The Realities of Work* (London: Macmillan).

Panitch, L. (1981) 'Trade Unions and the Capitalist State', *New Left Review*, 125, pp. 21–44.

Parker, M. and J. Slaughter (1988) *Choosing Sides* (Boston, Mass.: South End Press).

Purcell, J. (1993) 'Ideology and the End of Institutional Industrial Relations: Evidence from the UK', *Labour and Industry*, 5 (3), pp. 57–74.

Putnam, D. (2000) *Bowling alone: The Collapse and Revival of American Community* (New York: Simon & Schuster).

Sabel, C. (1982) *Work and Politics* (Cambridge: Cambridge University Press).

Schmitter, P. (1974) 'Still the century of corporatism?', *Review of Politics*, 36 (1), pp. 85–131.

Schmitter, P. C. and J. R. Grote (1997) 'The Corporatist Sisyphus: Past, Present and Future', paper presented at the conference on Plotting our Future: Technology, Environment, Economy and Society, European University Institute, Florence, 1997.

Smith, W. (1999) *The Left's Dirty Job: The Politics of Industrial Restructuring in France and Spain* (Pittsburgh, PA: University of Pittsburgh Press).

Stewart, P. (2004) 'Work, Employment, and Society today', *Work, Employment and Society*, 18 (4), pp. 653–62.

Stewart, P. and P. Garrahan (1995), 'Employee Responses to New Management Techniques in the Auto Industry', *Work, Employment and Society*, 9 (3), pp. 517–36.

Stewart, P. and M. Martínez Lucio (1998) 'Renewal and Tradition in the Politics of Production', in P. Thompson and C. Warhurst (eds), *Workplaces of the Future* (London: Macmillan).

Stuart, M. (1996) 'The Industrial Relations of Training: a Reconsideration of Training Arrangements', *Industrial Relations Journal*, 27 (3), pp. 253–66.

Valkenburg, B. (1995) 'Individualization, Participation and Solidarity', in B. Valkenburg and R. Zoll (ed), 'Two Perspectives on European Trade Unions Today', *European Journal of Industrial Relations*, 1 (1), pp. 119–144.

Waterman, P. (2001) 'Trade Union Internationalism in the Age of Seattle', in P. Waterman and P. Wells (eds), *Place, Space, and New Labour Internationalisms* (Oxford: Blackwell).

Weinstein, M. and T. Kochan (1995) 'The limits of diffusion: Recent developments in industrial relations and human resource practices in the United States', in R. Locke, T. Kochan and M. Piore, (eds), *Employment Relations in a Changing Economy* (Cambridge, Mass.: MIT Press).

Wills, J. (1998) 'Taking on the Cosmocorps: Experiments in Transnational Labor Organization', *Economic Geography*, 74, pp. 111–13.

# 14
# Flexible Rigidities: A Model for Social Europe?

*Richard Hyman\**

> We are left alone with our day, and the time is short, and
> History to the defeated
> May say alas but cannot help or pardon.
>
> (W.H. Auden, *Spain*, 1937)

Only connect… The contribution of social scientists is rarely to discover novel facts; it is more often to show what can plausibly be interpreted as patterns of causal association between what is already familiar. We attempt to discern the ways in which the elements in the jigsaw fit together; and not infrequently we must first show how conventional images of the ensemble are misleading before offering new and perhaps surprising alternatives. The essence of social analysis is the search for relationships. In the world of action, too, those who can make the strategic connections which are not normally self-evident are best placed to shape their – and our – futures.

In this chapter I will attempt to link four concepts which are probably well known to most of us but are not commonly treated in the same discourse: moral economy, risk society, multi-level governance and flexible rigidities. I believe it is important to make these connections, because flexibility has become the Leitmotiv of contemporary European industrial relations policy. Dismantling long-established regulatory standards is almost universally presented as an unavoidable response to the imperatives of competitiveness. By connecting my four very disparate themes we may perhaps be better placed to evaluate the nature and the limits both of the challenges and of the responses.

## Moral economy

The classic analysis of moral economy is Edward Thompson's account of popular resistance to the growing dominance of purely market principles over social relations in eighteenth-century England. He argues that the frequent upsurges of violent mass protest were an expression of a 'moral economy of the poor' which embodied 'a consistent traditional view of social norms and obligations' and supported a 'popular consensus [which] was so strong that it overrode motives of fear or deference' (1971, pp. 78–9). So, for example, the sharp increases in bread prices in periods of scarcity provoked riots fired by the fact that 'millers and... bakers were considered as servants of the community, working not for a profit but for a fair allowance' (ibid., p. 83). Society was deemed to rest on a stable network of established rights and obligations; and, in consequence, buying and selling should be governed by these established norms rather than by the vagaries of supply and demand.

While Thompson's discussion is not explicitly directed beyond the specificities of time and place which here concern him, there are evident implications of a more general character. Against the capitalist insistence that welfare is maximized where there is unfettered freedom to buy all commodities (including labour power) in the cheapest markets and sell in the dearest, popular opinion across nations and over centuries has tended to the view that there is a principle of fairness which should be set against the priorities of profit, and hence that there is a need for social control of markets.

The popular consensus (which has possible connections to contemporary references to civil society, a point I consider below) insists that economic actors must accept responsibility for the consequences of their behaviour; the pursuit of market advantage is no excuse or alibi. That there are norms of moral economy which should be imposed by force if necessary was fundamental to the socialist movements of the late nineteenth and twentieth centuries, but also to Christian-democratic tendencies which in some countries have exerted an important influence on labour movements. It remains an important element in contemporary industrial relations, as Swenson (1989) has shown in applying the notion of moral economy in his comparative study of trade union policy in Germany and Sweden. Does the almost universal genuflection at the altar of competitiveness indicate that this morality is now *passé*?

## Risk society

Ulrich Beck (1992) has given us the concept of risk society. I will not attempt to summarize his book as a whole, not all of which I find illuminating or persuasive, but concentrate on a few themes which I present with my own elaborations. In one sense, Beck argues, hazard and uncertainty have been perennial accompaniments of human existence; but in the past risks were to a significant degree calculable (hence to some extent open to actuarial assessment and cost-benefit analysis – the necessary foundation of any form on insurance). Today, increasingly, risk is different in character, both in terms of the size of potential disasters and the distance between cause and consequence. A nuclear reactor accident occurs in the Ukraine and must of north-west Europe is contaminated. Forests die from acid rain generated thousands of miles away. Antarctic penguins reveal high levels of insecticide poisoning – as, routinely, does human breast milk. American insistence on an orgy of fuel consumption threatens to drown much of Bangladesh and remove many inhabited Pacific islands from the map. While unpredictable (or sometimes all too predictable) hazards of these kinds are built into current capitalist normality, the aggressor, however, is now typically anonymous: for every Bhopal with a Union Carbide dripping blood from its corporate hands, there are a thousand cases of ecological victims unable to point the finger at the distant perpetrators.

Beck is primarily concerned with the Faustian pact between science and profit. The agents of capital, operating on an increasingly global scale, give overriding priority to short-term returns from high-risk products, materials and techniques; scientists are increasingly the well-funded servants of corporate power. This has obvious implications for employment, with workers – and not only in the Third World – being exposed to novel hazards. And there are much more general industrial relations implications, in terms of what Beck (1992, ch. 6) calls the 'destandardisation of labour'. He points to the familiar features of erosion of the traditional 'normal' employment relationship: the rise in unemployment, the growth of short-term and precarious contracts, the expansion of 'flexibility' in respect of working time and location of work, and linked to this an intensification of stress. 'One can say that a transition is occurring in industrial society from a uniform system of lifelong full-time work organized in a single industrial location, with the radical alternative of unemployment, to a *risk-fraught system of flexible, pluralized, decentralized underemployment*' (1992, p. 143).

We may see affinities here with the recent argument by Supiot (1999) that summarizes key themes from the EU report which bears his name. Part of his focus is the implication of this 'destandardisation' for systems of labour law based on a Fordist model of the 'normal' employment relationship. One element in the shift from the standard model of the past is the growing number of economically dependent workers who in legal terms are counted as self-employed and therefore lack the legal protections of traditional employees (one reason, of course, why this form of flexibility is attractive to many employers).

The Fordist employment model, Supiot argues, involved a trade-off with costs but also benefits for both sides. The worker accepted subordination to managerial authority and hence the employer's right to define the job, but in exchange for relative security of pay and status. The employer gained a normally loyal and predictable workforce, but at the cost of obstacles to discarding unwanted workers in times of difficulty or when more profitable options appeared. This reciprocity disappears in the risk society of industrial relations. The demands on workers multiply – they are increasingly held accountable for outcomes which they lack the time and resources to control – while their security diminishes. 'Thus, the terms of the quid pro quo that originally underpinned wage-employment status – i.e. subordination for security – have broken down' (1999, p. 36). Supiot's recommendations represent, in effect, a call for a new moral economy – or, perhaps, a redefinition of the old in relation to new circumstances – to underpin new patterns of regulation which enable a 'new occupational status' guaranteeing rights and dignity. As he eloquently poses the issue, what is required is 'a form of solidarity that would ensure individual and collective security in the face of contingencies that can arise at any time anywhere, because of the inescapable increase in insecurity' (ibid., p. 44).

I do not wish in this context to debate the details of Supiot's proposals or the (rather unspecified) means by which they might be realized. It is important that a semi-official EU investigation should acknowledge that the drive for competitiveness and flexibility has destructive consequences which can be mitigated only by a new and strengthened regulatory regime. Yet this need arises, as the Supiot report again recognizes, when the regulatory capacity of individual nation-states is constrained by economic internationalization ('globalization') and by the transfer of *de jure* and *de facto* authority to the level of the EU itself. How far is it possible for the EU to initiate such a regime? This clearly requires an assessment of the nature of the EU as a system of governance.

## Multi-level governance

The industrial relations literature has long been polarized between two views of the potential for effective employment regulation within the EU. An 'optimistic' perspective (which has affinities with more general 'spillover' theories of EU politics) sees an ever-consolidating structure of social policy, with the emergence of European-level actors whose status and capacity are enhanced by at first limited achievements and who thus are on the threshold of initiating a genuine European industrial relations system. Conversely, the 'pessimistic' perspective stresses that the 'negative integration' driving the European project involves economic liberalization, antagonistic to re-regulation at EU level; and that the continuing salience of national interests obstructs the emergence of a transnational policy consensus which would be a prerequisite of effective European rule-making in the industrial relations arena (Scharpf, 1999).

In some respects the debate has now moved on, as industrial relations analysis draws on more sophisticated concepts developed by political scientists. An important example is the notion of governance. Its meaning, if I understand correctly, is the *process* of control and regulation. While the more common term 'government' can have the same processual import, usually it refers to a specific set of institutions and agents. Bulmer (1998, p. 366) has argued that 'governance ... has particular value in examining the pattern of rule in the EU. The EU does not resemble, or have, a government, so governance offers some descriptive purchase on the character of the polity.'

To counterpose governance to government is to indicate the uncertainty of agency: who does what, and with which, and to whom? Again, in pessimistic mode it can be argued that a process of European integration driven by market liberalism has unleashed a dynamic of cut-throat competitiveness, a destructive genie which cannot now be put back in its bottle. The 'external coercive laws' of the European market impose a set of outcomes which governance can only ratify. More optimistically, however, it can be suggested that the dynamic can be channelled as a means at least of damage limitation; governance can provide a 'steering' of market forces.

Current analysis of EU governance has developed a repertoire of concepts such as soft law, thin policy integration and flexible regulation. The notion of 'steering' seems to imply a looser, less visible mode of control than is customary in economic regulation by national governments. But is it possible to steer a tiger? We may return to the idea of moral economy. The perspective of 'neo-institutionalism', which has become the dominant approach in political studies (March and Olsen, 1989), tends to emphasize that norms and values exercise an influence over policy; but it is less clear in indicating where these come from. Is the normative order merely an elite construction? Certainly this appears the case with much of the politics of the EU, with competitiveness and flexibility – as I already suggested – seemingly the decisive values. A popular consensus articulating an alternative 'moral economy of the poor' – and which might power an effort to steer against the stream – is notably absent.

This leads to the concept of multi-level governance (Marks *et al.*, 1996). This denotes the extent to which the locus of policy determination in the EU is diffuse: 'EU public policy-making is non-hierarchical, heavily bargained and fragmented in different institutional settings' (Laffan, 1998, p. 242). Once more, very different readings of this phenomenon are possible. Viewed negatively, the fragmentation of regulation favours non-decision-making, underwriting multiple bases of veto power and offering wide-ranging scope for economic actors to escape the regulatory net. Viewed more positively, it provides a framework for new types of regulatory initiative: 'new strategic alliances and loose neocorporatist arrangements' emerge that can exploit 'the fact that global capital is still organizationally and environmentally dependent on local political, economic and social contexts' (Martínez Lucio and Weston, 2000, p. 205). Here too the question arises: who participates in such strategic alliances, and around what type of agenda? To the well-worn rhetoric of social dialogue, the European Commission has more recently added the idea of civil dialogue: the structured interaction between policy-makers and the 'representatives of civil society'. But civil society is not a homogeneous entity: it is a terrain of actual or potential struggle. If multi-level governance is to mean more than merely finessing the main drift of a hegemonic market logic, it must articulate an alternative, overtly contentious economic morality, and empower the victims of current forms of economic integration to become subjects rather than objects of globalization.

## Flexible rigidities

The archetype of flexibility is the jellyfish: not necessarily the ideal model for an economic regime. Any system of social relations involves some element of relative fixity and others more open to variation. For social and economic actors, the ability to take certain contexual factors as stable and predictable provides a secure basis for innovation elsewhere. This is the central message of Ronald Dore's account (1986) of economic restructuring in Japan, with the provocative title *Flexible Rigidities*.

My aim is not to comment on the adequacy of Dore's analysis of Japanese experience (I have no special qualifications to do so), and it is certainly not to propose Japan as a model for Europe. Not simply because the Japanese economy has also succumbed to the global economic crisis; for, even in its period of signal success, this was founded on a highly segmented labour market (not least on the basis of gender), a management–worker relationship which could be characterized as soft authoritarianism, and a unique combination of intense work pressure and exceptionally long working time.

Nevertheless, what I find particularly significant in *Flexible Rigidities* is Dore's insistence (ibid., p. 1) that 'the Japanese... have never really caught up with Adam Smith'. In his interpretation there exists a firmly based moral economy in which 'trust relationships' are of greater importance than 'arm's-length contractual relationships' (ibid., p. 3). This creates 'a network of mutual confidence' (ibid., p. 66) which encourages both a long-term perspective and a secure framework for risk-taking (since a single misplaced risk should not have traumatic consequences). Thus certain types of institutionalized rigidity can prove a means to economic efficiency.

Streeck, drawing on German experience, has argued along similar lines: 'rigidity and flexibility are not mutually exclusive... To gain flexibility in one respect, one needs to create rigidities in another' (1988, p. 417). Here, an important distinction is between internal and external (or functional and numerical) flexibility. Where external flexibility is constrained (it is difficult for employers to hire and fire at will) they are obliged to pursue product and production strategies which stabilizes demand, while employees are more likely to cooperate in technical and organizational innovation than where external flexibility is greater. Here, firms can respond to falling demand by pursuing short-term cost reduction, and insecure employees have a rational incentive to resist change. This connects to the familiar contrast between contract and status. Streeck has argued (1987) that the employment relationship traditionally involved a complex mix of market exchange on the one hand, and a relationship embodying rights and responsibilities on the other. In hard times, he suggests, there are opposing options: to intensify the principle of hire-and-fire, or to reinforce employees' status within the organization as a platform for constructive adaptation.

Such options apply also at the macroeconomic level – both nationally and for Europe as a whole – hence Supiot's call for 'a new occupational status'. Current enthusiasm for flexibility and deregulation clearly expresses the logic of a strengthening of market principles – even if calls at the EU level for the pursuit of both flexibility and security imply that it is possible to square the circle. Security denotes a particular type of rigidity, albeit one which may form the basis for other kinds of flexibility. Whether the ideal of social Europe can be sustained thus depends in part on what is denounced as rigidity, and what is applauded as security; and hence which flexibilities are encouraged and which inhibited. This is at root an issue of values and ideologies: whether a norm of moral economy informs our vision of European integration. And it is also a question of *interests*: *whose* rights and status are to be protected? Whose rendered flexible? There can be no innocent recipe for flexible rigidity.

This brings me to a conclusion. For almost half a century, European integration has been primarily a project to construct a common market. Market-making at supranational level has itself reinforced the trends towards a risk society; and the elusive character of EU governance has provided little basis for countervailing social regulation. Such a re-regulation would require mobilization and struggle in support of a new moral economy, the construction of a European civil society, not as a bland etiquette but as a terrain of contestation.

The moral economy of which Thompson wrote inspired resistance, often violence, at times heroism. In today's Europe, unions and social movements have occasionally articulated powerful resistance to some of the cruelties which stem from the logic of market-making. From resistance to creative intervention is a major step, but not an impossible aspiration. It requires a new unity of theory and practice, a new alliance of scholars and activists. Only connect...

### Note

\* This chapter was originally published as 'La rigidez flexible ¿un modelo para una Europa social?', *Cuadernos de Relaciones Laborales*, 19, 2001, pp. 17–29.

### References

Beck, U. (1992) *Risk Society: Towards a New Modernity* (London: Sage).
Bulmer, S. (1988) 'New Institutionalism and the Governance of the Single European Market', *Journal of European Public Policy*, 5 (3), pp. 365–86.

Dore, R. (1986) *Flexible Rigidities: Industrial Policy and Structural Adjustment in the Japanese Economy 1970–80* (London: Athlone).
Laffan, B. (1998) 'The European Union: A Distinctive Model of Internationalization', *Journal of European Public Policy*, 5 (92), pp. 235–53.
March, J. and J. P. Olsen (1989) *Rediscovering Institution: The Organization Basis of Politics* (New York: Free Press).
Marks, G., L. Hooghe and K. Blank (1996) 'European Integration from the 1980s: State-Centric vs Multi-Level Governance', *Journal of Common Market Studies*, 34 (3), pp. 341–78.
Martínez Lucio, M. and S. Weston (2000) 'European Works Councils and "Flexible Regulation": The Politics of Intervention', *European Journal of Industrial Relation*, 6 (2), pp. 203–16.
Scharpf, F. (1999) *Governing in Europe: Effective and Democratic?* (Oxford: Oxford University Press).
Streeck, W. (1987) 'The Uncertainties of Management in the Management of Uncertainty', *Work, Employment and Society*, 1 (3), pp. 281–308.
Streeck, W. (1988) 'Comment on "Regidities in the Labour Market"', *Government and Opposition*, 23 (4), pp. 413–23.
Supiot, A. (1999) 'The Transformation of Work and the Future of Labour Law in Europe: A Multidisciplinary Perspective', *International Labour Review*, 138 (1), pp. 31–46.
Swenson, P. (1989) *Fair Shares: Unions, Pay and Politics in Sweden and West Germany* (Ithaca: Cornell University Press).
Thompson, E. (1971) 'The Moral Economy of the English Crowd in the Eighteenth Century', *Past and Present*, 50, pp. 76–136.

# Index

accreditation 78–9
accumulation 20, 111
Ackroyd, S. 44, 80, 122, 126, 130, 184, 185, 191–5
*Action for Employment in Europe: A Confidence Pact* 114
adaptability 92–3, 95–6, 109
Adkins, L. 146, 147
age
 entry to job market 60
 retirement 60
ageing of the population 177–8
agency working 12, 69–70, 72–5, 79–81, 144
 *see also* atypical workers/contracts
Aglietta, M. 6, 21, 90, 201
Albarracín, J. 90, 91, 94, 96, 98
Alonso, L.E. 62, 90, 92
Amin, A. 120
'amnesiac' consumption 160
Amsterdam Treaty 92, 93, 108, 114
 Employment Title 110
Arendt, H. 26
Arestis, P. 106, 107, 108, 115
ASEAN 89
assembly line 18, 19
Atkinson, J. 7, 43, 44, 70
Attali, J. 158
atypical workers/contracts 38, 38–9, 43, 43–8, 57
 *see also* employment agencies; part-time employment; temporary employment
Aucoin, P. 132
Australia 126
Austria 45
autonomy 193–5
Aznar, J. Maria 113

Bach, S. 121, 124, 125, 127
Bacon, N. 204
Bailey, T.R. 42
Balls, E. 140

Barnard, C. 107, 108, 110, 113
Bauman, Z. 161
Beck, U. 10, 110, 141, 142, 160, 169, 171
Becker, B.E. 42
Bell, D. 5
Berlusconi, S. 113
Bernhardt, A.D. 42
Beveridge welfare system 95, 148
Beynon, H. 202
Bilbao, A. 60–1
birth rate, decline in 143, 177–8
Blair, T. 113
Blyton, P. 37
Boltanski, L. 156
Boukaert, G. 120, 128, 131
Bouffartigue, P. 58
boundaryless organizations 71, 80
bourgeois hegemony 97
Bowles, S. 81
Boyer, R. 18
brands 158–9
Brandth, B. 143
Brannen, J. 143
Breton, A. 5
broken marriages, length of 173
Bruegel, I. 140, 141
bureaucracy 79
burn-out 8
Burrows, R. 120
Butler, R. 77

capitalism 110, 111, 121, 183–4
 consumer capitalism and production capitalism 26
 consumption and new spirit of 158–9
 disconnected 148–50
 ruptures in industrial logic of 5–6
capitalization principle 177
care management system 125
career progression 144–6
Carney, M.G. 77

Carré, F.   43
Castel, R.   54
Castells, M.   10
Castillo Mendoza, C.A.   98
centralization   80
　public services and   122, 127–8, 132
Chiapello, E.   156
children, number of   172, 173
citizenship   24
citizenship principle   175–6
Clarke, J.   123, 126, 127, 131, 132, 133
Coffield, F.   110, 116
cohabitation   171–2
coherent labour flexibility strategy   70
collective agency   10
collective bargaining   7, 105
　*see also* trade unionism
collectivism   14, 182–99, 202
　decline of and the rise of the subject   186–90
　individualism and in the labour process   191–5
Colling, T.   125, 128, 132
Collins, H.   78
communication   209, 210
communities   197
　workplace communities   146–7
competition   94
competitiveness   106
conflict   191–5, 208
consumer capitalism   26
consumer goods   26
consumption   7, 14, 153–68, 208
　Fordism   20–1, 22–4, 27, 28–9, 30, 155, 162–3
　fragmentation and lifestyles   154–8
　globalization and differential consumption   160–2
　and virtual society   158–60
contingent labour   12, 69–85, 97, 125, 149
　agency working   12, 69–70, 72–5, 79–81, 144
　flexibility debate   70–2
　Spain 97–8
　subcontracting   *see* subcontracting
　*see also* part-time employment; temporary employment
convergence criteria   107
Corby, S.   128
Corderi, J.   45
core and periphery model   7–8, 43–4, 70
corporatism   202–3, 211
cost reduction   19
coupledom   170
crisis of Fordism   21, 26–8
crisis of labour   206–7
critical social relations (CSR) approach   185, 195–8
Cully, M.   45, 46, 71, 140
cultural studies   205
Cutler, T.   128

Daly, G.   15
Darmon, I.   111
Day, P.   128
Deakin, N.   76, 77, 81
Deakin, S.   7, 76, 107, 108, 110, 113
decentralization   12, 69–85, 125, 132
　agency working   12, 69–70, 72–5, 79–81, 144
　flexibility debate   70–2
　outsourcing   38, 38–9, 43–5, 61, 97
　of production   40–1, 207–8, 210
　subcontracting   *see* subcontracting
decision making, standardization of   129
decommodification of work   57, 65
decommodifying state   25
defensive consumption   160
Della Rocca, G.   124, 127
Delors, J.   116
　White Paper   92, 108, 111
demand   19, 23
Denmark   99
Dent, M.   125
deregulation   40, 155–6
differential consumption   156–7, 160–2
disconnected capitalism   148–50
'dissipated' consumption   160

divorce 171, 173, 174
  challenges posed to the welfare state 179–80
  downsizing the welfare state 123–4
Drucker, P. 144
dual welfare system 123–4
Duncan, C. 128

Eastern Europe 100
economic growth 38, 90
education 126–7, 129
elder care 176, 179
Elger, T. 74
employability 12–13, 63, 66, 92, 95, 104–19
employment agencies 12, 69–70, 72–5, 79–81, 144
employment norms 12, 52–68
  economic activity and social norms 52–4
  entrepreneurial employment norm 58–61
  salaried employment norm 54–7
  salaried employment norm vs contested entrepreneurial norm 61–4
entitlements to welfare services 123–4
entrepreneurial employment norm
  during the globalization years 58–61
  vs salaried employment norm 61–4
entrepreneurship 92–3, 109
equal opportunities 92–3, 109
Esping-Andersen, G. 57, 131, 169
Essen plan 108
euro 92, 99, 107
European Central Bank (ECB) 107, 108
European Commission 94–5
European Council guidelines for member states' employment policies 111
European employment strategy (EES) 12–13, 91–6, 104, 107, 108–17
  and the cult of learning 114–17
  employability 92, 95, 112–13
  issues and connections 109–13
  pressure for change 111
  real politics and flexibility 113–14
  revision 94–6
  scope and limitations 93–6
  social partnership 107, 109–11, 113
European Monetary Union (EMU) 107, 114, 115
European Round Table of Industrialists (ERT) 106, 112
European Union (EU) 89–103, 104–19, 206–7
  constitution 100
  Directive 79/7/EEC 176
  economic policy 92–3, 96, 107–8, 110; contradictory nature of 115
  economics and employment 106–7
  employment rate 91, 92
  employment strategy see European employment strategy
  employment and wage relations 90–2
  institutional response to global pressures 107–8
  as a regulatory process 99–100
exploitation 8–9, 186–90, 197
Ezzy, D. 186

'facilitative' state 7
fair employment 55–6, 57
Fairbrother, P. 207–8
family 13–14, 169–81
  challenges posed to the welfare state by changes in 177–80
  demographic contribution to social security systems 177–8
  gender relations and family-work choices 141–3
  model underpinning the conservative welfare state 175–6
  size 172, 173
  transformation of family life 169–75
Faure, E. 116
feminization of work 140–1, 149–50, 206

Fergusson, R. 128
Fernández Duran, R. 90
Ferrara, M. 122, 126, 131
Fine, B. 206
fixed-term contracts 58, 61
  *see also* temporary employment
flexibility 14–15
  defining 37
  employability and the flexible economy 12–13, 104–19
  functional 43–8
  individualization and 141–3
  numerical 40, 43–8, 70, 125, 149
  public service provision 125
  real politics and 113–14
  and use of contingent labour 70–2
flexible enterprises 12, 35–51
  factors for change in production 35–8
  job flexibility 38–43
  labour relations and the job market 47–8
  organizational transformation and job fragmentation 43–7
flexible firm model 7–8
flexible manufacturing 7
flexible specialization 41
Flynn, N. 122, 123, 126, 131
Flynn, R. 129
Forde, C. 74
Fordism 6, 11, 18–31, 121, 148
  consumption 20–1, 22–4, 27, 28–9, 30, 155, 162–3
  crisis of 21, 26–8
  Fordist production 18, 19–21, 41–2
  golden age of 22–5
  interconnected levels 6–7
  public services and 126–7
  and the state 24–5, 121–2; crisis of Fordism 27–8
Foster, C. 123
fragmentation 29, 71
  job fragmentation 43–7
  labour 42–3, 188–9
  and lifestyles 154–8
  production 41–2
  public services 125
France 37, 100, 114, 128, 203
Freeman, C. 19

Freyssenet, M. 18
full employment 58
  European employment strategy 91–2, 110
  Spain and 54–5, 58
functional flexibility 43–8
functional Fordism 22–3

Gaebler, T. 130
García López, J. 98
Gardiner, J. 148
GDP growth 38
Geary, J. 75
Geddes, M. 122
gender 13, 57, 139–52
  and disconnected capitalism 148–50
  feminization 140–1, 149–50, 206
  individualization and flexibility 141–3
  new forms of work organization 143–7
general strikes 63
generational solidarity 177
Germany 100, 114, 147
Giddens, A. 105, 141, 142
Gintis, H. 81
globalization 7, 155, 156
  and differential consumption 160–2
  economic restructuring and political ideology 105–7
  entrepreneurial employment norm in Spain 58–61
  and trade unionism 203, 209–10
Glucksman, M. 192
Godard, J. 37
Goetschy, J. 108, 110, 113, 114
Gonos, G. 74–5
Gorz, A. 5–6, 202
Gottfried, H. 72
Gramsci, A. 20, 90
Great Depression 22
Green, F. 129
Greenwood, I. 104–19
Grimshaw, D. 73, 75
Grote, J.R. 203, 209
Growth and Stability Pact 92, 93, 107–8
Guest, D. 9

*habitus* 24, 154
Harris, J. 125, 126, 129
Harrison, S. 129
Harvey, D. 111, 197
health 126, 129
Henkel, M. 128
high employment 110
Hoggett, P. 123, 125, 126, 132
Holloway, J. 183
hollowed-out Schumpeterian workfare state 123
Hood, C. 124, 127, 128, 130, 132
Hudig, D. 106
Hugman, R. 127
human capital 48, 140
human resource management 196, 197, 204
Hunter, L.C. 70, 76
Huselid, M.A. 42
Hutton, W. 123
Hyman, R. 38, 107, 113, 202, 205, 210–11

Iglesias de Ussel, J. 178
immigration 60
inclusive job market 95
income inequality 59, 140, 141
indirect wages 25
individual responsibility 10
individualism 14, 182–99, 204
  and collectivism in the labour process 191–5
individualization 63, 156, 160, 202
  and family life 169, 170–1
  and flexibility 141–3
inflation 27
information society 93
information technology 8, 157–8
infrastructure costs 25
insecurity, job 8–9, 47–8, 55–6, 56, 189
insider–outsider syndrome 39
inspection 128
instability 14–15
institutional theory 131–2
institutions
  EU response to global pressures 107–9
  labour institutions *see* labour institutions
  internal labour markets 144–6

Ireland 99
irresponsible autonomy 193–4
Italy 100

Japan 7, 8, 147
Japanese relational contracting 77
Jenkins, S. 145
Jessop, B. 6–7, 89, 121, 123, 201, 202
job creation 38, 91, 92, 106
job flexibility 38–43
job fragmentation 43–7
job models 43
job security/insecurity 8–9, 47–8, 55–6, 56, 189
job stability 47–8, 55–6, 56
Joshi, H. 140
justice, social 53, 197

Kalleberg, A.L. 44
Kanter, R.M. 146
Kasselow, E.M. 105
Kaufmann, F.X. 177, 178
Kessler, I. 125
'Keynesian' pact 62
Keynesian welfare state 6, 27–8
Keynesianism 54, 62
Kickert, W. 124
Kingsmill, D. 144
Kirkpatrick, I. 120–36
Klein, N. 159
Klein, R. 122, 128
Knights, D. 183, 185, 186, 190
knowledge-based economy 106
knowledge-intensive production 146–7
Kochan, T.A. 204
Kvande, E. 143

labour costs 114
labour institutions 37, 42, 43
  *see also* collective bargaining; trade unionism
labour markets 11–12, 37–8
  fragmentation 42–3; organizational transformation and 43–7; labour relations and the job market 47–8
  internal 144–6
  *see also* decentralization; employment norms; flexible enterprises

labour standards 196
Lane, C. 130
Lasch, C. 157
Lash, S. 127, 146–7, 202
Lasierra, J.M. 45–7, 48
lawless consumption 157, 158–60
lean production 184, 189, 195–7
learning 104–19
Lefresne, F. 112
Lehmbruch, G. 202
liberalization 5
lifelong learning 104–19
lifestyles 154–8
Loader, B. 120
Lovering, J. 140–1
Lowe, J. 9

Maastricht Treaty 92, 107, 109
Macdonald, C. 126
MacInnes, J. 44, 47, 70, 76
MacKenzie, R. 76, 78, 79, 208, 209
Macneil, I.R. 81
management 9, 184, 196–7, 208, 210
managerialism 132
Maria Aznar, J. 113
marketization 5
of public services 124–5
marriage 169, 170, 171, 171–2
average length of broken marriages 173
Martin, B. 142
Martínez Lucio, M. 59, 183, 187, 190, 191, 204, 205, 208, 209, 212
Marx, K. 111
mass production 18, 19–21, 41–2
Mauss, M. 153
McCabe, D. 185, 186, 190
McDowell, L. 139
McHugh, D. 144
McLaughlin, K. 124
Meager, N. 70
mechanization 20–1
Meil, G. 178
*Memorandum on Lifelong Learning, A* 115
mercantilism 20–1
Mercosur 89
Michie, J. 76, 77
minimum guaranteed professional wages 56, 59

misbehaviour 14, 192–5
Montes, P. 91
Morgan, J. 38, 39
Morris, J. 37

NAFTA 89
national action plans (NAPs) 94, 109
National Institute for Clinical Excellence 129
neoclassical auction model 39
neocorporatism 202–3, 211
neo-Fordism 130–1
neo-Foucauldians 192
neoliberalism 4, 5, 12, 105–6, 195–7
neo-Taylorism 100–1
  EU and 99–100
  Spain 98
Netherlands, The 114, 126, 128
network organizations 71, 80
networks 10–11
new agendas of labour 207–10
new conjugal pact 170–1
new consumers 163–4
new economic systems 5–6
new order 9–11
new politics of production 14, 196, 208
new public management (NPM) 124–5, 127, 130
New Zealand 124
Newman, J. 126, 131, 132
Nice Treaty 99
Nichols, T. 197
Nolan, P. 9
non-market forms of organization 146–7
Nordic countries 132
Norway 143
numerical flexibility 40, 43–8, 70, 125, 149

obligational contracting 77, 79
O'Doherty, D. 185, 186–8, 189–90, 191
Offe, C. 122
Organisation for Economic Co-operation and Development (OECD) 45–7
organizational diversity 39–41

organizational misbehaviour  14, 192–5
organizational structure/form  71, 80
organizational transformation  43–7
  consequences for labour relations and job market  47–8
Osborne, D.  130
Osterman, P.  42, 43, 204
outsourcing  38, 38–9, 43–5, 61, 97
overaccumulation  111

Paci, P.  140
Panitch, L.  211
parental leave  143
part-time employment  8, 57
  Spain  59
  women  140
  *see also* atypical workers/contracts
partnership, social  107, 109–11, 113
*Partnership for a New Organisation of Work*  107
partnership sourcing relationships  77–8
pay-as-you-go social security systems  177–8
pay determination  127–8
pay inequalities  59, 140, 141
Paz, O.  5
Peck, J.  126
pensions  176
  widow's pension  179
performance measurement  128
Perrons, D.  142–3
Pierson, P.  114–15
Piore, M.  41
Plowden, F.  123
political dissonance  4
political ideology  105–7
political underpinnings of change  3–17
  arrival of a new order  9–11
  new economic systems  5–6
  Post-Fordism and its costs  6–9
Pollert, A.  114, 130
Pollitt, C.  120, 128, 131
population ageing  177–8
post-bureaucratic organizations  71, 80

Post-Fordism  3, 11, 28–9, 105, 210
  consumption  14, 153–68
  and its costs  6–9
  gender and the new economy  148–50
  Post-Fordist state thesis  121–5; changing organization of welfare state  124–5; changing role of welfare state  123–4; critique  126–9; current restructuring  127–9; public services and Fordism  126–7; towards a Post-Fordist state  122–5
  and state administration  13, 120–36
  and trade unionism  211–12; crisis of trade unionism  201–6
  virtual society  159
postmodernism  158
post-structuralism  183, 186–7
poverty  180
power  80–1
'preferred supplier' arrangements  74, 75
Primo de Rivera dictatorship  96
Pringle, R.  146
private insurance  59
privatization  155–6
  family life  170
procreation  171
Prieto, C.  52–68
Procter, S.  44
production
  decentralization of  40–1, 207–8, 210
  Fordist  18, 19–21, 41–2
  fragmentation of  41–2
  new politics of production  14, 198, 206
  reflexive  146–7
  specialization  40–1
productivity  27
professions
  reduction of autonomy  129
  regulation of  128
public choice theory  132
public sector  27–8
public services  *see* state administration; welfare state

Purcell, J. 204
Purcell, K. 140
purchaser–provider split 124–5

qualifications 47–8
qualitative intensification of labour 149
quality
  labour supplied by agencies 73
  subcontracting 78
quantitative flexibility 40, 43–8, 70, 125, 149

rationalization 20–1
recommodification 155–6
reflexive production 146–7
regulation
  EU as regulatory process 99–100
  and job flexibility 38–9
  state role 12, 209, 210
regulation theory 6, 29–30, 121, 130–1, 139
Reich, R. 105
remunerated work, employment and 52, 53
repeat workers 74
reserve army of labour thesis 141
resistance, workplace 193–5
responsible autonomy 193
restructuring
  globalization, political ideology and 105–7
  production 36
  public services 127–9, 130–2
  Spain 97
retirement age 60
Rhodes, M. 124
Rifkin, J. 8
rigidity, temporary workers and 75
risk 9–10, 81, 110–11
  individualization and flexibility 141–3
risk society 160
role culture 146
Roussel, L. 170
Rubery, J. 40, 143
Ruigrok, W. 105

Sabel, C. 41, 201
Sako, M. 79

salaried employment norm
  during the constitution years 54–7
  vs the contested entrepreneurial norm 61–4
salaries see wages/salaries
Santer, J. 114
Savage, M. 146
Sawyer, M. 106, 108
Schmitter, P. 202, 203, 209
Schumpeter, J.A. 93
scientific management 6, 18
Scott, A. 193
screening 74
self-organization 193–5
semiotization 158
Sennett, R. 142
service sector 36, 44
sexual labour 147
sexual relations 171
Shaoul, J. 123
Simpson, D. 204
Sinclair, J. 129
single interest rate policy 92
single market 92
single-parent families 175
'single-supplier' arrangements 74, 75
Skeggs, B. 155
skills 104
  development 47–8
  see also learning
Smith, A. 40
Smith, C. 74
Smith, W. 203
social change 36–7
social classes 54
  bourgeois hegemony 97
  working class 202
social dialogue 107
social justice 53, 197
social norms 52–4
  see also employment norms
social partnership 107, 109–11, 113
social protection 56, 59–60, 95
social reproduction 154
social responsibility 112
social security insurance principle 175–6
social usage 154
social work 126–7, 129

society 13–14
*see also* collectivism;
  consumption; family; gender;
  trade unionism
space 159–60
Spain 5, 37, 39, 45, 203
  divorce and separation 174
  Employment Act 1980 55
  employment norms 52–68;
    constitution years 54–7;
    globalization years 54,
    58–61
  employment rate 91, 92
  and EU 99, 100
  Industrial Relations Act 1976 56
  role of state in employment
    96–8
Sparke, M. 72
specialization in production 40–1
Stability and Growth Pact (SGP)
  92, 93, 107–8
stable employment 47–8, 55–6,
  56
stagflation 27, 28
standardization, public services and
  122, 129
state 12–13
  'facilitative' 7
  Fordism and 24–5, 121–2; crisis
    of Fordism 27–8
  inherent contradictions 7
  role in employment in Europe
    12, 89–103; employment and
    wage relations 90–2; EU as a
    regulatory process 99–100;
    Spain 96–8
  trade unionism and 202–3; state
    role and regulation 209, 210
  *see also* European employment
    strategy
state administration 13, 120–36
  Post-Fordist state thesis 121–5;
    critique 126–9
Stephenson, C. 195, 196
Stewart, P. 183, 187, 190, 191,
  195, 196, 208
Stinchcombe, A.L. 76
Stoker, G. 122, 125
Storey, J. 204
Streeck, W. 113
Strehl, F. 126

Stuart, M. 104–14
structural unemployment 95
subcontracting 97
  flexible enterprises 38, 38–9,
    43–8
  myth of decentralization 12,
    69–70, 71–2, 75–9, 79–81
subject, rise of the 186–90
supervision 76
supplier partnerships 77–8
supply teachers 73, 75
sustainable development 93
Sweden 110, 128

task culture 146
Taylor, F.W. 18
Taylorism 6, 18
*Teaching and Learning: Towards the
  Learning Society* 111
teamworking 8, 146
technology 36
  consumption and 157–8
  Fordism 22
temp-to-perm schemes 74
temporary employment 8, 57, 58,
  61
  employment agencies 12, 69–70,
    72–5, 79–81, 144
  *see also* atypical workers/contracts
third sector 93, 101–2
third way 105
Thompson, P. 9, 139, 144, 148–9,
  184, 185, 191–5
Tickell, A. 126
Tight, M. 111
time 159
time and motion studies 18
Tomlinson, J. 153
tourist industry 147
Toyotism 7
trade unionism 14, 25, 38, 105,
  182–3, 200–15
  new agendas of labour 207–10
  possibilities and limits of unions
    210–12
  Post-Fordism and the crisis of
    201–6
  rereading the crisis of labour
    206–7
  Spain 59, 63
  *see also* collective worker

training 39, 78–9, 104, 106
Trotsky, L. 5
trust 77

uncertainty 3
  manufactured 9
  see also risk
unemployment 35–6, 42, 95
  EU 90, 91, 93–4, 96, 106, 108, 114
  Spain 54, 58, 59–60, 63
UNICE 106, 112, 113
unification 188–9
United Kingdom 5, 37, 99, 114, 148
  atypical employees 45
  postal service 145
  public services 121, 122, 126, 131, 132; centralizing tendencies 127–8; changing organization of welfare state 124–5; changing role of welfare state 123–4; standardization of decision making 129
  trade unionism 203, 204
United Nations 100
United States (US) 25, 42, 74–5, 100, 124
universal access to services 175–6
Urry, J. 127, 202

Valkenburg, B. 202
Van Tulder, R. 105
Venturi, A. 177, 179
vertical integration 122, 124
Virno, P. 159
virtualization 156
  consumption and virtual society 158–60

wages/salaries 47–8, 206
  Fordism and 19–20
  indirect 25
  minimum guaranteed professional wages 56, 59
Waine, B. 128
Wajcman, J. 142, 146
Wallace, T. 121

Walsh, K. 76, 77, 81
Ward, K. 72, 74
Waterman, P. 209
Webb, J. 128
Weil, S. 21
welfare state 13–14, 62, 95, 148
  challenges posed to by changes in the family 177–80
  changing organization 124–5
  changing role 123–4
  family model underpinning the conservative welfare state 175–6
  Fordism and 121–2
  three regimes 131
  variety of policies and structures 126
Weston, S. 205, 209
White, G. 125, 127
widow's pension 179
Willmott, H. 183, 185, 186–8, 189–90, 191
Winchester, D. 125
Witz, A. 146
women 8, 13
  challenges posed to welfare state by women's participation in labour market 178–9
  employment rate 57, 174, 175
  European employment strategy 93, 95
  feminization of work 140–1, 149–50, 206
  in workforce in Spain 60
  see also gender
Wood, S. 9
Woodall, J. 145
work–life balance 141–3
work organization, new forms of 143–7
working class 202
working hours 56, 58–9
Working Time Directive 115
workplace communities 146–7
Workplace Employee Relations Survey (WERS) 71–2
world economy 25

Zeltin, J. 131, 133